ARGOPREP
GRE

2018-2019
GRE®
ARGOPREP

{ **3** **PRACTICE TESTS**

2 IN THE BOOK AND 1 ONLINE

+20%
OFF TO OUR FULL ONLINE
GRE COURSE

HIGHER SCORE
GUARANTEED

* Or money back. Condiions apply. See inside for details of our Higher Score Guarantee Policy.
*GRE is a registered trademark of the Educational Testing Service which is not affiliated with this book nor endurses this product.

ArgoPrep is one of the leading providers of supplemental educational products and services. We offer affordable and effective test prep solutions to educators, parents and students. Learning should be fun and easy! For that reason, most of our workbooks come with detailed video answer explanations taught by one of our fabulous instructors. Our goal is to make your life easier, so let us know how we can help you by e-mailing us at info@argoprep.com.

Higher Score Guarantee Policy

At ArgoPrep we know our test-taking strategies work. Our material reflects the most up-to-date content to best prepare you for your exam. If you are not satisfied with our book for any reason, you may return it for a full refund of the original purchase price (exclusive of sales tax and shipping). In order to qualify for a refund, you must return this book along with the sales receipt and provide a brief explanation for your return.

Please send to:

ArgoPrep Inc.
Attention: Customer Service Department
900 Lenox Road
Brooklyn, NY 11203

Please note, all claims for refunds must be submitted within 60 days of the date of the book purchase. Refunds are issued in four to six weeks. U.S. residents only.

TABLE OF CONTENTS

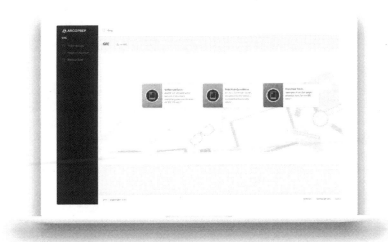

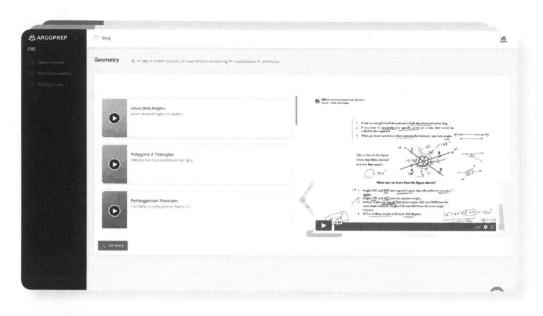

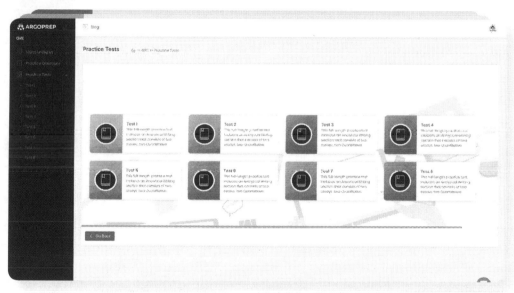

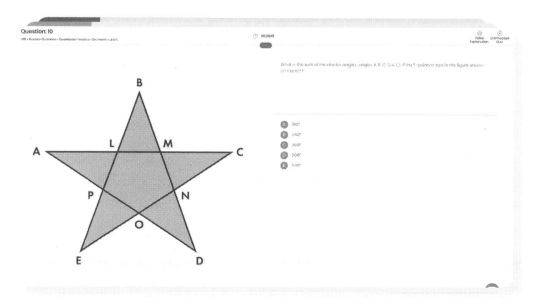

I | INTRODUCTION

About the GRE

The GRE® Revised General Test (GRE) is the most commonly accepted exam for many graduate programs. While the exam typically is required for many Master's and Ph.D. programs, many business schools are now starting to accept GRE scores in place of GMAT scores. The exam measures your aptitude for advanced graduate study using three core assessment areas: Verbal Reasoning, Quantitative Reasoning, and Analytical Writing. Each year, admissions committees receive applications from thousands of candidates with diverse educational backgrounds; the GRE provides a standard measure of candidates' educational qualifications that transcripts and other application materials are often unable to provide.

As the name of the exam itself implies, the GRE® Revised General Test is a general exam and tests your overall knowledge of reading comprehension, high school-level math, and critical writing. In addition to the general exam, there are also subject-specific exams. Depending on the program and institution you are applying to, the subject exams may be required in addition to, or in place of, the general exam.

The GRE is offered in more than 150 countries in two formats: computer-adaptive and paper-administered. In most locations, you can register to take the computer-adaptive exam any time during the year. In locations where the paper-administered exam is available, it is typically only offered three times a year. The GRE is administered by Educational Testing Service (ETS), the same organization that administers other standardized tests such as the TOEFL exam. The latest updates about the GRE Revised General Exam are available on the ETS GRE website at: www.ets.org/gre.

Computer-Adaptive Testing

The GRE is administered most often on a computer, though a paper-administered exam is available. There is often much confusion about the differences between the computer-adaptive exam and the traditional paper exam. Test-takers are often unsure of their options and which route might be best for them. The overhaul of the GRE in 2011 helped reduce some of this confusion by narrowing the options available to test-takers. Let us explore the characteristics of each of the exams.

Computer-Adaptive Exam vs. Paper Exam

- The **computer-adaptive exam** is the most common version of the exam and is the only option available in most of the more than 150 countries where it is offered. The exam is administered via computer and offered continuously throughout the year at testing centers around the world. The computer-adaptive exam requires you to input your answers into a computer and to type your Analytical Reasoning essay using a basic word processor. The exam has adaptive scoring based on your performance on the first sections of Verbal Reasoning and Quantitative Reasoning. We will dive into adaptive scoring shortly.

- The **paper exam** is only available to those testing in an area where the computer-adaptive exam is not available; not many testing locations fall into this category. The paper exam differs from the computer-adaptive exam in a number of ways. Of course, the exam is taken on paper as opposed to the computer. Because of this, adaptive scoring is not possible. Regardless of your performance on the first sections of Verbal Reasoning and Quantitative Reasoning, your second section will not change. Instead of the on-screen calculator, you will receive a calculator at the testing site for you to use during the Quantitative Analysis section.

The computer-adaptive exam has several advantages over the paper exam. Perhaps the biggest advantage those who take the computer-adaptive exam have over those who take the paper exam is the time frame for receiving scores. With the computer-adaptive exam, you will receive your unofficial scores at the end of the exam. The score will be an unofficial assessment of your Verbal and Quantitative Reasoning sections and will not include your Analytical Writing score. Your official scores are available 10–15 days after the exam. With the paper exam, you will not receive an unofficial score report at the end of the exam, and you may have to wait 5–6 weeks before receiving your score.

The GRE Revised General Test is section-adaptive, not question-adaptive. This means that your performance on the first Verbal Reasoning and Quantitative Reasoning sections determines the difficulty of the questions you will receive in the second sections.

Your performance in one assessment area is not linked to the other. It is possible to receive more difficult questions for the second Quantitative Reasoning section and not the Verbal Reasoning section. Test-takers who receive less difficult questions on the second section will encounter a scoring ceiling that can make it difficult to reach the top percentile ranks.

Only the Verbal Reasoning and Quantitative Reasoning sections are adaptive. Your performance on the first sections of both Verbal Reasoning and Quantitative Reasoning is assessed in real-time using a proprietary algorithm created by ETS. The Analytical Writing section is not adaptive; your response on the first prompt will not influence which prompt you receive for the second essay.

The computer-adaptive exam is meant to be test-taker friendly, allowing you to test however you feel most comfortable. You can skip questions and come back to them later, work within the section in any order you feel comfortable, and mark questions for review so you can revisit them. You are also always free to change your answers within the allotted time for each section. Even with the adjustments of adaptive testing, it is best to not worry too much about whether or not the questions have increased in difficulty. Just try your best on each of the questions to try to optimize your score.

Testing Instruments for Computer-Adaptive Testing

The computer-adaptive exam has several on-screen tools to help you navigate the exam with ease. You will be able to click through all of the questions for each section and approach them in any order you see fit. In each section, you will be able to scan the entire section, mark questions for later review, and change your answers within the given time period.

For the Quantitative Reasoning section, you also have an on-screen calculator available to assist you with computations. The calculator has basic functionalities and is not nearly as robust as a typical graphing calculator. Since the calculator only has the basic operation functions and a square root key, it is important to hone your understanding of concepts like exponent rules and simplifying expressions to better position yourself to calculate values.

> **Prep Fact:** Because a vast majority of the test-takers who register for the GRE will take the computer-adaptive exam, this text will focus primarily on the preparation for the computer-adaptive exam instead of the more rarely administered paper exam.

How to Register for the Exam

The computer-adaptive exam is offered continuously throughout the year in more than 800 locations worldwide. You can register for the exam by visiting the ETS website at www.ets.org/gre. You can also register via phone. In some areas, the computer-adaptive exam is not offered on a continuous basis, and test-takers must select one of the test administrations offered, which is usually twice per month.

Test-takers in areas where the computer exam is not available can still register online, via phone, or by mail in most locations. The options for test dates are more limited, however, with paper exams only being administered several times per year, usually in February, October, and November. For up-to-date information about the exam, including how to register and current fees, test-takers should consult the official ETS website at www.ets.org/gre.

Changing Your Exam Date or Canceling your Registration

If after you schedule your exam you need to cancel, reschedule, or change your testing location, you must do so at least four days prior to the exam, depending on your location. If you do not make the necessary changes within the allowable time window, you may forfeit your testing fees.

Taking the Exam Multiple Times

You are allowed to take the computer-adaptive GRE once every 21 days. It is important to note that you can only sit for the exam five times in any 12-month period. If you register for the paper exam, you are eligible to take it whenever it is offered without any restrictions.

Test-Takers with Disabilities

ETS provides additional resources for test-takers with documented disabilities. Special accommodations can be made for test-takers who need:

- Additional testing time or extended breaks
- Special medical or computer equipment at the testing site
- Recording devices
- Sign language interpreters
- Other special services or requests

In addition to arranging special accommodations, ETS also has its online study materials available in accessible formats. Test-takers requiring special accommodations should refer to the Bulletin Supplement for Test Takers with Disabilities, available as a download at www.ets.org. Review of submitted documents could take several weeks, so be sure to submit all of the required forms and information well in advance of your test date.

Test Day Expectations

The most important thing on test day is to be prepared to tackle the three core assessment areas. You also want to make sure that you have a clear understanding of what to expect on test day.

Registration on Test Day

- Be sure to arrive early to allow yourself time to find parking and the precise location. It is a good idea to do a test run prior to the exam to find the location and determine how long it will take you to get there, particularly if you are unfamiliar with the location.
- Make sure that you have the proper identification. Your ID should be valid, be signed, and be issued by a government agency. Examples of proper identification include a valid driver's license, a passport, or a student ID with a signature and expiration date.
- At some testing sites you can expect to be fingerprinted; refusal to comply may impact your ability to take the exam, and you may not receive a refund for your fees.
- If you are taking the computer-adaptive exam, be sure to bring the required admissions documents sent to you by ETS.
- Prior to the start of the exam, you will be required to complete a confidentiality agreement. Failure to completely write out the confidentiality statement will void your registration and you will not be able to sit for the exam. In this event, your fees will not be refunded.

Test Center Regulations

- Food and beverages are not allowed in the testing center. If you have a medical issue that requires you to bring food or beverages into the testing center, accommodations will need to be arranged ahead of time using the resources outlined on the ETS website for testing accommodations.
- Smoking is not allowed in the testing center.
- Aside from your identification and registration materials, no other items may be brought into the testing center. It is best to arrive with as few things as possible. The testing center assumes no responsibility for your personal items that may need to be left outside the testing area while you sit for the exam.
- Some testing centers have video surveillance equipment to monitor the administration of the exam.

- Personal calculators and watch calculators are not permitted during the exam. Some test sites may ask that you leave your watch outside the testing area.
- Cell phones and other electronic devices are not allowed in the testing area.
- At most test centers, you will be assigned a seat.
- Prior to the exam, you will be given scratch paper for use on each of the sections at your discretion. If you need more scratch paper you can obtain it from your test administrator. You are not allowed to bring your own scrap paper into the test center or take scratch paper out of of the test center.
- Be sure to dress in layers. The temperatures in the testing centers can vary widely. By dressing in layers, you have more control over your comfort level while taking the exam.

Breaks

- At the completion of each section, there is a 1-minute break before the next section begins. After the third section, there is a 10-minute break. This break is optional; you may choose to continue working if you would like.
- If you need a break outside of those provided, you may raise your hand and get the attention of the test administrator. Additional breaks other than those allotted will not stop the testing timer.
- Depending on your test site, you may be required to sign in and out whenever you leave the testing room.

Resources and Tools

ETS Exam Resources and Services Powerprep® II Software

Taking an exam on the computer can be awkward, especially if you have not had previous practice using the testing software. To help test-takers better prepare for the computer-adaptive testing environment, ETS has made available the PowerPrep® II Software. The software, which is Mac and PC compatible, allows test-takers to:

- Practice answering real test questions using all the options available on the actual exam
- Get accustomed to navigating the calculator and word processing functions
- Take timed exams to simulate actual testing conditions

The software can be downloaded from the ETS website and includes two full-length practice exams.

GRE Search Service®

ETS also offers the GRE Search Service to help graduate schools find students who fit the criteria they are looking for in a qualified candidate. When you register for the exam, you can opt-in to be included in the registry. You can also change your mind and register or hide your profile at any time by changing your preferences on your online applicant profile. Graduate schools and fellowship programs peruse the profiles of those who have registered, and may reach out to test-takers directly to introduce their programs. While this service is used primarily as a recruitment tool for schools and fellowship programs, there are many benefits for the test-taker. By registering, test-takers may gain awareness of various programs and scholarship opportunities, and may have the opportunity to connect with individuals directly involved in the admissions process.

GRE Subject Exams

The GRE is a general exam. It measures your understanding of broad concepts and your ability to reason logically. ETS does, however, administer GRE Subject Exams that test your in-depth knowledge in a particular subject area. These exams are meant for students with an extensive knowledge in a particular field, and scores can be used to supplement the General Exam scores. While some programs require the GRE Subject Exams in addition to the General Exam, other programs may only require the Subject Exam. Similar to the GRE General Exam, you can take the subject exam multiple times. Unlike the General computer-adaptive exam, however, the Subject Exams are only offered three times a year in

September, October, and April. These exams are not adaptive and are only administered in paper format. All subject exams are scored on a 200–990 scale.

Available GRE Subject Exams

Biochemistry, Cell, and Molecular Biology: 170 multiple-choice questions. Focused primarily on biochemistry, cell biology, molecular biology, and genetics.

Biology: 200 multiple-choice questions. Focused primarily on cellular, organismal, and molecular biology, as well as ecology.

Chemistry: 130 multiple-choice questions. Focused primarily on analytical, inorganic, organic, and physical chemistry.

Literature in English: 230 multiple-choice questions. Focused primarily on literary analysis, literary criticism, literary history, and identification of key literary periods, authors, and works.

Mathematics: 66 multiple-choice questions. Heavily focused on calculus while a significantly smaller portion of the exam tests knowledge of algebra, real and discrete analysis, and statistics.

Physics: 100 multiple-choice questions. Broadly focused on key physics concepts such as classical and quantum mechanics, optics and wave phenomena, relativity, laboratory methods, and thermodynamics, to name a few.

Psychology: 205 multiple-choice questions. Focused primarily on developmental, learning, abnormal, and clinical psychology, as well as psychometrics and research design.

About This Book

This book is your comprehensive guide to tackling the GRE. Studying for the GRE can be a daunting task. Figuring out where to start, what to study, and how to track your progress adds additional stress. The goal of this book is to eliminate that stress and provide you with a proven study outline and plenty of exercises and examples to help you build your proficiency in the core assessment areas. In addition to the chapters that provide you with an in-depth look at the content of the exam in each section, this book also includes a multitude of additional resources to help you:

- Understand the format and core assessment areas of the exam
- Identify your areas for improvement and work toward addressing them
- Refresh your math and vocabulary proficiency
- Simulate real testing conditions using full-length GRE practice exams

Preparation Resources in This Book

Diagnostic Exam: There are 2 full-length exams included in this book and 1 full-length exam online. We strongly recommend that you take one practice test as a Diagnostic Test before starting this book to help you ascertain your starting point and general understanding of the core assessment areas on the GRE. Do not take your score too personally, especially if the score falls below the score you are hoping to earn. Instead, use this exam to identify weak areas and to measure your progress as you become more familiar with the exam and complete other practice tests.

Math Primer: The Math Primer will help you dig up all that high school math you thought you would never use. From angles to fractions to algebra, this refresher will prepare you to navigate your way through the Quantitative Analysis section of the exam.

> ## Preparation Resources in This Book
>
> **Writing Primer:** The Analytical Writing section is usually the section students prepare for the least. Since graduate programs are keenly interested in your writing ability, it is best to spend some time preparing for this section. The Writing Primer will walk you through common writing mistakes and discuss the key characteristics of good, logically sound writing that essay graders are looking for in your essays.
>
> **Extensive Vocabulary Study List:** Having a strong vocabulary is key for the verbal section and plays a critical role in the Analytical Writing section as well. The vocabulary list provides you with commonly used words on the exams as well as an overview of prefixes, suffixes, and roots to help you better understand words you may not know.
>
> **Sample Analytical Writing Prompts and Essays:** When it comes to the Analytical Writing section, practice is key. In this text, you will not only find essay prompts to practice with, but you will also find example essays that model what a good essay looks like.
>
> **Practice Exams:** Monitoring your progress is a critical component of optimizing your performance on the exam. The practice exams will help you keep track of your progress and identify areas for improvement.

Chapter Overview

At the end of each chapter, you will find a recap of the key concepts presented. The Chapter Overview is a great way to review the material and serves as a good reference guide for material covered in a particular chapter.

Key Chapter Concepts

In this chapter, we have covered the basics of how to register for the exam, what to expect on test-taking day, and how to manage the distribution of your scores. We also walked through the resources available to you for exam preparation, both in this book and via ETS.

Computer-Adaptive Testing

Only the Verbal Reasoning and Quantitative Reasoning sections are adaptive. The Analytical Writing section is not adaptive; your response to the first prompt will not influence which prompt you receive for the second essay task.

Your performance on the first sections of both Verbal Reasoning and Quantitative Reasoning is assessed in real-time using a proprietary algorithm created by ETS. The GRE Revised General Test is **section**-adaptive, not **question**-adaptive. This means that your performance on the first Verbal Reasoning and Quantitative Reasoning sections determines the difficulty of the questions you will receive in the second sections. Your performance in one assessment area is not linked to the other. It is possible to receive more difficult questions for the second Quantitative Reasoning section and not the Verbal Reasoning section.

Score Reporting

At the conclusion of the exam, you can choose to have your scores reported or you can elect to cancel them. If you cancel your scores, you will not receive a report of them and they will not appear on your testing record. If you change your mind after canceling your scores, you have 60 days to submit a request for your scores to be reinstated.

For those taking the computer-adaptive exam, unofficial scores for all sections except the Analytical Writing section are

presented at the end of the exam. Official scores for both the paper and computer-adaptive exams are usually reported to the test-taker and your selected institutions within 10–14 days.

ETS Resources

ETS Resources	Benefits
GRE® Search Service	GRE® Search Service helps graduate schools and fellowship programs find students who fit the criteria they are looking for in a qualified candidate. When you register for the exam, you can opt-in to being included in the registry. Graduate schools and fellowship programs peruse the profiles of those who have registered and may reach out to test-takers directly.
PowerPrep® II Software	The software, which is Mac and PC compatible, allows test-takers to practice answering real test questions using all the options available on the actual exam, get accustomed to navigating the calculator and word processing functions, and take timed exams to simulate actual testing conditions.

Resources in This Book

This book is your comprehensive guide to tackling the GRE. A number of resources are included to help you better prepare for the exam and optimize your score. More specifically, the available resources can prepare you to:

- Understand the format and core assessment areas of the exam
- Identify your areas for improvement and work toward addressing them
- Refresh your math and vocabulary proficiency
- Simulate real testing conditions using full-length GRE practice exams

Resources in This Book	Benefits
Diagnostic Exam	We strongly recommend that you take one practice test as a Diagnostic Test before starting this book to help you ascertain your starting point and general understanding of the core assessment areas on the GRE.
Math and Writing Primers	The Math Primer will help you dig up all that high school math you thought you would never use and prepare you for the content you will encounter on the Quantitative section. The Writing Primer will walk you through common writing mistakes and discuss the key characteristics of good, logically sound writing that essay reviewers are looking for in your essays.
Vocabulary List	The vocabulary list provides you with commonly used words on the exams as well as an overview of prefixes, suffixes, and roots to help you better understand words you may not know.
Practice Exams	Monitoring your progress is a critical component to optimizing your performance on the exam. The practice exams will help you keep track of your progress and identify areas for improvement.

UP NEXT: The next chapter will cover the basics of the GRE format and scoring.

2 | GRE EXAM STRUCTURE

Exam Structure

The GRE is comprised of three core assessment areas:

- Analytical Writing
- Verbal Reasoning
- Quantitative Reasoning

These areas are designed to measure your aptitude for critical reasoning and quantitative analysis, and to assess your ability to write coherent, well-supported arguments based on provided evidence and instructions.

The core assessment areas are spread out across the exam in five scored sections: one Analytical Writing section of two essay tasks, two Verbal Reasoning sections, and two Quantitative Reasoning sections. You will have 30 minutes to complete each Analytical Writing essay task (60 minutes total) and Verbal Reasoning section, and 35 minutes for each Quantitative Reasoning section. The exam can take anywhere from three and a half to four hours depending on the version of the exam administered, any unscored sections that we will address later, and the amount of time you spend on the exam orientation tutorial.

The exam orientation tutorial is an untimed introduction to the computer system used to administer the GRE. Only those taking the computer exam will need to complete this tutorial. During the tutorial, you will walk through and familiarize yourself with the various functionalities of the system including the calculator and word processing functions.

It is important to take your time during this tutorial and make sure you are clear on how to operate the system in order to optimize navigation and avoid issues that could impact your score. You must demonstrate your ability to navigate the testing platform before being allowed to move on to the timed exam. Each section of the exam is scored and timed separately. You can only work on one section at a time.

GRE Core Assessment Areas

Time is a critical aspect of the GRE. It is important to monitor your time closely so that you are able to work through the section efficiently and attempt as many questions as possible. When taking the computer-adaptive exam, you will have an on-screen clock that shows how much time has elapsed and how much time you have remaining. While this can be a daunting tool, the on-screen clock allows you to track your pace and manage your time.

While time is an important aspect, your primary focus when beginning to study for the GRE should be solidifying your strategy and approach to each of the core assessment areas. First, get comfortable with your approach for each of the sections, then incorporate timing into your study plan.

Analytical Writing

In this section, you will be asked to write well-reasoned and supported responses to two separate topics chosen at random from the database of available questions. This assessment area is designed to test your analytical and critical thinking skills as well as your ability to both formulate and critique arguments.

Your exam will consist of **one** scored Analytical Writing section that includes **two** prompts:

1. Analyze an Issue Prompt

The Analyze an Issue prompt will present you with specific instructions on how to analyze a given topic. The topic lends itself to multiple perspectives, and there is no correct answer. What is important is that you construct a well-reasoned, cohesive argument that both supports your stance on the issue and closely follows the instructions given in the prompt.

2. Analyze an Argument Prompt

The Analyze an Argument prompt will present you with an argument and ask you to evaluate its merits and logical soundness. Unlike the Analyze an Issue prompt, you will not choose a side for this prompt. Instead, you will write a critical assessment of the argument presented.

The Analytical Writing section will always appear first on the exam. You will have 30 minutes to complete each essay task. The essay tasks are separately timed, and you can only work on one prompt at a time. The section is scored on a scale of 0–6, in half-point increments. A "6" is the highest possible score. The score reflects your combined Analytical Writing performance; you will not receive a separate score for each essay.

Verbal Reasoning

In the two Verbal Reasoning sections, you will be asked to read and synthesize information presented in various forms that range from short sentences to multi-paragraph passages. This assessment area is designed to test your ability to comprehend and evaluate written material. The Verbal Reasoning sections also measure your understanding of sentence structure, punctuation, and proper use of vocabulary.

Your exam will consist of two scored Verbal Reasoning sections that include the following question types:

Reading Comprehension

Reading Comprehension questions require you to read the given passages and select the answer choice that best completes the question task. Content of the the passages can come from a wide range of subject matter, and there is often more than one question that corresponds to each passage.

Text Completion

Text Completion questions require you to identify the appropriate term (or terms) that best completes a given sentence. Text Completion questions can have anywhere from one to three terms that need to be identified. A strong vocabulary and the ability to understand context clues are both essential in this section.

Sentence Equivalence

Sentence Equivalence questions require you to identify two terms for a single blank in a sentence that will create two similar sentences that express the same main idea. Similar to the Text Completion questions, this section requires a strong vocabulary and a command of context clues.

The Verbal Reasoning sections can appear in any order on the exam following the Analytical Writing section. You will have 30 minutes to complete each section. Each section on the computer-adapted test consists of 20 questions. The sections are separately timed, and you can only work on one section at a time. The sections are scored on a scale of 130–170, in one-point increments. A 170 is the highest possible score. The score reflects your combined Verbal Reasoning performance; you will not receive a separate score for each verbal section.

Quantitative Reasoning

In this section, you will be asked to solve mathematical problems drawn from the subject areas of arithmetic, geometry, algebra, and data analysis. This section tests your ability to solve quantitative problems, understand real-world applications of mathematical principles, and interpret statistical data from charts and graphs.

Your exam will consist of **two** scored Quantitative Reasoning sections that include the following question types:

Quantitative Comparisons

Quantitative Comparison questions require you to analyze the relationship between two given quantities and select the answer choice that best describes the relationship. These questions focus more on understanding mathematical relationships and less on actual mathematical calculations.

Mathematical Problem-Solving

Mathematical Problem-Solving questions require you to use various mathematical formulas and processes to solve for the correct answer to the given problems. These are multiple-choice questions that can have either one or multiple correct answers. These questions may also require you to input your own answer without being provided any answer choices to select from.

Data Interpretation

Data interpretation questions require you to interpret data from charts and graphs in order to solve for the correct answer. These questions are a subset of the Mathematical Problem-Solving questions and occur as part of a set where you will use one chart or graph to answer multiple questions.

The Quantitative Reasoning sections can appear in any order on the exam following the Analytical Writing section. You will have 35 minutes to complete each section. Each section on the computer-adaptive test consists of 20 questions. The sections are separately timed, and you can only work on one section at a time. The sections are scored on a scale of 130–170, in one-point increments. A 170 is the highest possible score. The score reflects your combined Quantitative Reasoning performance; you will not receive a separate score for each quantitative section.

Unscored Experimental and Research Sections

Your exam may also include one or two unscored sections. The unscored sections can either be an unidentified experimental section, an identified research section, or in rare instances, both. The unscored experimental section can occur at any point after the Analytical Writing section, and will be either a Verbal Reasoning or Quantitative Reasoning section. The unscored research section will always be identified as such and will always occur last. Both these sections are used by ETS to assess the current test methods and to try out new question types and material.

It is important to approach every section as if it is a scored section. Do not try to outsmart the test by figuring out which section, if you have one, is an unscored section. A miscalculation can seriously impact your overall score.

GRE Scores and Score Reporting

As we have already touched on, the GRE test is divided into three core assessment areas: Verbal Reasoning, Quantitative Reasoning, and Analytical Writing. The score range for the Verbal and Quantitative Reasoning sections is 130–170 points, in one-point increments. The score range for the Analytical Writing is 0.0–6.0, in half-point increments. Your official score report will reflect three separate scores:

Score	Score Range
Cumulative Analytical Reasoning	• 0.0–6.0 in half-point increments • Essays that are off-topic or in a language other than English may receive a score of "0"
Cumulative Verbal Reasoning	• 130–170 in one-point increments • Sections where no responses are recorded will be notated "No Score (NS)"
Cumulative Quantitative Reasoning	• 130–170 in one-point increments • Sections where no responses are recorded will be notated "No Score (NS)"

The maximum score you can receive on the Verbal and Quantitative Reasoning sections combined is a 340. For the Analytical Writing section, the maximum score you can receive is a 6.0. If you fail to enter any responses for any of the Verbal or Quantitative sections, you will not receive a score. If you fail to submit a response for an essay prompt, you will not receive a score. If your essay is off-topic or in a language other than English, you may receive a "0" for that essay task.

Raw Scores and Scaled Scores

For the Verbal and Quantitative Reasoning sections, your raw score is simply the number of correct responses you entered. Your raw score on these sections is converted into a scaled score that takes into account the difficulty of your second section based on the adaptive nature of the exam. The calculation of the scaled score ensures that the scores reflect your performance in comparison to all test-takers and provides an accurate picture of your overall performance.

Guessing on the Exam

Often times students are confused about how guessing might impact their score. When you take exams in school, wrong answers often detract from your overall score.

Good news! There is **no penalty for guessing** on the GRE. You will not be penalized for incorrect answers; your raw and scaled scores are solely based on the number of correct responses you submit. However, even though there is no penalty for guessing, you should do your best to make an educated guess. This is especially true in the first Verbal Reasoning and Quantitative Reasoning sections, given the adaptive nature of the exam. Try to eliminate 2-3 incorrect answer choices if possible before making a guess.

Unofficial and Official Test Scores

Those taking the computer-adaptive exam will receive their unofficial Verbal and Quantitative Reasoning scores at the completion of the exam. These scores may not be your final score. Official scores are typically available 10-15 days after the test administration. To view your scores, log into the online account you established when you registered for the exam. Your Analytical Writing score will be included in your official score report. If you take the paper exam, you will not receive an unofficial score report. Instead your official scores will be available within 5-6 weeks of your test date.

Score Validity

GRE scores are only valid for five years. If you are applying to graduate schools and/or fellowships and your scores are more than five years old, they may not be accepted and you may need to sit for the exam again.

Sending Your Scores to Institutions

Your exam registration allows you to send your official GRE scores to four institutions at no additional cost. At the testing center, after you have completed the exam and reviewed your unofficial scores, you can select the institutions you would like to receive your scores. Scores will be received by the institutions within 10-15 days of your test date. If you need to send additional score reports, you can do so by logging in to your online account and selecting the institutions you would like to receive a score report. Score reports above the four included reports incur an additional fee. If you take the paper exam, you can select your institutions when you register or when you submit your admissions ticket at your test site.

ScoreSelect® Service

ScoreSelect® is an additional service offered by ETS, the administrators of the GRE, that allows you more flexibility in how you report your scores to institutions. This is an optional service that carries an additional fee. With ScoreSelect®,

you decide which scores you send to which institutions. After your test administration, you can decide to send institutions your most recent scores, all of your scores, and any single exam score earned within the past five years. Regardless of which scores you choose to report, it is important to remember that your scores on all three sections for any single test administration will be reported. This means you cannot mix and match scores from different exams, or elect to exclude a score on a particular section on an exam while including another. ScoreSelect® is available for both the General and Subject Exams and only allows you to select from valid scores reported within the past five years.

Canceling Your Scores

At the end of the exam, you will be given the option to cancel your scores. You will be prompted to cancel your score before the unofficial score is displayed on the screen. Once you view your scores at a computer-delivered exam, you cannot cancel them.

Canceling your score ensures the score is not reported to any institution and does not become a part of your testing record. When you cancel your score, you cancel all section scores for the entire exam. It is not possible to cancel a score from a particular section while keeping the others. Although you will not receive a score for the exam and the exam will not appear on your test record, you are not entitled to a refund for a canceled score.

With available options like ScoreSelect® that allow you more control over your score reports, and the option to have your scores sent only to you, you should strongly consider whether or not you want to cancel your score.

Score Reinstatement

If you cancel your scores and later decide you want to have them reported, you can request your scores be reinstated up to 60 days from the date of your exam. All requests must be submitted via fax or mail and require a $50 reinstatement fee. When you request a reinstatement of scores, you can request to have your scores sent to up to four recipients, the same option available on test day. You are still eligible to use ScoreSelect® once your score is reinstated.

Once a reinstatement is requested, it can take up to 14 days for scores to be reported. If you have selected institutions to receive your scores, your scores will be sent shortly after they are reported to you.

Chapter Overview

In this chapter, we covered the basics of the GRE format and scoring, as well as information on how to manage the distribution of your scores.

Core Assessment Areas and Scoring

The **computer-adaptive exam** consists of three core assessment areas:

Analytical Writing: One section with two 30-minute essay tasks: Analyze an Issue and Analyze an Argument.

Verbal Reasoning: Two 30-minute sections; 20 questions per section.

Quantitative Reasoning: Two 35-minute sections; 20 questions per section.

Core Assessment Area	Sections/Questions	Time Allotted	Score Range
Analytical Writing	One Section Two Essay Tasks	30 minutes per essay task	0.0–6.0
Verbal Reasoning	Two Sections 20 questions each section	30 minutes per section	130–170
Quantitative Reasoning	Two Sections 20 questions each section	35 minutes per section	130–170
Unscored Experimental and Research Sections	Varies	Varies	Unscored

Computer-Adaptive Testing

Only the Verbal Reasoning and Quantitative Reasoning sections are adaptive. The Analytical Writing section is not adaptive; your response to the first prompt will not influence which prompt you receive for the second essay task.

Your performance on the first sections of both Verbal Reasoning and Quantitative Reasoning is assessed in real-time using a proprietary algorithm created by ETS. The GRE Revised General Test is **section**-adaptive, not **question**-adaptive. This means that your performance on the first Verbal Reasoning and Quantitative Reasoning sections determines the difficulty of the questions you will receive in the second sections. Your performance in one assessment area is not linked to the other. It is possible to receive more difficult questions for the second Quantitative Reasoning section and not the Verbal Reasoning section.

Score Reporting

At the conclusion of the exam, you can choose to have your scores reported or you can elect to cancel them. If you cancel your scores, you will not receive a report of them and they will not appear on your testing record. If you change your mind after canceling your scores, you have 60 days to submit a request for your scores to be reinstated.

For those taking the computer-adaptive exam, unofficial scores for all sections except the Analytical Writing section are presented at the end of the exam. Official scores for both the paper and computer-adaptive exams are usually reported to the test-taker and your selected institutions within 10–14 days.

ETS Resources

ETS Resources	Benefits
ScoreSelect®	With ScoreSelect®, you decide which scores you send to which institutions. After your test administration, you can decide to send institutions your most recent scores, all of your scores, and any single score earned within the past five years.

UP NEXT: The next chapter will introduce the Analytical Writing section of the exam and provide you with an overview of the section's scoring and the characteristics of a good essay.

GRE® PREP

3 | # INTRODUCTION TO
ANALYTICAL WRITING

Analytical Writing: The Basics

The Analytical Writing section is designed to test your ability to think critically and formulate cohesive, analytical arguments on a given topic. This section will always appear first on the exam. Each essay prompt is presented separately, and you will not be able to switch between the two or use remaining time from one essay for the other. You will have 30 minutes to complete each essay. For those taking the computer-adaptive exam, responses are typed using basic word processing software. While basic functions like cut and paste are available, common features like spelling and grammar check are not.

Do I Really Need to Prepare for the Analytical Writing Section?

The Analytical Writing section is of particular importance to graduate and business schools. The section was introduced specifically to ascertain the writing skills and abilities of candidates. Across the board, test-takers spend less time preparing for the Analytical Writing section than the other sections on the exam. In many cases, students are underprepared for this section, relying on their perceived writing ability and feeling like they can easily master the essays with little preparation. However, it is important to familiarize yourself with the specific essay tasks and understand what GRE essay reviewers are looking for in a top-rated essay.

Even if you are a strong writer, you should still devote some time to preparing for the Analytical Writing portion of the exam. This chapter will discuss the Analytical Writing section in general, explore the key strategies for approaching the section, distinguish the fundamental difference between the two prompts, and cover the rubrics for a logically sound essay that scores well.

In the Analytical Writing section, you will be presented with two essay tasks and given 30 minutes for each task:

> **Analyze an Issue:** The Analyze an Issue prompt will present you with specific instructions on how to analyze a given topic. The topic lends itself to multiple perspectives, and there is no "correct" answer. What is important is that you construct a well-reasoned, cohesive argument that both supports your stance on the issue and closely follows the instructions given in the prompt.
>
> **Analyze an Argument:** The Analyze an Argument prompt will present you with an argument and ask you to evaluate its merits and logical soundness. Unlike the Analyze an Issue prompt, you will not choose a side for this prompt. Instead, you will write a critical assessment of the arguments presented.

About the Prompts

The prompts for the Analytical Writing section are drawn from a wide range of subject areas. You can expect to see topics from the social sciences, humanities, and physical sciences, for example. While the prompts are drawn from a broad pool of subjects, no content knowledge is expected. If you encounter a physical science prompt on the exam, for instance, rest assured that you will not need to be a science expert in order to write a well-reasoned response.

Sample Analyze an Issue Prompt

Colleges and universities should require their students to spend at least one semester studying in a foreign country.

Write a response in which you discuss your views on the policy and explain your reasoning for the position you take. In developing and supporting your position, you should consider the possible consequences of implementing the policy and explain how these consequences shape your position.

Sample Analyze an Argument Prompt

A recent sales study found that consumption of beef dishes in New York City dine-in restaurants has increased by twenty percent during the past three years. But there are currently no operating city restaurants whose specialty is beef. Moreover, the majority of families in New York City are dual-income families, and a nation-wide study has shown that such families eat significantly fewer home-cooked meals than they did five years ago, though they are more concerned about healthy eating. Therefore, the new Moo-Town Steakhouse that specializes in premium beef should be quite popular and profitable in New York City.

Discuss the questions that need to be asked about the argument to determine if the proposed outcome is likely. In your response, explain how these answers will aid in evaluating the argument.

Prompts on the ETS Website

Unlike other exams you have taken, all of the possible Analytical Writing essay prompts are provided for you ahead of time to review. ETS makes available all the possible topics you can have for each prompt on the exam. This is an excellent resource and opportunity to practice with real essay questions. You can view the prompts on the ETS website, or you can request a copy by mail. There are lots of possible prompts with no real way to determine which ones you might have on your exam. With the prompts available, however, you at least have the opportunity to work with real exam material and get a clear idea of the phrasing of questions and their accompanying instructions. Even though you have access to all the prompts, that does not mean you need to work through all of them. Working through all the prompts would be a huge undertaking, and your time could be better used honing your writing skills or spending time reviewing the Writing Primer or the Vocabulary List. The subsequent chapters will outline some key strategies to help you make the most of practicing with the available prompts and developing an effective approach to the essay tasks.

Plagiarism

It is important to remember that the work you submit for each essay is your own work. ETS uses proprietary software to scan submitted essays for similarities to other published print and electronic material. The software also detects similarities between essays submitted by other test-takers. If ETS determines your work is too similar to other submitted essays or published material, they may cancel your score. If your score is canceled because similarities are detected, you will not receive a refund of fees paid. Under certain circumstances, you may file an appeal with ETS by contacting them directly.

> **Prep Tip:** You can find the prompts for the exam on the ETS GRE website at: https://www.ets.org/gre/revised_general/prepare/analytical_writing/

How Essays Are Scored

Essays are scored based on your demonstrated ability to logically construct an argument from the provided evidence, use appropriate examples, and adequately defend your position. Only one score, scaled from 0.0–6.0 in half-point increments, is assigned to reflect your combined performance on both essays; you will not receive a separate score for each essay task. Essays that are off-topic or written in a language other than English will receive a score of "0."

Two reviewers will evaluate each of your prompts. Essay reviewers are typically faculty members at colleges and universities with a broad range of specialties. Each reviewer will assign you a score of 0–6 based on your demonstrated ability to formulate a logical argument and appropriately respond to the essay task.

To arrive at your cumulative section score, the scores assigned by both reviewers for each essay are averaged, then the average of those figures is taken to arrive at your cumulative score.

For example, if your Analyze an Issue essay receives a score of "3" from one reviewer and a score of "4" from the other, your final score for the Analyze an Issue essay would be "3.5." Let us suppose that for your Analyze an Argument essay, you then receive a score of "4" from one reviewer and a score of "5" from the other. Your final score for the Analyze an Argument essay would then be "4.5." To arrive at your cumulative section score, you would simply average the final scores for each essay—in this case, "3.5" and "4.5." The cumulative section score in this example would be calculated using the following equation: (4.5 + 3.5)/2. This leaves us with a final cumulative score of "4."

Scoring Discrepancies

If the two reviewers assign you scores that differ by more than one point, a third reviewer will review your essay. In this case, the third reviewer, who is typically a more senior and experienced reviewer, will simply assign your essay a score. No averaging will happen for that particular prompt. The score assigned by the third reviewer will be averaged with the score from your other essay task to derive your cumulative section score.

Score Reporting

Only one score—the average of your scores for the two essay tasks—will be reported on your official score report. Unlike the Verbal and Quantitative Reasoning sections, the Analytical Writing section will not appear on your unofficial score at the end of your test administration. Your Analytical Writing section scores will be available when your official scores are released, usually 10–15 days after your test administration. Institutions that receive your scores will not receive a copy of your essays; they will only receive your cumulative section score.

Scoring Rubric

The Analytical Writing essay reviewers use a holistic approach to scoring essays. Essentially, they assess the essay on its overall cohesiveness and argumentation instead of assigning points based on set criteria. However, there are certain elements that reviewers consider when calculating an overall score. So, what are the characteristics of an essay that receives a score of 6? The following general rubric outlines the typical characteristics that correspond to each possible whole score on the section. In the subsequent chapters, we will explore the scoring rubric specific to each essay task.

Top to Mid-Range Percentile Analytical Writing Scores

6.0 – Outstanding

- Essay is well-structured, logically sound, and demonstrates a clear understanding of the essay task and analysis of the evidence/argument.
- Essay is well-organized, ideas are presented clearly, and transitions are smooth.
- Key components of the argument/issue are addressed and essay reflects clear insight and understanding.
- Strong support is offered for arguments, and evidence is used appropriately to support or critique the position advanced by the writer.
- Essay demonstrates an excellent command of writing, sentence structure, and vocabulary.
- Essay contains minimal grammatical and spelling errors.

5.0 – Strong

- Essay offers a well-developed and organized assessment of the issue/argument and demonstrates strong writing and understanding of the prompt and evidence.
- Ideas are clearly developed and articulated, transitions are smooth, and the essay flows logically.
- Evidence is used appropriately to support or critique the present issue/argument.

- Essay demonstrates a strong command of writing though it may contain minor grammatical and spelling errors.

4.0 – Satisfactory

- Essay offers a satisfactory assessment of the issue/argument and demonstrates an understanding of writing and the essay task.
- Essay identifies the main issues and addresses most of the key components of the prompt.
- Essay offers sufficient support for or critique of the argument and presented evidence.
- The writing is structured but contains little complexity and some minor and critical grammatical flaws.

3.0 – Limited

- Essay is generally organized but offers a flawed critique of the issue/argument. Essay demonstrates a limited understanding of the evidence and a below-average command of writing.
- Essay fails to marshal evidence to form cohesive and well-supported arguments.
- Essay demonstrates a limited range of complexity in sentence structure and vocabulary.
- Writing contains grammatical, spelling, and syntax errors.

2.0 – Seriously Flawed

- Essay demonstrates a clear disconnect from the main components of the issue/argument and is generally disorganized and illogical.
- Evidence is not leveraged to support argument and critique is not well-supported.
- Essay demonstrates a limited analysis of main components and little to no insight and understanding.
- Essay contains critical grammatical, spelling, and syntax errors and exhibits limited vocabulary and sentence structure variation.

1.0 – Fundamentally Deficient

- Essay demonstrates poor understanding of the main components of the argument and fails to provide a logical, organized analysis.
- Essay contains limited analysis and insight on the issue/argument and an inability to clearly express ideas.
- Writing contains critical grammatical, usage, and mechanical errors, and lacks cohesiveness.

0.0 – Unscorable

- Essays are completely off-topic, contain only random keystrokes, are written in a language other than English, or simply copy the essay prompt without providing an answer.
- A score of "0" is rarely assigned. It is not to be confused with a score notation of No Score (NS), which is assigned to essays where the input field is left completely blank.

Prep Fact: According to ETS, 90% of all Analytical Writing essays earn scores in the 2.0–6.0 range.

Characteristics of a Top-Scoring Essay

In order to make your essay stand out and increase your chances of earning a top score, your essay needs to not only be well-written, but also fully address the prompt and align with the essay tasks. If the essay asks you to choose a side and you write a well-developed essay that argues the merits of both sides and how both options are a good idea, then you are not going to score well, even with a well-written essay. The key to scoring well on the Analytical Writing section is more than writing well; you need to follow instructions, use the provided evidence, and adequately support your claims.

Organization and Clarity

Essay reviewers have lots of essays to review and do not have time to re-read your essays in order to grasp your point. As such, it is critical that your essay is well-organized and clearly articulates your argument and analysis of the prompt. Essay reviewers should not have to guess your position or search for your supporting evidence. Your position should be clearly stated and supported by both the provided evidence and the relevant evidence you choose to introduce. The flow of the essay should be logical and easy to follow. Make sure you divide your essay into paragraphs, grouping together ideas that are directly related to each other and ensuring that your transitions make sense. In the next chapters we will discuss some strategies on how to organize your essay logically and align with the key elements that essay reviewers are looking for when deriving your score.

Appropriate Use of Evidence

Creating a well-organized, logically sound, and clear essay largely depends on how you use evidence to support your argument. A well-written essay will marshal not only the provided evidence in support of your position, but will also include relevant evidence introduced by you to further strengthen your argument and support your position. The use of examples, real-world occurrences, and logical assumptions can all be helpful in constructing a well-supported, logical essay.

Vocabulary, Grammar, and Sentence Variety

Though content is the most important factor that essay reviewers consider when scoring your essay, it is important to ensure your essay is grammatically sound and that it demonstrates a strong command of written English. With the computerized exam, you will not have access to the typical word processing functions, like grammar and spell check, that you are likely accustomed to using. You will need to be diligent and ensure that you leave a few minutes at the end of each essay to proofread and correct mistakes.

While minor issues may not count against you, major issues or a lack of variety and complexity in your writing may significantly impact your cumulative score. Reviewers want to see that you understand proper syntax and grammar, and can use a variety of complex sentence structures and vocabulary. However, this is not an invitation to break out all your championship spelling bee words. Use vocabulary that is appropriate and makes sense in the context. Remember that there are ample opportunities in the Verbal Reasoning section for you to demonstrate your vocabulary prowess.

Critical Analysis and Logical Reasoning

Having an essay that is logically sound and that provides a critical analysis of the issues and evidence is an important component if you want to score in the upper percentile for the Analytical Writing section. Your goal is to convince your reader of your point of view by providing a well-supported case. Having a logically sound argument also means that you have avoided common logical pitfalls and interpreted the issue and evidence without the use of fallacious reasoning.

A Note on Essay Length

You may have noticed that essay length was not listed as one of the key characteristics of a high-scoring essay. While there is no prescribed length for your essay, you should ensure that your essay is comprehensive enough to address the prompt. Your essay length is certainly important, but it should be a secondary focus. If you are thinking about how to articulate logical arguments in an organized and cohesive manner by using sufficient evidence to support your position, the length will likely happen organically.

The essay reviewers know that you have a limited amount of time to construct a well-reasoned, complete essay; they understand that you can only do so much in the 30 minutes you are given and that the final product won't be the most polished and extensive analysis of the presented issue or argument. What is expected is that your writing will demonstrate an understanding of the main concepts and sufficiently address the major components of the section according to the prompt. Covering all these bases is rather hard to do in a few sentences.

So, while there is no specific length that is required, an essay that includes a brief introduction, two to three body paragraphs, and a conclusion stands a greater chance of receiving a 5 or 6 than one with just a paragraph or two. Essays should generally be between 400–600 words. But make sure you are going for quality over quantity and not just adding superfluous information to make your essay seem longer. Doing so can adversely affect your score.

Chapter Overview

In this chapter, we covered the basics of Analytical Writing, scoring, and the characteristics of a strong essay. The Analytical Writing section is designed to test your ability to think critically and formulate cohesive, analytical arguments on a given topic. Even if you are a strong writer, it is important to spend an adequate amount of time preparing for the section and understanding the essay tasks.

Analytical Writing Essay Tasks and Scoring

Essay Task	About the Prompt	Scoring
Analyze an Issue	The Analyze the Issue prompt will present you with specific instructions on how to analyze a given topic. The topic lends itself to multiple perspectives and there is no "correct" answer.	Essays are scored on a scale of 0.0–6.0 in half-point increments. Your scores on both essays are averaged to arrive at your cumulative Analytical Writing score.
Analyze an Argument	The Analyze an Argument prompt will present you with an argument and ask you to evaluate its merits and logical soundness. Unlike the Analyze an Issue prompt, you will not choose a side for this prompt.	

Key Components of a Good Essay

Organization and Clarity: Your essay should be organized and your position clearly articulated and supported.

Vocabulary, Grammar, and Sentence Variety: Use a variety of sentence structures and appropriate vocabulary. Be mindful of grammar and spelling.

Appropriate Use of Evidence: Use the evidence provided to offer support or critique of the issue/argument. Introduce relevant evidence of your own when appropriate.

Critical Analysis and Logical Reasoning: Offer a critical analysis of the main components of the prompt and ensure your reasoning flows logically and avoids common logical flaws.

Appropriate Length: Ideally, your essay should be between 400–600 words, though there is not a specified length. Ensure you write enough to fully address the essay tasks and provide a well-supported argument.

Prompts Available on the ETS Website

Remember that all the prompts for both essay tasks are available on the ETS website. Use these prompts to practice writing essays and to gain greater insight into the prompts themselves and the specific instructions for each essay task.

UP NEXT: In the next chapter, we will discuss how to study and prepare for the Analytical Writing section, and how to lay out a strategic approach to outlining and writing your essay on test day.

4 | HOW TO PREPARE: ANALYTICAL WRITING

How to Prepare for the Analytical Writing Section

In the previous chapter, we discussed how test-takers are often underprepared for the Analytical Writing section, devoting significantly less time to studying for it compared to the Verbal and Quantitative Reasoning sections. Having reviewed the criteria for scoring and the key characteristics that essay reviewers look for when assigning scores, hopefully you now understand the importance of spending an adequate amount of time building your proficiency in this section.

How do you prepare to write organized, logical, and well-supported essays? There are several tools included in this text and offered by ETS that will help you hone your approach to the Analytical Writing section and position you to be able to produce strong, high-scoring essays.

Writing Primer

Before launching into the Analytical Writing chapters on the Analyze an Issue and Analyze an Argument prompts, it is recommended that you work through the Writing Primer in the back of this book. The Writing Primer will:

- Walk you through common writing mistakes.
- Discuss key characteristics of good, logically sound writing that essay graders are looking for in your essays.
- Provide a review of grammar, mechanics, sentence structure, punctuation, and other critical technical areas of writing.
- Provide an overview of logical constructs and common reasoning errors, as well as examples of solid writing that demonstrate the characteristics of high-scoring GRE Analytical Writing essays.

In terms of structuring your study plan for this section of the exam, the Writing Primer should be your first step even if you are a strong writer. It will best situate you to avoid costly mistakes and draft essays that resonate with the essay reviewers, thus increasing your chances of earning a high score.

Essay Prompts

As we discussed in the last chapter, you have access to all the Analytical Writing prompts used for the GRE. They are the perfect resource for you to get direct exposure to prompts you will encounter on the exam. Try to tap into your network of professors or peers to read your essays and provide you with feedback since errors are not always apparent when reading your own work.

ScoreItNow!™

ScoreItNow!™ is an online scoring service offered by ETS that allows you to submit your practice essays to be graded by an e-grader. The scoring service will simulate testing conditions for you, present you with a test prompt, and provide you with an immediate score once you are done with your essays. The system is fee-based depending on the number of essays you wish to have scored.

ScoreItNow!™ is a useful practice tool that allows you to see how your writing measures up to the guidelines that essay reviewers use to score your essay. None of the scores earned in the system are valid to be sent to schools; they are also not recorded or stored in any database. You can use the confidential scoring system and not have to worry about your scores being seen by anyone but you.

> **Prep Tip:** While ScoreItNow!™ is a great tool, it is fee-based and may not be accessible to everyone. Tapping into your network and asking professors, colleagues, or peers to review your essays using the outlined criteria is also a helpful way to get feedback on your essays.

Developing a Strategy

You only have 30 minutes to write each essay in the Analytical Writing section. With such limited time, your approach is crucial and above all things, it must be strategic. With the time limit, you simply do not have the luxury of digging deeply into the material and spending lots of time exploring all the possible angles from which to approach the essay. You have to dive in and attack the essay, and to do that, you must have a comfortable strategy.

A strategic approach to the Analytical Writing section merits attention to several key areas:

Time Management

Understanding how to best use the allotted time to strategically approach the essays

Essay Format

Structuring your essay so that it is organized, it contains a proper introduction and conclusion, and it addresses the main components of the prompt

Critical Writing Components

Clearly articulating your position in an appropriate tone, ensuring that you proofread for errors

Key Differences Between the Prompts

Understanding that the Analyze an Issue and Analyze an Argument prompts are very different in terms of the type of response they require and ensuring your essays align with each essay task

You should work to implement your strategy while preparing for the exam and continue to refine it as you practice with the sample prompts; test day is not the time to try out new strategies! Let us look at some of the key strategic areas more closely.

Time Management

Managing your time on the entire exam is critical. However, the Analytical Writing section arguably presents the greatest challenge in this area. Your time limit starts when the prompt is displayed on the screen. You are tasked with writing a cohesive essay that offers critical analysis and insight into a randomly generated topic...all within a 30-minute time limit!

As you begin to work through prompts and write your sample essays, you should first focus on constructing logical arguments without much worry about the time constraints. It is important to spend some time refining your writing and making sure you understand key logical constructs and how to avoid common errors first. Then incorporate the element of time into your study plan. Once you have practiced a few essays focused on writing, then it is time to start exploring how to put together a high-scoring essay under time constraints.

Your time should be divided among four key tasks:

- Reading
- Brainstorming and Outlining
- Writing your Essay
- Proofreading

Read: 2 minutes

Make sure you fully read the presented argument or issue and the instructions that follow. You want to read the prompt and form a clear understanding of the essay task. Underline key terms and instructions as you read. It may seem like 2 minutes is not enough time, but remember, since you have access to the prompts ahead of time, you have likely seen most of the instructions, even if the argument and issue presented are not familiar to you. Practicing with the provided prompts and familiarizing yourself with the essay tasks will allow you to spend less time reading and trying to understand the prompt.

Brainstorm and Outline: 5 minutes

After you have read the prompt and are clear on the essay task, spend the next couple of minutes brainstorming and outlining your essay. The first step here is to decide your position. Once you know what direction you are going in, you can then brainstorm some counterpoints and supporting evidence before outlining how to lay out your essay. As you work through the Analyze an Issue and Analyze an Argument prompts, you will find useful tools to help you refine and systemize your approach to the essay tasks. The more you practice writing sample essays using a strategic approach, the easier it will likely be on the exam.

Write: 18 minutes

Writing the essay is, of course, the most important task. Spend about 18 minutes writing your essay using your outline as a guide. Your essay should include a brief introduction, 2–3 body paragraphs, and a conclusion.

Proofread: 5 minutes

You are not expected to produce a flawless essay in 30 minutes. But you should reserve some time at the end to look over what you have written and correct any grammar, punctuation, spelling, or other critical errors discussed in the Writing Primer.

> **Prep Tip:** Since the word processing software does not include grammar or spell check, it is a good idea to practice typing your essays with those functions disabled on your computer. Practicing without these tools helps you better simulate actual testing conditions and spot errors on your own while proofreading.

Essay Format

Organization is a critical aspect of the Analytical Writing essay. If you want to score in the higher percentiles, your essay needs to be well-organized and flow logically. There is no specific format outlined for the test. However, going into the exam, you should have a general idea on how to best structure your essay for both the Analyze an Issue and Analyze an Argument prompts. While each prompt will require a slightly different approach, there are some key components of the essay format that should be present in both essays.

Introduction

Your introduction should clearly state your position on the issue or argument. It should be succinct and to the point; you should try to avoid long-winded introductions with superfluous information and phrases. You should avoid addressing the reader directly ("What would you do if this happened to you?"), or including an otherwise instructive phrase ("Imagine a world without crime.") Demonstrate that you understand the presented issue or argument, state your position, firm up your thesis statement, and move on to the body of the essay.

Body

This is the meat of your essay. You want to craft two to three paragraphs based on your outline that critically analyze the main components of the prompt. You should start a new paragraph for each key point you introduce, making sure to support your viewpoint with the appropriate evidence. Your transitions between paragraphs should be clear and logical so the essay reviewer can easily follow along.

Conclusion

For the conclusion, you want to drive your point home. Re-emphasize your thesis, and close out your argument. Avoid phrases like "As I have shown" or "As you can see." If you have clearly articulated your argument, these types of statements will not be necessary.

Critical Writing Components

Clarity of Position

Your essay should very clearly articulate your position. Be certain to take a firm stance on the issue and make your point. Particularly with the Analyze an Issue prompt, you want to make sure that you do not straddle the fence and try to address the merits of both sides of the argument. A key consideration for scoring is your ability to clearly defend your position. If you have not taken a clear stand, it will be hard to meet this expectation. Taking time to outline your essay will help you construct an organized and logical argument. Avoid broad statements and generalizations that cannot be supported by evidence or that add little value to your argument. Relevant examples, coherent analysis, and proper use of evidence will play a major role in helping you draft an essay that clearly states and defends your position.

Logical Flow of Ideas

Having a logically sound argument is also a critical component of a good essay. Essay reviewers want to see that you have solid critical thinking skills and that you understand the basic principles of a logical argument and logical fallacy. For the Analyze an Argument prompt, you will often need to address logical flaws in the prompt. To do so, you will need to have a clear understanding of such flaws as well as the ability to form a logical rebuttal.

Tone

Essay reviewers expect that your essays may not be as polished as they would be if you had more time. However, you should still treat the essay as a piece of formal writing. You should ensure that your language is appropriate, vocabulary is used correctly, and that you avoid the use of informal speech. While there is no articulated preference for first-person or third-person narrative voice, third-person is your safest choice to ensure your essay flows well and accurately advances your argument.

Key Differences Between the Prompts

The Analytical Writing section has two distinct essay tasks that both require their own approach. One of the most common mistakes test-takers make is devising a single approach and applying it to both essays. While the essays have some similar characteristics and will have some of the basic key elements, their differences do need to be accounted for when you are writing.

The differences between the two essays lend themselves to much discussion. We will take a detailed look at the different expectations and approaches for each of these essays in their respective chapters that follow. First, let us briefly explore the key differences between the Analyze an Issue and Analyze an Argument prompts.

Primary goals for the **Analyze an Issue** prompt:

- Choose one side of the issue. This is the most critical aspect of this essay. It is important to clearly argue for one side of the issue or the other.
- Provide an analysis of a general issue that is often presented without comment or additional information. The issue is usually derived from some aspect of politics, popular culture, the arts, or history.
- Use your own evidence and appropriate examples to support your thesis.

Primary goals for the **Analyze an Argument** prompt:

- Provide critical analysis of the position presented in the prompt. Unlike the Analyze an Issue prompt, you will not be picking a side. Instead, you will analyze the presented argument.
- Assess the logical soundness of the prompt and highlight any logical fallacies.
- Analyze the given evidence and comment on the effectiveness of the evidence in supporting the argument.

Chapter Overview

In this chapter, we covered the key preparation strategies to prepare you for the Analytical Writing section, including available resources to help you prepare, timing strategies, and critical writing components that will help you develop a good essay.

Prep Resources for the Analytical Writing Section

Resource	Benefits
Writing Primer	The Writing Primer should be your first step, even if you are a strong writer. It will best situate you to avoid costly mistakes and draft essays that resonate with the essay reviewers, increasing your chances of earning a high score.
Essay Prompts	You have access to all the Analytical Writing prompts used for the GRE. They are the perfect resource for you to get direct exposure to prompts you will encounter on the exam. Try to tap into your network of professors or peers to read your essays and provide you with feedback, since errors are not always apparent when reading your own work.
ScoreItNow!™	ScoreItNow!™ is a useful practice tool that allows you to see how your writing measures up to the guidelines that essay reviewers use to score your essay. The scoring service will simulate testing conditions for you, present you with a test prompt, and provide you with an immediate score once you are done with your essays.

How to Manage Your Time When Writing Your Essay

Task	Objective	Time Allotted
Read	Read the presented issue and the essay task. Underline key pieces of evidence and important information included in the instructions.	2 minutes
Brainstorm and Outline	Decide your position and chart your pros and cons. Briefly outline your paragraphs and the evidence you plan to use to support your argument.	5 minutes

Task	Objective	Time Allotted
Write	Write your essay using the outline you drafted.	18 minutes
Proofread	Proofread your essay, checking for grammar, spelling, logical flaws, and glaring errors.	5 minutes

UP NEXT: In the next chapter, we will discuss the fundamentals of the Analyze an Issue essay prompt and outline an approach to the prompt.

5 | THE ANALYZE
AN ISSUE PROMPT

The Analyze an Issue Prompt: The Basics

The Analyze an Issue prompt will always appear first in the Analytical Writing section. The prompt expresses a particular viewpoint or viewpoints about a general issue. For the Analyze an Issue essay task, you will write a concise, well-reasoned response to the presented prompt. Your task is to develop your own argument, provide supporting evidence for your position, and use the additional instructions to further explain various aspects of your decision. You will have 30 minutes to complete the Analyze an Issue essay. For those taking the computer-adaptive exam, the essay is typed using the word-processing functionality.

Components of the Prompt

The Analyze an Issue prompt is broken into two distinct parts: the issue and the instructions. The issue is typically very brief, presented in only a sentence or two. The topics are general in nature and require no advanced or specialized knowledge for you to draft a response. The instructions will provide you with specific points to address in your argument outside of simply choosing a side of the issue.

There is no right or wrong answer for the prompt. Since this essay task measures your ability to choose a position on the issue and use appropriate and convincing evidence to support your position, it is absolutely essential for you to choose a clear side: do not straddle the fence. Make a decision and explain the merits of your choice!

Essay Task Directions

At the start of the Analyze an Issue essay task, you will see directions that outline your task and explain how your essay will be evaluated. Let us look at an example of the directions you may see on the exam:

> **Directions:** You will be presented with a brief statement that addresses a particular topic of interest and specific instructions on how to respond. No specific knowledge of the topic is needed to answer the question. Your response will be evaluated based on your ability to:
>
> - Clearly articulate and support your point of view using specific, relevant examples
> - Organize your response so that it flows logically
> - Analyze and address complex nuances of the issue
> - Articulate your point of view using standard English and a demonstrated understanding of proper grammar, usage, and mechanics

The directions are straightforward and consistent. Given the time constraints on the exam, it is best to familiarize yourself with the directions prior to the exam so that you do not have to spend valuable time re-reading them on test day.

The Issue and Writing Instructions

A sample prompt includes the presentation of the issue and the specific writing instructions. It may read as follows:

Issue

Homeschooled students often miss out on critical social interactions that lead to the development of important social skills and competencies.

Instructions

Write a response in which you discuss the extent to which you agree or disagree with the claim. In developing and supporting your position, be sure to address the most compelling reasons and/or examples that could be used to challenge your position.

On the actual exam, the prompt will be presented without the **Issue** and **Instructions** labels used above. As you can see, the additional instructions move beyond you simply stating your position on the issue. The prompt is designed for you to go a step further and address several other elements of the issue in your argument including:

- Instances when your position might not prove to be true
- Circumstances under which your position may not have the intended outcome
- Possible consequences of acting based on your position
- Possible challenges to your position
- Additional arguments that support your position

Analyze an Issue Writing Instructions

While the presented issues will run the gamut of topics, you will be asked to approach the essay according to one of six sets of instructions. The wording may vary slightly from what you see on the actual exam but the instructions below closely reflect the instructions you will encounter for the Analyze an Issue essay task:

- Discuss the extent to which you agree or disagree with the statement and explain your position. Also discuss instances when the statement may or may not be true and how these instances impact your viewpoint.
- Discuss the extent to which you agree or disagree with the statement and explain your position. Citing specific examples, explain how the circumstances under which the recommendation could be adopted would or would not be advantageous in developing and supporting your view point.
- Discuss the extent to which you agree or disagree with the claim and cite the most compelling reasons someone could use to dispute your stance.
- Ensuring you address both viewpoints provided, discuss which more closely aligns with your own views. Be sure to use specific evidence to support your position.
- Discuss how much you agree or disagree with the claim and the support offered in defense of the claim.
- Discuss your viewpoint on the proposed policy and the reasons for your perspective. Consider potential consequences of implementing the policy and the extent to which these consequences influence your stance.

Analyze an Issue Scoring Rubric

In Chapter 3, we looked at the general scoring rubric for the Analytical Writing essays. That rubric outlined the holistic characteristics that essay reviewers look for when scoring an essay. The rubric below and the rubric found in the next chapter outline the essay-specific characteristics that reviewers look for when scoring your individual essays.

6.0

- Essay takes a clear stance on the issue and provides a complete response to the issue.
- Essay is organized and contains sufficient connections between presented ideas.
- Essay uses persuasive evidence to support the position and incorporates specific examples and other appropriate premises.
- Every sentence is structured and uses appropriate vocabulary.
- Essay contains only minor grammatical, usage, and spelling errors.

5.0

- Essay takes a clear stance on the issue and presents a cogent and focused response.
- Essay is clearly organized and proper connections are drawn between presented ideas.
- Proper evidence is used to support the selected position and includes appropriate examples, insight, and a

persuasive argument.
- Essay exhibits varied sentence structures, proper word choice, and a clearly advanced understanding of writing.
- Essay contains only minor grammatical, usage, and spelling errors.

4.0

- Essay takes a clear stance on the issue and presents a near-complete response to the prompt.
- Essay is logically organized and utilizes appropriate evidence.
- Sentences and vocabulary usage are clear and appropriate.
- Essay generally adheres to grammatical, usage, and spelling conventions, though some errors do exist.

3.0

- Essay takes a generally clear stance on the issue but addresses the prompt in a manner that may be unclear or incomplete.
- Ideas in the essay are not clearly linked and evidence is inadequate or unrelated.
- Essay is loosely organized and does not flow in a manner that is easily understood.
- Sentence structure and vocabulary choices sometimes hinder rather than help organization and flow.
- Writing exhibits occasional grammatical, usage, and spelling errors that impact the flow and clarity of the essay.

2.0

- Essay takes a position that is unclear or poorly articulated and does not sufficiently address the prompt.
- Evidence used is incomplete, illogical, or unclear; ideas of the passage do not connect to each other.
- Organization is lacking and the overall flow of the essay is without clarity and understanding.
- Sentence structure and vocabulary use negatively impact the flow of the essay.
- Consistent grammatical, usage, and spelling errors significantly impact the flow and clarity of the essay.

1.0

- Position taken on the issue is uncertain and the prompt is unaddressed.
- Evidence is poorly marshaled, is illogical and/or irrelevant.
- Essay is poorly organized and reflects no clear structure.
- Sentence structure and vocabulary significantly impact the flow of the essay.
- Consistent grammatical, usage, and spelling errors significantly impact the flow and clarity of the essay.

0.0

- The response is written in a language other than English.
- The response includes nothing but a copy of the question task or the issue.
- The response is not legible (paper exam) or contains only non-English characters (computer-adaptive exam).

Developing a Strategy

With only 30 minutes to write your essay, you want to be strategic in your approach. During your preparation for the exam, it is wise to outline some key elements that should be part of your essay regardless of what the prompt may be. This minimizes the time you spend thinking about how to organize your essay and allows you to test out your format since you have the prompts available to you ahead of the exam.

Having a plan going into the essay helps you create a cogent, organized essay that addresses the issue and the instructions. In turn, you increase the chances of your essay earning a high score. Let us look at some of the key concepts you should keep in mind when responding to the Analyze an Issue prompt.

Clear Statement of Your Position

The most critical element of the Analyze an Issue essay is the statement of your position. The reviewer should not have to guess what side of the issue you have taken. Remaining neutral is not an option; doing so will significantly impact your score. A clear thesis that directly states your position should be included in the first paragraph. An effective approach to ensure the reader is clear on your position is to clearly articulate your position in the first sentence of your essay and then follow up with content that both supports your stance and addresses the additional instructions provided in the prompt.

Address the Essay Prompt

Make sure you answer the prompt. With limited time allocated to finish your response, you might hurry to get all of your ideas down. Remember to go back to the prompt to make sure you are doing what the task asks of you, addressing all points of view, bringing up possible objections, and not just agreeing or disagreeing with the stated issue.

Get Organized

Having a clear structure for your response will allow the reviewer to easily follow your line of reasoning. Once you have an outline, organize your paragraphs so that they logically flow from one to the next as you build upon your main idea and accompanying evidence.

Use Strong Supporting Evidence

Developing adequate support is crucial to your success. Begin with a clear and concise statement of your opinion in your introduction and follow a clear line of reasoning as you develop each additional paragraph.

Connect Your Ideas

The organization of your essay does not need to be based on a rigid formula. However, it needs to be logical and concise. Make sure your ideas are linked together logically with supporting evidence.

When writing your paragraphs, do not begin them with phrases like "The first reason the argument is flawed is," or "My second support is." You should also avoid demonstrative phrases like "In conclusion," or "As I have shown." Instead, use transitional words and phrases like "Thirdly," or "With these arguments in mind." Transitional words and phrases allow paragraphs to flow from one to the next by pinpointing the connections in your writing.

Organizing Your Essay

Similar to the characteristics we just reviewed as part of your strategic approach to the prompt, having an idea of how you want to organize your essay regardless of the prompt will help you best utilize your time and optimize your score. The outline below models a layout that addresses the essay task and presents your position in an organized manner.

Opening Paragraph

- Make a clear and concise statement of your position. Do not straddle the fence.

First Body Paragraph

- Explain and support your first reason for taking the side of the issue you have chosen.

Second Body Paragraph

* Explain and support your second reason for taking the side of the issue you have chosen.

Third Body Paragraph

* This paragraph is best reserved to address the additional directions from the prompt. If you have been asked to consider counter-arguments to your position, address specific parts of the prompt in more detail, or consider potential consequences or outcomes, then this is the paragraph to do so.

Concluding Paragraph

* This is your last paragraph to make your point. Try to reserve your strongest point for this paragraph and fully support it using appropriate evidence. Reiterate your position and close your argument.

Do I Have to Use This Format?

While there is no standard organization expected by ETS, it is advantageous to practice using a standard organizational structure to ensure that your essay on the exam flows well, communicates your position, and fully addresses the prompt.

Each paragraph should provide support for your point of view. In addition to stating and supporting your position, the body paragraphs should address the specific instructions in the prompt. Everything you argue should be explained and supported.

> **Prep Tip:** Whether you are taking the computer-adaptive exam or the paper exam, you will have access to scratch paper to jot down notes, outline your essay, and organize the points you plan to present in your body paragraphs. Be sure to use this valuable resource to your advantage. While you cannot bring your own scratch paper into the exam, if you run out, you can request more.

Key Ingredients

If you are aiming for a top score, it is not enough to just organize your paragraphs logically. Each sentence you write in each paragraph must be organized logically and provide support for your position. In addition, we suggest you think through and practice with the following key ingredients for organizing your essay. You should have a command of where to best use each of these elements in a well-organized essay.

Topic Sentence

Your topic sentence should give the reader an idea of what the rest of your essay is about. The sentence should present your point of view, introduce the counter-argument, or address the specific directions of the prompt. For example, if you are arguing that zoos should be shut down because of their mistreatment of animals, your topic sentence might suggest that keeping animals locked in cages at zoos is bad for their well-being.

Evidence and Examples

Once you have your topic sentence and first paragraph, there are several ways you can develop the rest of your essay. Your goal in these paragraphs is to make your topic sentence persuasive by including supporting evidence. In discussing

the well-being of animals in zoos, for instance, you might talk about the quality of care provided for the animals, and you could emphasize the number of deaths of animals at zoos. Make sure your examples are both relevant and compelling.

Compelling Conclusion

Your conclusion should be compelling. In your conclusion, you should clearly reiterate your point of view and use your strongest piece of support to solidify your stance on the issue. You do not want to leave the reviewer with a lackluster feeling, so make sure you leave a lasting impression. You can state your main point of view again, summarize your main points, or make the reader aware of a larger issue.

Analyze an Issue Practice Writing Exercise

At the end of this chapter you will find a practice essay prompt. On one page we have provided a series of questions and a basic outline structure to help you think through the elements needed for a successful Analyze an Issue essay. The questions will help you solidify your position on the issue, organize your argument, and draft your essay. Practicing with these questions in mind can help you firm up your strategic approach to writing the Analyze an Issue essay. As you work through the ETS prompts, try to answer these questions as you outline your practice essays.

Chapter Overview

The Analyze an Issue task measures your ability to respond to a general issue by taking a clear stance and using appropriate examples to support your decision. The Analyze an Issue essay always appears first in the Analytical Writing section. You will have 30 minutes to complete the essay.

Essay Writing Instructions

In addition to responding to the issue, you will also be presented with specific writing instructions that require you to go a step further than simply stating and defending your position. Pay close attention to these instructions and familiarize yourself with the six common sets of instructions ahead of the exam.

Scoring

Essays are scored on a scale of 0.0–6.0 and your Analyze an Issue essay score is averaged with your score from the Analyze an Argument essay to derive your cumulative Analytical Writing score. You will not receive a separate score for the Analyze an Issue essay.

Tips for a Solid Analyze an Issue Essay

- Ensure your essay takes a clear stance on the issue, is well-organized, and addresses all components of the essay task.
- Your overall essay organization is important, but make sure each paragraph is also well organized.
- Take a few minutes to proofread your essay and check for missing words, awkward sentence constructions, and grammatical errors.

Issue Prompt

When we know our history, we are less likely to repeat it.

Discuss the extent to which you agree or disagree with the statement and explain your position. Also discuss instances when the statement may or may not be true and how these instances impact your viewpoint.

Brainstorm and Outline Your Ideas

Do you agree or disagree with the presented issue?

What are some specific examples that can help support your position?

What are some possible counter-arguments against your position?

Using your strongest points from above, briefly outline the evidence or counter-argument you will address in each paragraph.

Opening Paragraph:

First Body Paragraph:

Second Body Paragraph:

Third Body Paragraph:

Concluding Paragraph:

Using your outline, write an essay in response to the prompt.

Prep Tip: When writing your response for the Analyze an Issue and Analyze an Argument prompts, use a computer and turn off the spell-check feature to simulate real testing conditions. You may use this space for note-taking or brainstorming.

GRE® PREP

6 | THE ANALYZE AN ARGUMENT PROMPT

The Analyze an Argument Prompt: The Basics

The Analyze an Argument prompt always appears at the end of the Analytical Writing section. For the Analyze an Argument prompt, your task is not to develop your own opinion, but rather to write an essay that analyzes the presented argument and its evidence and to evaluate its persuasiveness and logical soundness. You will have only 30 minutes to complete this essay. For those taking the computer-adaptive exam, the essay is typed using the word-processing functionality.

Components of the Prompt

Like the Analyze an Issue prompt, the Analyze an Argument prompt is broken into two distinct parts: the argument and the instructions.

The **argument** is a brief statement, usually a couple of sentences, with supporting evidence that advances a specific conclusion on a topic drawn from a wide range of subjects. No specific knowledge on the topic is needed to draft a response. The **instructions** will provide you with specific points to address in your argument and prompt you to evaluate the evidence and the overall logical merits of the argument.

The arguments presented for this prompt will **always** be flawed in some way. We will explore common flaws in logical reasoning and argumentation in this chapter. While there is no right or wrong answer to this prompt, it is important to be able to clearly outline the weaknesses in the argument and respond to the specific essay task.

Essay Task Directions

At the start of the Analyze an Argument essay task, you will see directions that outline your task and explain how your essay will be evaluated. Here is an example of the directions you may see on the exam:

> **Directions:** You will be presented with a brief statement that addresses a particular topic of interest and specific instructions on how to respond. No specific knowledge of the topic is needed to answer the question. Your response will be evaluated based on your ability to:
>
> - Clearly articulate and support your point of view using specific, relevant examples
> - Organize your response so that it flows logically
> - Analyze and address the evidence used in the passage
> - Examine assumptions and assess the logical soundness of the argument
> - Articulate your point of view using standard English and a demonstrated understanding of proper grammar, usage, and mechanics

The directions are straightforward and consistent. Given the time constraints on the exam, it is best to familiarize yourself with the directions prior to the exam so that you do not have to spend valuable time re-reading them on test day.

The Argument and Writing Instructions

A sample prompt includes the presentation of the issue and the specific writing instructions. It may read as follows:

Argument

The results of a four-year study of the common cold examined the possible therapeutic effects of a vegan diet. While many foods are naturally rich in antioxidants, food processing companies also sell isolated antioxidants. The four-year study found a strong correlation between a vegan diet and a significant decline in the average number of colds reported by participants.

A control group that increased its antioxidant intake using supplements did not have a decrease in the number of colds. Based on these results, some health experts recommend a vegan diet over the use of packaged antioxidants.

Instructions

Discuss the questions that must be answered in the argument to determine if the advice provided is reasonable. As part of your response, explain how the answers would help in evaluating the validity of the argument.

On the actual exam, the prompt will be presented without the **Argument** and **Instructions** labels used above. As you can see, the additional instructions ask you to analyze the merits of the argument, identify fallacious reasoning, and/or present cogent counter-arguments that challenge the articulated position. While reading the argument, it is important to pay close attention to and examine:

- The evidence used to advance the argument.
- Additional evidence that can be used to weaken or strengthen the argument.
- Assumptions the author makes and whether the provided evidence supports them.
- The logical soundness of the overall argument.
- Alternate explanations that could realistically compete with the explanation.

You will need to examine the structure of the argument and the way that the author forms the line of reasoning. You will need to identify the flow of logic in the passage and consider whether or not the movement from each step makes sense. In order to do this, look for transition words that reveal the author's attempts to make a logical connection.

For the Analyze an Argument task, it is also important to remember what you are **not** being asked to do:

- You are **not** being asked to examine whether the argument is true or false.
- You are **not** being asked to agree or disagree with the argument.
- You are **not** being asked to discuss your personal opinion on the matter.

Analyze an Argument Writing Instructions

The second part of the prompt lists the instructions to follow in order to complete your response to the argument successfully. You must be specific in explaining your evaluation of the argument while reviewing the evidence and examples provided. As you prepare your response, remember the goal is to identify problems in the argument's reasoning. The sets of instructions below are examples of what you can expect on the exam.

- Discuss the evidence needed to fully assess the argument. Include examples and an explanation of how the evidence provided strengthens or weakens the argument.
- Discuss the stated and unstated assumptions in the argument. Identify the relationship of these assumptions to the argument and discuss what the consequences might be if those assumptions are shown to be unwarranted.
- Discuss the questions that must be answered to determine if the advice provided is reasonable. As part of your response, explain how the answers would help in evaluating the validity of the advice.
- After reviewing the author's argument, examine any alternate explanations that could reasonably compete with the proposed explanation. In your response, explain how your analysis explains the facts provided in the argument.

Analyze an Argument Scoring Rubric

6.0

- Essay provides a logically sound, well-supported response to the prompt.
- Evidence is appropriate and persuasive, provides insight, and makes way for in-depth analysis of the argument presented in the prompt.
- Essay reflects a high-level of organization and clearly and concisely draws connections between the main ideas and the evidence used to support those ideas.

- Sentence structure and vocabulary reflect a level of complexity characteristic of strong writing skills.
- Essay contains only minor grammatical, usage, and spelling errors, if any.

5.0

- Essay provides a logically sound and well-supported response to the prompt.
- Evidence is appropriate, logical, and flows well.
- Essay is well-organized and logically flows.
- Sentence structure and vocabulary are varied and complex.
- Essay contains only minor grammatical, usage, and spelling errors.

4.0

- Essay provides a response that adequately addresses the prompt.
- Evidence is generally sound, though some evidence introduced may not adequately support the main ideas of the essay.
- Essay is generally organized, though the connection between some of the main ideas may not be particularly clear.
- Sentence structure and vocabulary are sufficient but not always properly used.
- Essay contains grammatical, usage, and spelling errors.

3.0

- Essay does not adequately address all components of the prompt.
- Evidence used is illogical and/or unrelated to the key points of the essay.
- Essay is loosely organized and does not flow in a manner that is easily understood.
- Sentence structure and vocabulary choices sometimes hinder rather than help clarify the intended meaning.
- Occasional grammatical, usage, and spelling errors impact the flow and clarity of the essay.

2.0

- Essay does not adequately address the prompt.
- A lack of evidence supports the main ideas of the essay and/or the evidence used is irrelevant, incomplete, or illogical.
- Essay is poorly organized and reflects no logical structure.
- Sentence structure and vocabulary negatively impact the flow of the essay.
- Significant grammatical, usage, and spelling errors impact the flow and clarity of the essay.

1.0

- The prompt is unaddressed.
- Evidence is poorly marshaled, is illogical and/or irrelevant.
- Essay is poorly organized and reflects no clear structure.
- Sentence structure and vocabulary significantly impact the flow of the essay.
- Consistent grammatical, usage, and spelling errors significantly impact the flow and clarity of the essay.

0.0

- The response is written in a language other than English.
- The response includes nothing but a copy of the prompt or the instructions.
- The response is not legible (paper exam) or contains only non-English characters (computer-adaptive exam).

Developing a Strategy

Having a plan going into the essay helps you create a cogent, organized essay that addresses the argument and the instructions. In turn, you increase the chances of your essay receiving a high score. Let us look at some of the key concepts you should keep in mind when responding to the Analyze an Argument prompt.

Read Actively

A well-organized essay should begin with a careful reading of the prompt. As you read, write key points on your scratch paper as well as your ideas about their validity. Do not simply evaluate individual statements; consider how all these statements interact with each other. Determine whether the conclusions flow logically from the statements made earlier in the prompt or if the prompt relies on logical fallacies or biased assumptions. The prompt will generally contain significant flaws, and your task is to address these problems in your essay.

Curb Your Opinion and Analyze

For the Analyze an Argument essay, you are analyzing an argument, not creating a new argument of your own. Your opinion on the topic is not relevant. Instead, evaluate the logic and content of the argument given to you. Read the prompt carefully and identify errors in reasoning and the use of evidence.

Structure Your Response

The GRE essay reviewers have no particular preference for how you organize your essay. However, your essay should flow logically and address all aspects of the essay task. Before you write your essay, create a brief outline to organize your ideas.

In the Analyze an Argument section of the writing exam, there are a few crucial elements that must be included as you construct your response. Your goal is to create a clear and concise response that analyzes the argument thoroughly and demonstrates the ability to identify the main parts of the argument, missing information and evidence, and assumptions that the prompt makes.

The argument will **always** be flawed. A passage containing only a few sentences is hardly going to provide solid, logical evidence and go in-depth on the topic. Do not be distracted by the one or two valid points in the argument. Your goal is to analyze, not agree with the argument. Be prepared for the argument to have several flaws for you to dissect.

Be specific with your argument, examples, and evidence. When you bring up an idea or state an objection to the argument, you need to follow that up with specific evidence to support your statement. Evidence can come from the prompt and/ or real world sources or personal experiences, as long as they directly relate to the topic. Stick to evidence that directly supports your point. The weaker your evidence, the harder it will be for you to argue your point.

Remember, the GRE does not expect you to have advanced knowledge on a topic. This essay is to evaluate your analytical writing capabilities and your rhetorical logic. They want to see critical thinking, not research. Successful responses use 3–5 paragraphs to dissect the argument, review the assumptions and evidence, offer alternate explanations and evidence, and bring up possible objections that arise out of developing the argument.

Before you begin writing your response, it is important to structure your essay clearly. Having an outline will keep you from going off on a tangent. Let us review how to organize your essay.

Organizing Your Essay

Similar to the characteristics we just reviewed as part of your strategic approach to the prompt, having an idea of how you want to organize your essay regardless of the prompt will help you best utilize your time and optimize your score.

The outline below lays out an essay that addresses the Analyze an Argument prompt and presents your position in an organized manner.

Introduction

- Briefly describe the author's point of view and and make a clear statement that the author's argument has flaws that you are going to analyze.

First Body Paragraph

- Discuss your first point of analysis of the argument and assess its validity and what assertions can weaken or strengthen the argument.

Second Body Paragraph

- Discuss your second point of analysis of the argument and assess its validity and what assertions can weaken or strengthen the argument.

Third Body Paragraph

- This paragraph is best reserved to address the additional directions in the essay task that have not been addressed in the previous two paragraphs. If you have been asked to address a question, examine alternate explanations, or discuss potential consequences that result from acting according to the presented reasoning, this is the place to do so.

Conclusion

- This is your last paragraph to make your point. Reiterate your position and evaluate the strength of the argument based on the analysis you presented.

Paragraph Structure

If you are aiming for a top score, it is not enough to just organize your paragraphs logically. Each sentence you write in each paragraph must be organized logically and provide support for your position. Paragraphs should follow a logical structure in the body of your response, one that takes into account the same key ingredients discussed in the last chapter: a topic sentence, evidence and analysis, and a compelling conclusion (see pp. 46-47).

Using a Standard Format

As mentioned in the previous chapter, there is not a standard way to organize your essay. However, as with the Analyze an Issue essay, it works to your advantage to develop a standard format for responding to the Analyze an Argument prompt. The prompts, which are made available to you before the exam, are consistent in their presentation, and the Analyze an Argument essay tasks do not change. You have the opportunity to hone your approach to your essay before the exam and to practice with real GRE prompts.

For the Analyze an Argument essay, you want to reflect your understanding of the logical shortcomings of the essay and demonstrate your ability to follow instructions by answering all components of the prompt. If you go into the exam with a solid foundation in analyzing an argument, garnered from practicing with the prompts and refining your essay structure, you can position yourself to earn a top score.

Logical Flaws and Errors in Reasoning

The arguments you encounter in the prompts for the Analyze an Argument essay will be flawed in some way. Logically, it is important to understand the common flaws in logic so that when you encounter them on the exam, you cannot only recognize them, but also articulate why the reasoning is not sound. This is the crux of the Analyze an Argument essay. You will also see these logical flaws arise in the Verbal Reasoning section of the exam, especially in Reading Comprehension passages. A majority of the body of your essay will be spent addressing the flaws in the reasoning that you have identified. In order to draft an essay that meets the expectations of the essay reviewers, it is imperative that you provide a clear and accurate analysis of the argument's flaws.

There are nearly one hundred logical flaws. Do not panic. We could not possibly cover them all here, and most of them will not occur on the exam. However, let us take a look at the most common logical flaws that you may encounter in the Analyze an Argument prompt.

Part of the Whole/Whole of the Part

These types of flaws occur when the author assumes that because something is true of the part it is also true of the whole. Conversely, the author may also erroneously assume that whatever is true of the whole is true of the part. For example, if the author asserts that he read a page in a book and it was good and then concludes that the book must be good, his reasoning is flawed. He has assumed that because a part of something was good (a page), then the entire thing must be good (the book). Similarly, if the author asserted that because the book was good, then every page in the book must be good, his reasoning is also flawed. You cannot attribute the characteristics of part of something to the whole or characteristics of the whole of something to each of its individual parts without proper evidence to establish the veracity of your claim.

Errors in Conditional Reasoning

Conditional reasoning is the logical relationship characterized by "if-then" statements where "if" is the sufficient and "then" is the necessary. Conditional reasoning is also commonly symbolized as A $\longrightarrow$ B, which is written as "If A, then B." Errors in conditional reasoning occur when the author fails to properly understand the sufficient/necessary relationship and makes inappropriate conclusions based on an erroneous understanding. Conditional reasoning has many complex nuances; many of these will not occur on the exam. But you will need to understand the basics. If you encounter a conditional relationship in the argument prompt, you should always examine it closely to ensure that it conforms to the conditional reasoning conventions. If it does not, then the argument is flawed and you will need to explain why. Let us look at a conditional reasoning statement and examine both the logical and illogical conclusions that can subsequently be made.

> If it rains tomorrow, then the store will be closed.
> The sufficient is "If it rains" while the necessary is "the store will be closed."

The only correct conclusions that you can draw from this statement are:

- If it rains, the store will be closed. Whenever the sufficient happens, the necessary **always** happens. If the author asserts that it rained but also asserts that the store is open, the argument is flawed since the necessary **must** occur whenever the sufficient occurs.
- If it does not rain, the store can be open or closed. The necessary can occur without the sufficient. If the author concludes that since the store is closed, it must have rained, the argument is flawed since it fails to consider that the necessary can occur without the sufficient.

Faulty Analogies

Reasoning by analogy functions by comparing two similar things. The faulty analogy flaw occurs when the author assumes that because similar things or people are alike in some way, they then share the same characteristics or outcomes in every instance. Here is an example of a faulty analogy flaw:

> Ted and Jim excel at both football and basketball. Since Ted is also a track star, it is likely that Jim also excels at track.

Here, similarities between Ted and Jim are the basis for the erroneous inference that they share additional traits.

Biased Sample

A biased sample occurs whenever an inadequate sample is used to justify the conclusion drawn. Here is an example:

> I have worked with 3 people from New York City and found them to be obnoxious, pushy, and rude. It is obvious that people from New York City have a bad attitude.

The data set for the inference in this argument—experiences with 3 people—is insufficient to support the conclusion.

Source Argument

The source argument flaw, also known as an ad hominem flaw, occurs when an argument is rejected because of irrelevant characteristics of the person presenting the argument. These types of flaws are common and are usually easy to spot. Here is an example:

> Governor Bates' new DUI law should be repealed since he was himself recently caught driving under the influence.

While Governor Bates being caught driving under the influence is certainly not a good thing for a number of reasons, in this case the argument provides no reasoning relevant to the suggested repeal of the law. The author only offers an assessment of Governor Bates, the person responsible for the law.

Appeal to Authority

Another type of fallacious reasoning is appeal to authority. Sometimes an author will cite the opinion of an expert or other authority on an issue as the only means of support. Some appeals to authority are logical, like citing the research of the foremost expert in Dissociative Identity Disorder to support an argument about the most effective psychological interventions for the disorder. A **fallacious** appeal to authority either appeals to an irrelevant authority or improperly assumes that citing the position of the authority figure is the only justification needed. Here is an example:

> Leonardo DiCaprio spoke about climate change in his Oscar speech. This should put to rest the ill-informed arguments of those who contend that global warming does not exist.

Leonardo DiCaprio is not an expert on climate change. While he is a celebrity who may have some influence, his speaking on the issue in no way validates or invalidates the global warming argument.

Analyze an Argument Practice Writing Exercise

At the end of this chapter you will find a practice essay prompt. On one page we have provided a series of questions and a basic outline structure to help you think through the elements needed for a successful Analyze an Argument essay. The questions will help you solidify and organize your responses to the argument and draft your essay. Practicing with these questions in mind can help you firm up your strategic approach to writing your essay.

Chapter Overview

The Analyze an Argument task measures your ability to analyze a presented argument and its evidence to evaluate its persuasiveness and logical soundness. The Analyze an Argument essay always appears last in the Analytical Writing section; you will have 30 minutes to complete the essay.

Essay Task Directions

In addition to assessing the argument, you will also be presented with specific writing instructions that require you to both understand and explain the errors in logical reasoning and potential weaknesses in the argument. Pay close attention to these instructions and familiarize yourself with the prompts ahead of the exam.

Scoring

Essays are scored on a scale of 0.0–6.0, and your Analyze an Argument essay score is averaged with your score from the Analyze an Issue essay to derive your cumulative Analytical Writing score. You will not receive a separate score for the Analyze an Argument essay.

Tips for a Solid Analyze an Argument Essay

- Evaluate the argument and identify logical flaws, areas of weakness, and/or issues with data.
- Analyze the merits of the argument and leave your opinion out of the equation.
- Your overall essay organization is important, but make sure each paragraph is also well organized.
- Take a few minutes to proofread your essay and check for missing words, awkward sentence constructions, and grammatical errors.

Common Flaws

- Assuming that characteristics of a group apply to each member of that group, and vice versa
- Assuming that a certain condition is necessary for a certain outcome
- Drawing a weak analogy between two things
- Relying on inappropriate or potentially unrepresentative statistics
- Relying on biased or tainted data (methods for collecting data must be unbiased and poll responses must be credible)

UP NEXT: In the next chapter, we will switch gears and look at the Verbal Reasoning section to explore the kinds of questions asked, some general strategies, and resources for helping you prepare for the section

Argument Prompt

The following was issued by a local community housing board:

In the last decade, our county has seen a dramatic decrease in population, with many properties now standing empty. Over the same decade, we have experienced a 50% rise in drug overdoses and a 20% rise in short-term renters. Therefore, we recommend that abandoned properties be demolished as quickly as possible to stem our growing attraction to criminals and drifters.

Discuss the questions that must be answered to determine if the advice provided is reasonable. As part of your response, explain how the answers would help in evaluating the validity of the argument.

Brainstorm and Outline Your Ideas

What logical flaws appear in the argument?

How does the evidence the author uses weaken or support the argument?

What questions need to be answered for the presented argument to flow logically? What holes are in the author's argument?

Using your strongest points from above, briefly outline the evidence or logical flaw you will address in each paragraph.

Opening Paragraph:

First Body Paragraph:

Second Body Paragraph:

Third Body Paragraph:

Concluding Paragraph:

Using your outline, write an essay in response to the prompt.

Prep Tip: When writing your response for for the Analyze an Issue and the Analyze an Argument prompts, use a computer, and turn off the spell-check feature to simulate real testing conditions. You may use this space for note-taking or brainstorming.

7 INTRODUCTION TO VERBAL REASONING

Verbal Reasoning: The Basics

The Verbal Reasoning section is designed to test your ability to read, comprehend, and evaluate written material using your logical reasoning and critical thinking skills. This section also measures your understanding of sentence structure, punctuation, and proper use of vocabulary.

The questions are presented in various forms, from short sentences to multi-paragraph passages. Two scored Verbal Reasoning sections will appear in any order on the exam following the Analytical Writing section. You will have 30 minutes to complete each section. Each section on the computer-adapted exam consists of 20 questions.

Why Is This Section Important?

Graduate programs use your performance on the Verbal Reasoning section to evaluate your critical thinking ability, analytical skills, and aptitude for using context and logical reasoning to infer meaning from written material. These skills are critical to successfully navigating graduate-level work. Graduate programs use your scores along with your application materials to assess whether you are a fit for graduate-level study.

Scoring and Computer-Adaptive Testing

The Verbal Reasoning section is scored on a scale of 130–170, in one-point increments. A 170 is the highest possible score. The score reflects your combined Verbal Reasoning performance. You will not receive a separate score for each verbal section.

When taking the computer exam, you are able to answer questions in each section in any order you wish. You can skip questions or use the built-in system tools to mark a question for review. You can then come back to it later as time permits. As we discussed earlier, the difficulty of your second scored section of Verbal Reasoning is determined by your performance on your first section. The Verbal Reasoning chapters of this book will outline strategies to help you manage your time, understand the question tasks, and deploy various strategies to optimize your Verbal Reasoning score.

Question Types

Your exam will consist of **two** scored Verbal Reasoning sections that consist of three question types. Each question type typically appears at the same frequency across exams. The chart below details the question types and the approximate number of questions you are likely to encounter on each of the two Verbal Reasoning sections.

Question Type	Question Task	Approx. # of Questions
Reading Comprehension	Reading Comprehension questions require you to read the given passages and select the answer choice that best completes or answers the question. Content of the passages can come from a wide range of subject matters, and there is often more than one question that corresponds to each passage.	9–10 questions
Text Completion	Text Completion questions require you to identify the appropriate term (or terms) that best completes a given sentence. Text Completion questions can have anywhere from one to three terms that need to be identified. A strong vocabulary and the ability to understand context clues are essential.	5–6 questions

Question Type	Question Task	Approx. # of Questions
Sentence Equivalence	Sentence Equivalence questions require you to identify two terms for a single blank in a sentence in order to create two sentences that express the same main idea. Similar to the Text Completion questions, this question type requires a strong vocabulary and a command of context clues.	4–5 questions

Timewise, answering 20 questions in 30 minutes allots you 1.5 minutes per question. This does not mean you need 1.5 minutes for each question, or more than 1.5 minutes on some questions, especially Reading Comprehension. While you are preparing for the exam, you should first focus on text-taking strategies and understanding the content. Then gradually incorporate timing into your study plan to work toward getting to all the questions in the allotted time frame.

Reading Comprehension

Reading Comprehension questions appear in some form on all standardized exams. You may be familiar with them from the SAT or other graduate entrance exams you may have taken. These questions make up a majority of the questions on the Verbal Reasoning section, with about nine to ten questions per section.

Reading Comprehension questions contain passages taken mostly from actual textbooks, articles, and books in the humanities, social sciences, arts, and the sciences. Passages are a minimum of one paragraph while some are more robust. While some passages will only have one question that corresponds to it, most passages will have several.

Sample Reading Comprehension Question

A popular publishing house in California estimated that 60 to 80 thousand people in the United States would be interested in an anthology that includes all of William Shakespeare's works. The publishing house and literary scholars who study Shakespeare's work attribute this interest to the complex psychological nature of Shakespeare's characters, which they assert still intrigue people in the present day.

The paragraph above best supports which one of the following assertions?

Ⓐ Shakespeare was an expert in psychology
Ⓑ Californians are particularly inclined to enjoy Shakespeare's work
Ⓒ Shakespeare's characters are more interesting than characters of more recent works
Ⓓ Shakespeare's characters play a major role in people's interest in his work
Ⓔ Academic scholars agree on the reason people tend to enjoy Shakespeare's work

---

Text Completion

Text Completion questions focus heavily on your understanding of advanced vocabulary. Each section of the Verbal Reasoning assessment will contain 5–6 Text Completion questions that will require you to select **one, two,** or **three** answers to fill in the corresponding blanks. You will have 3–9 answer choices to select from depending on the number of blanks in the sentence.

Like the Reading Comprehension questions, the specific content runs the gamut of subjects. You do not need to be an expert. Instead, your task is to use context clues to choose the appropriate word that best completes the sentence.

Sample Text Completion Question

He _____ the article's ideas with current events to demonstrate how closely they were related.

- (A) nixed
- (B) aligned
- (C) juxtaposed
- (D) juggled
- (E) merged

Sentence Equivalence

Similar to the Text Completion questions, Sentence Equivalence questions also rely heavily on vocabulary and your ability to use context clues to identify the correct answer. Each section of the Verbal Reasoning assessment will contain 4–5 Sentence Equivalence questions.

Sentence Equivalence prompts are usually one sentence long and contain one blank. Your task is to identify **two** separate answer choices that can be inserted into the blank and have the sentence retain the same meaning.

Sample Sentence Equivalence Question

You cannot become a certified personal trainer without completing the _____ fitness test and client contact hours.

- (A) typical
- (B) requisite
- (C) optional
- (D) mandatory
- (E) physical
- (F) staid

How to Prepare for the Verbal Reasoning Section

In addition to the strategies we will explore in the subsequent chapters, there are several tools included in this text to help you hone your approach to the Verbal Reasoning section.

Vocabulary Lists

Having a strong vocabulary is key as it plays a critical role in the Verbal Reasoning section. The vocabulary lists in Appendix 1 of this text provide you with commonly used words on the exams. Appendix 2 provides an overview of prefixes, suffixes, and root words to help you better understand words you may not know.

Practice Sets and Explanations

Use this book's practice tests and chapter sets to apply the strategies discussed in the Verbal Reasoning chapters. Then review the explanations given in each answer key to help you gain a better understanding of how to arrive at correct answer choices while avoiding tricky answer choices meant to distract you.

Chapter Overview

Your performance on the Verbal Reasoning section depends heavily on the breadth of your vocabulary and your ability to critically analyze written text. It is essential to have a solid vocabulary and a good understanding of root words, suffixes, and prefixes. You must also be able to draw inferences and use critical analysis to examine passages.

It is important to note that vocabulary alone, however, will likely not be enough to achieve a high score on this section. You must understand how to use and analyze information in context to identify the correct word or words missing from the Text Completion and Sentence Equivalence questions and to understand the content of the Reading Comprehension passages.

The subsequent chapters and the vocabulary resources in the appendices will provide you with tools to bolster your vocabulary, strengthen your reasoning skills, and develop a strategic approach to optimize your test performance.

FAST FACTS: Section Breakdown

- Two scored Verbal Reasoning sections per exam
- Can occur in any order after the Analytical Writing section
- 30 minutes per section
- 20 questions per section, appearing in a randomized order
- Depending on your exam, you may have an additional unscored section of Verbal Reasoning. Remember to approach all sections as if they are scored.

Question Breakdown

Question Type	Question Task	Approx. # of Questions
Reading Comprehension	Reading Comprehension questions require you to read the given passages and select the answer choice that best completes or answers the question. Content of the passages can come from a wide range of subject matters, and there is often more than one question that corresponds to each passage.	9–10 questions
Text Completion	Text Completion questions require you to identify the appropriate term (or terms) that best completes a given sentence. Text Completion questions can have anywhere from one to three terms that need to be identified. A strong vocabulary and the ability to understand context clues are essential.	5–6 questions

Question Type	Question Task	Approx. # of Questions
Sentence Equivalence	Sentence Equivalence questions require you to identify two terms for a single blank in a sentence in order to create two sentences that express the same main idea. Similar to the Text Completion questions, this question type requires a strong vocabulary and a command of context clues.	4–5 questions

UP NEXT: In the next chapter, we will discuss Reading Comprehension questions, which comprise a majority of the questions in the Verbal Reasoning section. We will explore the anatomy of a Reading Comprehension passage, common question types, and strategies to help you navigate these oftentimes long and complicated questions.

GRE® PREP

8 | **READING**
COMPREHENSION
QUESTIONS

Reading Comprehension: The Basics

Reading Comprehension questions require you to read the given passages and select the answer choice that best completes the question task. Content of the passages can come from a wide range of subject matters, and there is often more than one question that corresponds to each passage. Each section of Verbal Reasoning has 3–5 Reading Comprehension passages with 1–5 accompanying questions. With a total of 9–10 questions, Reading Comprehension accounts for about half of the questions on each of the scored Verbal Reasoning sections.

The passages are generally one paragraph but can be up to five paragraphs in length. They are drawn from a range of sources like journals, academic texts, and literature. You can expect to see passages related to the sciences, humanities, social science, and art, to name a few. The passages are intentionally complex and are often replete with complex vocabulary and complicated sentence constructions. Because of this, Reading Comprehension questions can be some of the most difficult in the Verbal Reasoning section.

This chapter will help you understand the types of passages and questions you will encounter on the exam. It will also outline some useful strategies on how to best approach reading and outlining the passages.

> **Prep Fact:** You will have a maximum of two longer passages; the rest will be one paragraph long.

Reading Comprehension and the Computer-Adaptive Exam

Reading passages and trying to answer corresponding questions are daunting tasks on their own. But having to read the passages and answer the questions on a computer screen can complicate the section even further. The creators of the computer-adaptive exam try to make the section as seamless as possible by utilizing a split-screen model. The passage will always be displayed on the screen alongside the question you are currently working on. As we discussed in the Introduction chapter, ETS offers its free PowerPrep II Software so you can walk through the elements of the section like practice reading, selecting answer choices, and navigating the section. Utilize this resource to not only familiarize yourself with the material, but to also get accustomed to the built-in functions of the exam and with reading long passages using the scroll function on a split-screen.

Since you cannot annotate the passage on the screen, you want to allow yourself time to practice with alternative methods to notate the information in the passage. As you work on this chapter, practice taking notes on your scratch paper instead of growing accustomed to writing on the passages. This way, on exam day, you can easily use this method.

Components of a Reading Comprehension Question

Reading Comprehension questions are comprised of three key components: the **passage**, the **question stem**, and the **answer choices**.

> ### Components of a Reading Comprehension Question
>
> **Passage:** This is the meat of the Reading Comprehension question. The passage will be 1–5 paragraphs in length with content drawn from a wide range of sources like journals, academic texts, and popular literature.
>
> **Question Stem:** The question stem provides you with a specific task based on the passage. There are several question stems that occur frequently on the exam, each of which test different aspects of your critical reading and analytical reasoning skills. We will explore these stems in greater detail later in this chapter.

Components of a Reading Comprehension Question

Answer Choices: You will have 3–5 answer choices for each Reading Comprehension question or be asked to select a specific sentence in the text. For those with answer choices, be sure to read them all before selecting your answer, as Reading Comprehension questions are notorious for having tricky, nearly true answer choices included.

Sample Reading Comprehension Question

Let us look at an actual Reading Comprehension question:

Question 1 corresponds to the following passage. Select one answer unless otherwise indicated.

Passage

Scientists know very little about the eating habits of our ancestors who lived over 2.5 million years ago. To solve this problem, scientists have started examining chimpanzees' hunting behavior and diet to find clues about our own prehistoric past. It is not difficult to determine why studying chimpanzees might be beneficial. Modern humans and chimpanzees are actually very closely related. Experts believe that chimpanzees share about 98.5 percent of our DNA sequence. If this is true, humans are more closely related to chimpanzees than they are to any other animal species.

Question Stem

1. The main purpose of the passage is to:

Answer Choices

Ⓐ explore biological and physiological similarities between humans and chimpanzees
Ⓑ assert that scientists can understand past human activity through studies of chimpanzee behavior
Ⓒ discuss the health benefits of eating and hunting meat while simultaneously predicting the effect of this behavior on chimpanzee offspring
Ⓓ bring attention to the pioneering research of Dr. Jane Goodall in Tanzania
Ⓔ educate the public on the impact that tool use had in early human societies

About the Passages

GRE passages are usually complex excerpts from a wide range of scholarly texts. The passages mirror the complexity of reading materials you will encounter at the graduate level. Regardless of the passage length, Reading Comprehension passages can be overwhelming as they contain intentionally complex language and require you to understand the presented information. In many cases, you are asked to make inferences based on the information provided. The author of each passage will express a viewpoint and/or state a series of facts that outline an argument. You can expect questions that test your understanding of the logical flow of the passage, the organization, the author's tone, and weaknesses in the argument.

Common Elements of Passages

Though GRE passages are organized in a number of ways and vary in content, they all share some common elements that you will need to identify and understand in order to accurately answer the questions. Let us look at some key characteristics you can expect to find in all GRE passages.

Main Point

Each passage will have a main point (sometimes referred to as the conclusion). The main point is always the author's point of view and answers the question, "Why did the author write this passage?"

Note that the main point is not limited to the opening paragraph or closing sentence; it is a common misconception that main points are always found in one of these two locations. The main point can be found anywhere in the passage and requires you to carefully consider what the author is trying to convey. In the example above, the main point is found in the second sentence: *To solve this problem, scientists have started examining chimpanzees' hunting behavior and diet to find clues about our own prehistoric past.*

Premises

The main point is supported by premises in the passage. Premises are statements that provide evidence for the author's argument. In some cases, premises provide evidence against a position that conflicts with the author's assertion. Premises can support the main point independently or work together with other premises to support the author's main point.

On the exam, premises are often correct answer choices for questions. You should also be able to distinguish between the main point and evidence that supports the main point, as some questions will ask you to do just that. In the example above, the sentence describing humans' and chimpanzees' shared DNA is a premise that supports the author's argument of the scientific validity of studying chimpanzee behavior to understand humanity's past.

Applying Main Points and Premises

Your ability to dissect Reading Comprehension passages into their Main Point and Premises will allow you to understand how the content of the passage is put together. Let us examine this passage as an example:

> Scientists have hypothesized that disturbing rainforests to gain access to fossil fuels may alleviate the country's impending energy crisis. This is nonsense. While fossil fuels may temporarily alleviate some energy issues, the larger problem of deforestation will not only exacerbate the energy crisis, but will also create an entirely new set of issues.

First, find the main point of this passage. Why did the author write this passage? What is her stance on the issue being discussed? To identify the main point of this passage, it is important to identify the author's perspective. This is particularly important in this example, since there are two perspectives expressed: the author's and the scientists'.

The main point of the passage is that disturbing the rainforests to gain access to fossil fuels is not a viable solution to the impending energy crisis. This is the **author's** assertion. It is important not to confuse what the scientists are assuming with what the author is arguing.

Then locate the premises. The author directly responds to the scientists' claims by stating, "This is nonsense." She then goes on to explain why: fossil fuels are a temporary fix and deforestation will only create more issues. These premises support her argument.

Reading Comprehension Question Tasks

The Reading Comprehension questions are not meant to test your knowledge or opinion about a particular subject. You should answer questions based only on the information presented in the passage, and not on any prior knowledge that you might have of the subject. You might be asked to draw a conclusion or make an inference, but you should do so based only on what the author actually states or implies.

Main Idea Questions

Main Idea questions ask you to identify or infer the main idea of the passage. Main Idea questions may also ask you to draw other inferences based on the main point of the passage. Main Idea questions account for a large portion of the questions in the Verbal Reasoning section. It is important to remember that the main idea is not geographically defined; you will not always find it in the concluding sentence or the opening paragraph.

Examples of Main Idea Question Stems

- Select the sentence that best represents the author's central argument.
- The primary purpose of the passage is to...
- Given the author's point of view, which one of the following would be an appropriate title for the passage?

Supporting Idea Questions

Supporting Idea questions ask you to identify premises and evidence in the passage that support the main idea. Supporting Idea questions may also ask you to infer supporting ideas not explicitly mentioned in the passage, or to select an answer choice that explains why a particular supporting idea was included.

Examples of Supporting Idea Question Stems

- The author mentions the "think-tank" experience in order to...
- The passage lists all of the following consequences of the regulations except...
- Select the sentence that best supports the author's main point.

Author's Attitude Questions

Author's Attitude questions ask you to describe the author's tone about various issues presented in the passage or to use information presented in order to infer how the author might feel about similar situations. It is important to be able to separate the author's point of view from other viewpoints presented in the passage.

Examples of Author's Attitude Question Stems

- The author's attitude toward contemporary art can best be described as...
- The author would most likely agree with which of the following policies relating to copyright laws?

Specific Reference Questions

These questions ask you to respond based on information in a specific location of the passage. The question will often direct you to a particular sentence or term. In this case, it is best to read a few lines before and after to get some context and to avoid missing critical connections or transitions that may impact your understanding of the specific line or term in question. This type of question can also ask you to identify points specifically addressed or not addressed in the passage.

Examples of Specific Reference Question Stems

- The author most likely uses the term "precarious" in line 14 to communicate...
- The passage mentions each of the following as reasons for the policy, EXCEPT:

Strengthen/Weaken Questions

These questions ask you to identify answer choices that will either strengthen or weaken the presented argument. An answer choice that strengthens an argument might add to an assumption that the author has made but has not explicitly stated. Or the answer choice may add additional information that clears up problematic statistics presented in the argument. These answer choices will add relevant value to the passage and make the argument stronger, if only by a smidge. In contrast, an answer choice that weakens an argument will address holes in the reasoning, such as unjustifiable assumptions, issues with data, or a lack of evidence. The answer choice in this case must hurt the argument, but it is not necessary for the choice to completely invalidate the argument to be correct.

Examples of Strengthen/Weaken Question Stems

- Which of the following, if true, would most **weaken** the author's argument?
- Which of the following, if true, would most **strengthen** the conclusion drawn in the passage above?

Passage Organization Questions

These questions test your understanding of how the passage is organized and how the organization impacts the author's argument. As you read through the passage, pay close attention to how the paragraphs flow, whether the author uses enumerations (first, second, third) or any chronological information like dates. Understanding the organization of the passage is not only helpful in answering Passage Organization questions, but will also help you better understand the author's point of view, refer back to the passage quickly to locate information, and answer other types of questions.

Examples of Passage Organization Question Stems

- Which of the following best outlines the organization of the passage?
- Which of the following best describes the organization of the third paragraph?

Parallel Questions

These questions test your understanding of the reasoning in the passage. Because of this, they can be both lengthy and complicated. Oftentimes, these questions require you to make inferences not explicitly stated in the passage, or to apply the reasoning and/or structure to similar, parallel situations unrelated to the passage.

Examples of Parallel Question Stems

- Which one of the following is most similar to the process described above?
- Which of the following would best match the reasoning outlined in the passage?

Reading Comprehension Answer Choices

For Reading Comprehension passages you can expect to see questions that ask you to select **one or more** answer choices. Some questions will ask you to select specific text within the passage. Let us look more closely at these answer choice types.

Multiple Choice: Choose One Answer Choice

These questions ask you to select the **one** answer choice that best answers the question stem. You will be presented with five answer choices and must select only one. This question type is the most popular type on the exam. In order to select the best answer, you must read all the answer choices. The GRE is commonly littered with attractive answer choices that are not correct. Read all the answer choices to be sure.

Multiple Choice: Select All that Apply Answer Choices

These questions ask you to "select all that apply" to answer the question stem. There is no partial credit for these questions; you must select all and only the correct answers in order to receive credit for your response. Assess each answer choice on its own to determine if it answers the questions. As with the previous multiple-choice scenario, make sure you read all the answer choice options.

Select-in-Passage

These questions ask you to select the sentence in the passage that best addresses the question stem. On the computer-adaptive exam, you will use your mouse and cursor to highlight the appropriate sentence.

Incorrect Answer Types

Having an understanding of the common types of incorrect answers you may encounter in the Reading Comprehension section can help you avoid falling for many of the tricky answer choices and psychometrics built into the exam. One of the most important components of Reading Comprehension questions is the understanding that because you are making inferences from the provided passages, most of your answers must be true based on the passage. Reading Comprehension questions will ask you about the main point, the author's point of view, and inferences you can draw from the passage. You will always be able to map the correct answers to these questions directly back to the passage. Do not be enticed by answers that could be true. Instead, look for the answer choice(s) that, based on the passage, absolutely **must** be true.

The test writers create intentionally misleading but attractive answer choices and co-mingle them with the correct answer. These answer choices typically fall into several consistent categories. Let us explore some common incorrect answer types.

Out of Scope

These answer choices introduce information that is not included in the passage, though it may be closely related. Since you are looking for answers that **must** be true, it will be difficult to prove that something not mentioned in the passage or inferred from the passage must be true. Out of Scope answers occur in a myriad of ways. Some of the trickier instances occur when dates are involved. For instance, a passage may address events that happened in the 1900's and an answer choice may make an assertion about what happened in the previous century. While it may be tempting to make common sense assumptions or incorporate your personal knowledge on the matter, remember that your task is to use **only** the information presented in the passage to guide you to the correct answer.

Partially Correct

Your correct answer choice will accurately and completely answer the question. You will sometimes encounter answer choices that are mostly true or that only address part of the question. Make sure your answer choice addresses all aspects of the question and is correct in its entirety

True but Not Correct

Not all answer choices that are true are correct. Just because you can map it directly back to the passage and confirm its validity does not mean it properly answers the question. Before selecting an answer choice, be sure you are clear about what the question stem is asking of you and that your answer both responds to the question stem and is drawn from and supported by the passage.

Too Extreme

Be wary of answer choices that use words like always, never, everyone, and so on. While the use of these terms does not always signify an incorrect answer, their inclusion does merit additional attention. When you encounter this type of absolute language in an answer choice in Reading Comprehension (example: all the neighborhoods will be affected by the drought), you want to be sure that you can map it directly back to the passage. If the passage indicates that **most** of the neighborhoods have experienced some negative consequences as a result of the drought, you cannot logically conclude that **all** of them have.

> **Prep Tip:** Reading Comprehension questions are concerned with your ability to critically analyze written information, not your ability to express your personal opinion on the passage. Keep your opinion under wraps and ensure you are only using the information in the passage and logical inferences drawn from that information to select your answer choices.

Developing a Strategy

Many people fail to prepare adequately for the Reading Comprehension questions because they mistakenly equate their ability to "read" and "comprehend" with their ability to tackle this section. Reading Comprehension questions require more than simply being able to recap what you have read. You must be able to critically assess the reasoning, understand the structure, and pinpoint why particular evidence, vocabulary, and counter-examples are introduced—all within a short time period.

Developing an effective approach to answering these questions is of critical importance. The first two sections below walk you through how to read the exam and process your answers in order to maximize your time. Other parts of developing an approach involve honing your vocabulary and, most importantly, the pace at which you are able to read, process, and correctly answer Reading Comprehension questions.

Read the Questions First

When to read the passage questions is a common point discussed among test-takers. Often there are differing opinions and rationale presented to justify one side or the other. When thinking about how to strategically approach Reading Comprehension questions, taking into account the limited amount of time you have for each question and the amount of information you are usually required to read, we suggest you read the questions after you read the passage.

There is a reason the Reading Comprehension tasks are organized the way they are: the passage, the question stem, and then the answer choices. This is because it makes logical sense to read the passage, understand the various question tasks, then approach the answer choices. Aside from simply reading the passage as it is presented, there are some other key justifications for reading the questions after you read the passage:

- You have 30 minutes to answer 20 questions. Every second is valuable. Oftentimes, when people read the questions first, they then read them again after reading the passage. That time could be better spent navigating the answer choices or referring back to the passage for additional information if needed.

- A common justification for reading the questions first is that it helps you identify what you are looking for in the passage. While this may ring true in some instances, given the complex reasoning included in many of the passages, this typically has the opposite effect. When you read the question first, it primes you to look only for specific information, often at the expense of overlooking other critical premises and supporting evidence that is necessary to consider in order to get to the correct answer.

- Sometimes the question stems introduce new information that is not in the actual passage. If you are looking specifically for that information, you may be confused when going back to the passage and may end up spending more time trying to re-read and understand each question than if you had simply read the passage first.

Read ALL the Answer Choices

In order to select the best answer choice and avoid enticing but incorrect answers, you should make a habit of reading all of the answer choices before making a selection. As you work through the answer choices, some will immediately stand out as incorrect. You can eliminate those and move on to the next answer choice.

If you find yourself considering an answer choice for more than a few seconds, mark it as a possible answer and move on to the next answer choice. Using your scratch paper, you can jot down your eliminated and possible answer choices using a t-chart:

Eliminated	Possible
A	B
C	D
E	

In the example above, A, C and E were eliminated in the first pass. Once you have eliminated several answer choices and narrowed your options, carefully consider the remaining options in your second pass.

With only 30 minutes for the entire section, you will need to manage your time effectively. Since you cannot simply mark out the eliminated answer choices on the computer-adaptive exam, keeping track of the answers you already eliminated on your scratch paper allows you to focus on the possible answers.

Reading Comprehension and Vocabulary

While you will not be explicitly asked to outline definitions of words or fill in missing words in the Reading Comprehension questions, a strong vocabulary is critical for these questions. The passages require no specific knowledge on the subject matter presented, but they do use complex language that models the level at which a graduate-level student should be able to read and understand.

Study the vocabulary lists in the back of this text along with the root words, prefixes, and suffixes to help build your vocabulary and make better educated guesses about the meaning of a word you have not seen before.

Improve Your Reading Pace

The passages are typically replete with complex vocabulary, and sometimes the facts are buried in a dense web of rhetoric. Luckily, some of the passages are quite straightforward. But dealing with the dense and long passages can greatly impact the amount of time you have for the rest of the section, which of course affects your overall score. Reading at a good pace while also retaining information often presents the largest challenge with Reading Comprehension questions. However, there are ways that you can actively work to improve your reading speed.

One of the most effective ways to improve your pace is to incorporate reading complex material into your study plan. For example, many people find science-related passages daunting even though the subject matter of the passage should be a non-issue. Nonetheless, they struggle to process the unfamiliar terms and grow anxious about retaining the information, often re-reading and losing valuable time. Whether this describes you or not, try to increase your reading speed and your ability to clearly understand a passage by regularly reading material that is unfamiliar to you. Great examples include the abstracts of scientific and social science articles; academic journals; and newspapers and editorials from reputable journalism outlets. All these sources include the types of passages you might see in Reading Comprehension questions.

One of the key misconceptions about reading passages in the Verbal Reasoning section is that when you are finished with the Reading Comprehension passages, you should have an in-depth understanding of what was discussed so that you can answer the questions without referring back to the passage. This is absolutely not the case. You can and should always refer back to the passage to ensure you are selecting the correct answer choice. When reading the passage, prioritize using your scratch paper to annotate the main point of the passage, key transitions, tone, and the general structure of the passage. Understanding these key things will give you the necessary information to navigate the passage for those questions that require a bit more investigation.

Approach the Passages Methodically

Though the lengths of short and long passages can vary significantly, your approach to them should be the same. Your main goals are to **Read**, **Assess**, and **Predict and Answer**.

Read

Read the entire passage and look for the key components discussed above: main point, key transitions, tone, and general organization of the passage before moving on to the various question stems and answer choices. You should commit to reading the entire passage so you do not miss critical information that may be integral to answering the questions. Some strategies suggest you should read only the topic and concluding sentences. This is generally not an effective strategy and will oftentimes cause you to have to go back and re-read the passage again. As a result, you spend more time re-reading than actually answering questions, a situation that can significantly impact your score.

Assess

Once you have read the passage, take a quick second to assess and process. What is the main point? What type of attitude does the author have about whatever is being discussed in the prompt? Are there any weaknesses in the argument? If you have a shorter prompt, not all of these considerations may be relevant. However, every passage **will** have a main point. You should pinpoint that before moving on to the questions.

Predict and Answer

After you have read a particular question stem, take a second to pause and think about what the answer might be. Remember that your answers should be based on the information stated in or inferred from the passage. Predicting your answer can help you avoid tricky incorrect answer choices and save you time when you are eliminating incorrect answers. Once you have evaluated all the answer choices, however, select the answer(s) that best address the question stem.

Chapter Overview

Reading Comprehension questions require you to read the given passages and select the answer choice that best completes the question task. Content of the passages can come from a wide range of subject matters, and there is often more than one question that corresponds to each passage. Each Verbal Reasoning section has 3–5 Reading Comprehension passages with 1–5 accompanying questions. With a total of 9–10 questions, Reading Comprehension accounts for about half of the questions on each of the scored verbal sections.

Components of a Reading Comprehension Question

Passage: The passage will be one to five paragraphs in length with content drawn from a wide range of sources like journals, academic texts, and literature.

Question Stem: The question stem provides you with a specific task based on the passage. There are several question stems that occur frequently on the exam that test different aspects of your critical reading and analytical reasoning skills.

Answer Choices: You will have three to five answer choices for each Reading Comprehension question or be asked to select a specific sentence in the text.

Reading Comprehension Question Tasks

There are seven main types of question tasks that you will be given for Reading Comprehension passages (see pp.70–72). Developing a familiarity with the types of questions you are most likely to see can help you hone both your approach to reading the passage and time management. If you are reading and annotating key points and are familiar with the question tasks, you can use your time effectively and stand a better chance of selecting the correct answer choices.

Reading Comprehension Answer Choices

For Reading Comprehension passages you can expect to see questions that ask you to select one or more answer choices. Some questions will ask you to select specific text within the passage. Becoming familiar with the specifics of your expected answer choices before test-taking day is key to a successful exam. See the in-depth discussion in this chapter (pp.72–73) and use the Practice Exams to give yourself hands-on knowledge of how these answer choices work.

Incorrect Answer Types

Having an understanding of the common types of incorrect answers you may encounter in the Reading Comprehension section can help you avoid falling for many of the tricky answer choices and psychometrics built into the exam. One the most important components of Reading Comprehension questions is the understanding that because you are making inferences from the provided passages, most of your answers must be true based on the passage. Reading Comprehension questions will ask you about the main point, the author's point of view, and inferences you can draw from the passage.

Approaching the Passage

Though the length of short and long passages can vary significantly, your approach to them should be the same. Your main goals are to Read, Assess, and Predict and Answer.

UP NEXT: In the next chapter, we will discuss Text Completion and Sentence Equivalence questions. We will explore the different types of questions as well as strategies to help you select the proper words to complete the sentences.

Reading Comprehension Practice Set

In this chapter we have explored how to read and analyze Reading Comprehension passages, reviewed the types of questions you might encounter, and discussed how to select your answer choice while being careful to avoid common incorrect answer choice types. Now let us put those strategies to the test and get some practice with both short and long Reading Comprehension passages.

Questions 1–2 refer to the following passage.

Obesity is a serious medical condition that affects millions of people across the globe. The condition is characterized by an excess of body fat and a high body mass index (BMI), which is a proportional measurement of a person's height and weight. People with a BMI that reaches a certain threshold are considered obese and can be prone to a variety of health complications as a result of their excess body weight. People diagnosed as obese often are more at-risk for debilitating diseases likes diabetes, heart disease, and cancer.

While there are many causes of obesity, the combination of poor dietary habits and a sedentary lifestyle are often responsible for the onset and progression of the disease. However, active individuals who normally eat a healthy diet can also be obese as a result of genetics, thyroid or other endocrine disorders, medication, or poor lifestyle habits like lack of sleep or alcohol abuse. There are several pharmacological and surgical interventions to help individuals reduce their body weight to a healthy weight. However, experts contend that regardless of the cause of the onset of obesity, the best way to curb the progression of the disease and thwart some of the negative consequences of carrying excessive body weight, is to get active and to make smart dietary choices.

Obesity can be deadly, and healthcare providers throughout the world continue to coach their patients to make smarter choices and live healthier lives. In parts of the world where weight is often conflated with prosperity and wealth, healthcare providers have a harder time convincing patients to make what could be life-saving changes to their diet and exercise regime.

1. What is the main point of the passage?

    (A) To discuss the parameters and warning levels for BMI
    (B) To discuss obesity, its causes, and the long-term impact being overweight has on individuals
    (C) To caution people against surgical interventions for weight-loss

2. The author would most likely agree with which one of the following?

    (A) Lack of exercise is the primary reason people are obese
    (B) There are no effective treatments currently available for obesity
    (C) Even a person who exercises regularly, eats a proper diet, and gets proper sleep may be obese

---

Question 3 refers to the following passage:

Out of all the farm animals, farm goats make the best pets because of their co-dependence on and affection for human connection. Even as they grow old, goats display no interest in branching off and being independent.

3. The writer implies that most farm animals:

    (A) are generally hard to train
    (B) have an affinity for human interaction
    (C) become independent as they age
    (D) are communal only within their own species

Questions 4–6 refer to the following passage:

Cities across the world are essentially blends of smaller cultural environments that lead people to have vastly different experiences. Each city typically contains a broad spectrum of dining establishments along with various art institutions like museums and theatres. Yet with all these blends of dining, art, and night lives, what is the one characteristic that can distinguish a city? History. The undeniably unique history of each city provides rich traditions and a bond between the local people that overshadows any city's mélange of dining and art institutions.

4. Which of the following would the author likely agree is the most important city attraction or characteristic?

    Ⓐ An Italian fine dining restaurant in the European district
    Ⓑ The Museum of Natural History
    Ⓒ Ruins from the Berlin Wall in the center of a local community
    Ⓓ Wrigley Field
    Ⓔ A democratic government

5. Based on its use in the passage, which word most closely defines "mélange"?

    Ⓐ history
    Ⓑ variety
    Ⓒ tradition
    Ⓓ unique
    Ⓔ scarcity

6. Choose the sentence that conveys the author's main point.

Questions 7–9 refer to the following text:

Beyond the great prairies and in the shadow of the Rockies lie the Foothills. For nine hundred miles, the prairies spread themselves out in vast level reaches, and then begin to climb over softly-rounded mounds that ever grow higher and sharper till, here and there, they break into jagged points and at last rest upon the great bases of the mighty mountains. These rounded hills that join the prairies to the mountains form the Foothill Country. They extend for about a hundred miles only, but no other hundred miles of the great West are so full of interest and romance. The natural features of the country combine the beauties of prairie and of mountain scenery. There are valleys so wide that the farther side melts into the horizon, and uplands so vast as to suggest the unbroken prairie.

Nearer the mountains the valleys dip deep and ever deeper till they narrow into canyons through which mountain torrents pour their blue-gray waters from glaciers that lie glistening between the white peaks far away. Here are the great ranges on which feed herds of cattle and horses. Here are the homes of the ranchmen, in whose wild, free, lonely existence there mingles much of the tragedy and comedy, the humor and pathos, that go to make up the romance of life. Among them are to be found the most enterprising, the most daring, of the peoples of the old lands. The broken, the outcast, the disappointed, these too have found their way to the ranches among the Foothills. A country it is whose sunlit hills and shaded valleys reflect themselves in the lives of its people; for nowhere are the contrasts of light and shade more vividly seen than in the homes of the ranchmen of the Albertas.

7. Based on the context, what is the best definition for "pathos"?

    Ⓐ shade
    Ⓑ hunger
    Ⓒ passage
    Ⓓ sadness

8. What two types of landscapes comprise the Foothill Country?

   (A) mountains and coastline
   (B) prairies and mountains
   (C) prairies and foothills
   (D) foothills and valleys

9. Which word best describes the author's feelings about Foothill Country?

   (A) admiration
   (B) indifference
   (C) incredulity
   (D) unhappiness

Reading Comprehension Practice Set Answers

1. **B.**

2. **C.**

3. **C.**

4. **C.**

5. **B.**

6. The undeniably unique history of each city provides rich traditions and a bond between the local people that overshadows any city's mélange of dining and art institutions.

7. **D.**

8. **B.**

9. **A.**

9 | TEXT COMPLETION AND
SENTENCE EQUIVALENCE QUESTIONS

Text Completion: The Basics

Text Completion questions require you to read short passages that have words omitted from them. Your task is to use the context of the passage to correctly identify the missing word or words. For each Text Completion question, there will be 1-3 blanks and you will have 3-6 answer choices from which to select each answer. You can expect to see about 4-6 Text Completion questions per each section of Verbal Reasoning.

A strong vocabulary is essential for the Text Completion questions. It is not enough to study the definition of common words found on the exam. You must also understand how to use them in context and how to use context clues to properly identify the correct word that fits with the rest of the sentence.

Regardless of the number of blanks, each Text Completion question is worth one point, like every other question on the exam. For questions with multiple blanks, you must answer all of them correctly to receive credit for your response. There is no partial credit.

Question Formats

Aside from the number of omitted words, there is not much variation in how Text Completion questions are presented. The questions will be shorter than Reading Comprehension questions, containing a couple of sentences at most.

For each blank, you will have a corresponding column of answer choices. The blanks do not need to be answered in any particular order; you should make your choices in the way that best makes sense to you. For example, if the correct answer to the third blank is immediately obvious to you, selecting the answer choice for that blank first can make it easier to identify the remaining blanks. Some blanks are designed to test vocabulary, while others are more concerned with comprehension. Be sure to spend some time studying the vocabulary and root word lists in the back of this book to help strengthen your vocabulary and ability to surmise the meaning of words that you may not know.

As mentioned above, Text Completions will have 1-3 blanks. You must select all of the correct answers for a question in order for your response to be credited. Let us take a closer look at these question variations.

Text Completion Questions with One Blank

Text Completion questions with one blank will present you with a sentence and 5 answer choices. You are to select the answer choice that best completes the sentence.

> The celebrity designer is known for her outlandish and over-the-top formal wear, but her new line of gowns seems to be more _____ than her previous works.
>
> Ⓐ transparent
> Ⓑ lackluster
> Ⓒ fancy
> Ⓓ succinct
> Ⓔ extravagant

In this one-blank Text Completion question, there is a transition word ("but") that sends the argument in a different direction. So instead of looking for an answer choice that describes something similar to over-the-top and outlandish, you are looking for an opposite answer choice, one that connotes less "wow" factor than the designer's previous work. The logical answer here is B. The line is more *lackluster* compared to her previous works. *Lackluster* is a logical contrast to *outlandish*. When you plug *lackluster* into the sentence, it nestles in perfectly with the transition and sensibly completes the thought.

Text Completion Questions with Two or Three Blanks

Text Completion questions with two or three blanks are similar to their one-blank companions. However, when there is more than one blank, each blank will have its own corresponding set of three answer choices. You are to select an answer choice for each blank. Remember there is no partial credit. You must select the correct answer for each blank in order for your response to be credited.

Lacking any sense of (i)_____, David had no problem (ii)_____ credit for work that was not his own.

Blank (i)	Blank (II)
Ⓐ ethics	Ⓓ providing
Ⓑ urgency	Ⓔ claiming
Ⓒ dishonor	Ⓕ assigning

ANSWER: A, E

Although many new discoveries in quantum physics are often (i)_____ shortly after being accepted as valid, physicists do not shy away from hasty conclusions, (ii)_____ that the (iii)_____ nature of what is considered fact impedes innovation and rapid discoveries.

Blank (i)	Blank (ii)	Blank (iii)
Ⓖ purged	Ⓙ forbidding	Ⓜ hostile
Ⓗ disproved	Ⓚ denying	Ⓝ illusory
Ⓘ heralded	Ⓛ examining	Ⓞ predictable

ANSWER: B, E, H

Approaching the Blanks Strategically

Text Completion questions are rather straightforward: find the missing word or words that best complete the sentence. Instead of just diving into them, however, you still want to be strategic about your approach. Keep these strategies in mind as you work through the Text Completion questions in the Verbal Reasoning section.

Read and Understand

Read the entire sentence before moving on to the answer choices. Do not confuse yourself by oscillating back and forth between the sentence and the answer choices before you actually have an understanding of what is happening in the

sentence. Look for transition words like "but" or "however" that might change the direction of the sentence, or words like "moreover" or "since" that continue the same thought. Even the use of a semicolon can indicate the relationship between the two clauses. Pay close attention to the language of the sentences before considering what the missing word(s) might be.

Predict and Answer

Once you have an understanding of the flow of the sentence, think about what word could feasibly fill the blank and make sense in the sentence. If the questions have more than one blank, consider each blank individually and in an order that makes the most sense to you. If the second blank in a question jumps out as obvious to you early on, you can start there and begin the process of looking for the answer. This may help you complete the other blanks with greater ease. Once you have predicted your answer, scan the answer choices and select the word that best completes the blank. If your question has more than one blank, repeat this process until you have selected an answer for all the blanks.

Re-Read

Once you have an answer selected for each blank, re-read the sentence with your answer choice(s) to make sure it makes sense and flows logically.

Sentence Equivalence: The Basics

Sentence Equivalence questions require you to identify two answer choices from a slate of six that best complete the sentence. When inserted into the sentence, both words will form their own unique sentences but the sentences will be close in meaning. Like the multi-blank Text Completion questions, there is no partial credit for these questions. You must select two answers, and both answers must be correct in order for you to receive credit. Each question is worth one point, the same as every other question on the exam. You can expect to see 4–5 Sentence Equivalence questions per Verbal Reasoning section.

A strong vocabulary is essential for the Sentence Equivalence questions. But it is not enough to study the definition of common words found on the exam. You must understand how to use them in context and how to use context clues to properly identify the correct word that fits with the rest of the sentence.

All Sentence Equivalence questions will look the same. You will always have one sentence, with one blank, followed by six answer choices. You will need to identify the correct two answer choices for the blanks. Both choices, when plugged into the sentence, will communicate a similar thought.

As start-ups continue to proliferate, the success of a business is dependent upon two things: the degree to which it can _____ borrowed money, and its ability to endure uncertainty and fluctuations in the market.

- [A] capitalize
- [B] repudiate
- [C] collect
- [D] leverage
- [E] expend
- [F] reallocate

ANSWER: A, D

It is important to note that just because the answer choice yields two similar sentences, it does not mean the words will be synonyms. Likewise, avoid automatically selecting synonyms from the answer choices just because they are alike. You will often see pairs of words that are similar in meaning in the answer choices that are not the correct answer.

Also keep in mind that even though a word may fit into the sentence, that does not mean that the word is the correct answer choice. You are not looking for two words that make sense; you are looking for two words that both make sense **and** create a sentence that is similar in reasoning.

Approaching the Blanks Strategically

Sentence Equivalence questions are rather straightforward: find the missing words that best complete the sentence. Instead of just diving into them, however, you still want to be strategic about your approach. Keep these strategies in mind as you work through the Sentence Equivalence questions in the Verbal Reasoning section.

Read and Understand

Read the entire sentence before moving on to the answer choices. Do not confuse yourself by oscillating back and forth between the sentence and the answer choices before you actually have an understanding of what is happening in the sentence. Pay close attention to the language of the sentences before considering what the missing words might be.

Predict and Answer

Once you have an understanding of the flow of the sentence, think about what word could feasibly fill the blank and make sense in the sentence. Once you have predicted your answer, scan the answer choices and select the two words that best completes the blank. Remember, just because two answer choices are similar does not mean they fit into the sentence. Make sure the words you choose actually make sense and create two similar sentences.

Re-Read

Once you have your two answers selected for the blank, re-read the sentence with your answer choices to make sure it makes sense and flows logically.

Chapter Overview

Text Completion Questions

Text Completion questions require you to read short passages that have words omitted from them. Your task is to use the context of the passage to correctly identify the missing word or words. A strong vocabulary is essential for the Text Completion questions. It is not enough, however, to study the definition of common words found on the exam. You must understand how to use them in context and how to use context clues to properly identify the correct word that fits with the rest of the sentence.

Quick Facts About Text Completions

- Text Completions will have 1-3 blanks.
- For questions with multiple blanks, you must answer all of them correctly to receive credit for your response. There is no partial credit.

Sentence Equivalence Questions

Sentence Equivalence questions require you to identify two answer choices from a slate of **six** that best complete the sentence. When inserted into the sentence, both words will form their own unique sentences but the sentences will be close in meaning.

Quick Facts About Sentence Equivalence Questions

- Sentence Equivalence questions will always have one blank and two correct answer choices.
- Some answer choices may complete the sentence but still be incorrect. Remember that the sentences created from both chosen words must be similar.
- You must select both correct answers to receive credit for your response. There is no partial credit.

Strategy Overview

Read and Understand

Read the entire sentence before moving on to the answer choices. Do not confuse yourself by oscillating back and forth between the sentence and the answer choices before you actually have an understanding of what is happening in the sentence.

Predict and Answer

Think about what word could feasibly fill the blank and make sense in the sentence. Look for the answer choice(s) that closely match your prediction.

Re-Read

Once you have selected your answer choice(s), plug the word or words back in to the sentence(s) to see if they make sense.

Text Completion and Sentence Equivalence Practice Set

Choose the word that best completes the blank(s).

1. Tony was (i)_____ when he discovered Martin had erased Game of Thrones from the DVR. He (ii)_____ him for almost a week.

Blank (i)	Blank (ii)
Ⓐ pungent	Ⓓ flouted
Ⓑ incensed	Ⓔ eschewed
Ⓒ desperate	Ⓕ upbraided

2. Since losing her prestigious internship after a run-in with the law, Gina avoided family gatherings, afraid that her conservative and religious family would _____ her.

- Ⓐ begrudge
- Ⓑ pervade
- Ⓒ vex
- Ⓓ deride
- Ⓔ embrace

3. Chiang Mai has earned the _____ "Digital Nomad Capital of the World" since so many location-independent computer programming professionals tend to flock there.

- Ⓐ veneration
- Ⓑ repeal
- Ⓒ sobriquet
- Ⓓ syncopation
- Ⓔ misnomer

4. In 2008, The American Geological Society initiated The Living History of Geology Project to chronicle senior members who have made (i)_____ contributions during their career to the (ii)_____ of the discipline and profession of geology. Each esteemed geologist will be interviewed for (iii)_____, and the footage will remain on file at the American Geological Society Headquarters.

Blank (i)	Blank (ii)	Blank (iii)
Ⓐ remarkable	Ⓓ progression	Ⓖ corroboration
Ⓑ belabored	Ⓔ continuation	Ⓗ posterity
Ⓒ ostensible	Ⓕ thwarting	Ⓘ practicality

5. Brand loyalty plays a(n) (i)_____ role in a consumer's purchasing habits. Market research supports the notion that consumers are likely to spend more on a product they grew up using rather than try a generic brand that offers the same (ii)_____ at a lower price point. How much more are shoppers willing to spend for (iii)_____?

Blank (i)	Blank (ii)	Blank (iii)
Ⓐ marginal	Ⓓ quality	Ⓖ familiarity
Ⓑ appreciable	Ⓔ composition	Ⓗ paranoia
Ⓒ speculative	Ⓕ accolades	Ⓘ exposure

Select the two answers choices that when inserted into the sentence create two sentences that are similar in meaning.

6. Kristen was a(n) _____ new employee, eager to take initiative and perform up to standard. Unfortunately, her lack of industry knowledge made it impossible for her to move beyond her probationary period.

    A prudent
    B assiduous
    C enthusiastic
    D sullen
    E punctilious
    F garrulous

7. Everyone agreed that the Valedictorian's speech was profound and _____ in its delivery; it was enjoyed and understood by the audience overall.

    A pernicious
    B pellucid
    C majestic
    D perspicuous
    E regal
    F berated

8. Against her advisors' opinions, Mellie continued to run campaign ads that _____ her competitors' personal shortcomings to the media.

    A expressed
    B expunged
    C divulged
    D propagated
    E elevated
    F ameliorated

9. Despite receiving an outstanding performance review for his work and an impressive raise, Sean still felt _____ about his job security in the unstable economy.

    A confident
    B solid
    C anxious
    D apprehensive
    E suspicious
    F perspicacious

10. Valerie looked absolutely _____ when all of her children surprised her for her 55th birthday.

    A ecstatic
    B pensive
    C ebullient
    D lugubrious
    E morose
    F eclectic

Text Completion and Sentence Equivalence Practice Set Answers

1. **B, F.**
   Tony was *incensed*, which means angry. The second blank is tricky. *Flouted* and *eschewed* both mean avoid, which is a very plausible reaction for Tony. However, *flouted* means to avoid or disregard, usually in terms of a law or convention, and *eschewed* typically means to refrain or abstain from something and is often used in a religious context. Neither of these fit into the sentence. *Upbraided* means to reprimand or scold, which works in this context.

2. **D.**
   To *deride* is to ridicule, which is ostensibly what Gina is trying to avoid.

3. **C.**
   "Digital Nomad Capital of the World" is a nickname of sorts for Chiang Mai. *Sobriquet* means assigned name or title.

4. **A, D, H.**
   You are looking for a positive word that describes the senior members' contributions and explains why they would be honored; *remarkable* covers that base. Since the geologists have made remarkable contributions, it makes sense that those contributions *progressed* the field of study and that their interviews should be available for *posterity*, or for future reference.

5. **B, D, G.**
   For blank one, *appreciable* is measureable, like consumer studies. Blank two equates the *quality* of both name brand and generic products, while blank 3 asks how much *familiarity* means to consumers.

6. **B, E.**
   Kristen was eager and took initiative to meet the job's standards, regardless of her skill level. Both *assiduous* and *punctilious* refer to an attention to detail and working to meet standards.

7. **B, D.**
   The speech was profound and everyone understood it. *Pellucid* and *perspicuous* fit, with both words meaning clearly expressed.

8. **C, D.**
   You are looking for words that suggest Mellie may not have acted with good will towards her opponents. *Propagated* and *divulged* corroborate that she intentionally made her opponents' personal business public.

9. **C, D.**
   Look for the transitions. While Sean performed well and received positive reinforcement in the form of a raise, he still felt the opposite, with "still" indicating a move in the opposite direction. *Anxious* and *apprehensive* both yield sentences that express wariness or stress when plugged into the blank.

10. **A, C.**
    You are looking for a positive word to express the joy Valerie felt when she had the chance to see all of her children. *Ebullient* means high-spirited while *ecstatic* means thrilled or excited.

10 | INTRODUCTION TO
QUANTITATIVE REASONING

Quantitative Reasoning: The Basics

In this section you will be asked to solve mathematical problems drawn from the subject areas of arithmetic, geometry, algebra, and data analysis. This section tests your ability to solve quantitative problems, understand real-world applications of mathematical principles, and interpret statistical data from charts and graphs.

The Quantitative Reasoning sections can appear in any order on the exam following the Analytical Writing section. Your exam will consist of two scored Quantitative Reasoning sections that include the following question types: Quantitative Comparisons, Problem Solving, and Data Interpretation. We will discuss the question types in more detail later.

This section of the book will help you refresh your understanding on tested math concepts, manage your time, understand the question tasks, and deploy various strategies to optimize your Quantitative Reasoning score.

> **Prep Tip:** You can use the on-screen calculator for the Quantitative Section to help you solve expressions. The calculator includes basic functions like addition, subtraction, division, and multiplication. You can also use the calculator to solve square roots.

Why Is This Section Important?

Graduate programs use your performance on the Quantitative Reasoning section to evaluate your ability to solve quantitative problems, interpret data, and apply mathematical principles to a wide range of commonplace situations. Depending on the program to which you are applying, your Quantitative Reasoning scores may be of less concern. Nonetheless, you should try to do your best as your Quantitative Reasoning scores factor into your overall exam score.

In this chapter, we will discuss the format of each question type and provide you with specific strategies for successfully answering the GRE quantitative questions. The Math Primer in the following chapter provides a comprehensive overview of the topics tested in the Quantitative Reasoning section and will help you address gaps in your mathematics knowledge.

Scoring and Computer-Adaptive Testing

The section is scored on a scale of 130–170, in one-point increments. A 170 is the highest possible score. The score reflects your combined Quantitative Reasoning performance; you will not receive a separate score for each verbal section.

When taking the computer exam, you are able to answer questions in each section in any order you wish. You can skip questions or use the built-in system tools to mark a question for review and come back to it later as time permits. As we discussed in the section on computer-adaptive testing, the difficulty of your second section of Quantitative Reasoning is determined by your performance on your first section.

Question Types

Your exam will consist of two scored Quantitative Reasoning sections that consist of three question types. Each question type typically appears at the same frequency across exams. The list below details the question types and the approximate number of questions you are likely to encounter on each of the two Quantitative Reasoning sections.

Quantitative Comparison

Quantitative Comparison questions ask you to compare two quantities in two columns and determine whether one is greater, they are equal, or if there is not enough information to determine the relationship between the two quantities.

Some questions include additional information that is centered above the two columns that concerns one or both of the quantities. These questions may not require that you solve for every value. Instead, you are assessing the relationship between the expressions or quantities in the two columns. There is only one correct answer for each Quantitative Comparison question. Below is an example.

$$\frac{x}{y} = \frac{3}{4}$$

Quantity A	Quantity B
$\frac{2x - y}{y}$	$\frac{x}{x + y}$

Ⓐ Quantity A is greater
Ⓑ Quantity B is greater
Ⓒ The two quantities are equal
Ⓓ The relationship cannot be determined from the information given

In this sample problem, you are given additional information to consider when analyzing the relationship between Column A and B: $\frac{x}{y} = \frac{3}{4}$. This given should be applied to both quantities before you make a comparison. Remember, you are not necessarily looking for a value, but rather an understanding of how the two columns relate. In this case the answer will be A.

Problem Solving

Problem Solving questions are the catch-all questions on the GRE. These questions draw from any of the math content areas and are presented as either word problems, finding the angle of a geometric figure, or pure calculations of algebraic expressions. You will have access to the on-screen calculator to help you with any necessary calculations, though some of the questions will require scratch paper to work out the expression. Unlike the Quantitative Comparison questions, your answer for Problem Solving questions will be a value or expression.

Problem Solving questions have a variety of options when it comes to answer choices and there may be more than one correct response to the question. You will have to select **all** of the correct answer choices in order to receive credit for the problem.

What is the value of the following expression?
$$(2\sqrt{2})(\sqrt{6}) + 2\sqrt{3}$$

Ⓐ 20
Ⓑ $6\sqrt{8}$
Ⓒ $6\sqrt{3}$
Ⓓ $4\sqrt{2} + 2\sqrt{3}$
Ⓔ $12\sqrt{3}$

For this problem, you will need to solve the equation and select the corresponding answer choice. In this case the correct answer is C.

Data Interpretation

Data Interpretation questions are more of an extension of Problem Solving questions than a unique question type. For these questions, you will interpret data from charts, graphs, and other images and use this information to solve for the

99

correct answer. Like Problem Solving questions, these questions have a variety of answer choices and you may be directed to select more than one. Remember, you need to select **all** the correct answers in order to receive credit for the question.

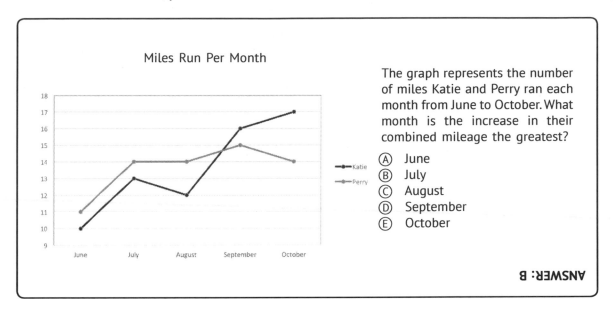

The graph represents the number of miles Katie and Perry ran each month from June to October. What month is the increase in their combined mileage the greatest?

(A) June
(B) July
(C) August
(D) September
(E) October

ANSWER: B

Answer Choice Types

You will encounter a number of different answer choice types on the Quantitative Reasoning section. You can expect to see questions that ask you to select one or multiple answer choices, and questions that will not provide any choices but will instead prompt you to fill in your own. Let us look more closely at these various answer choice types.

Multiple-Choice: Choose One Answer Choice

You will be presented with up to five answer choices, of which only one will be correct. Quantitative Comparison questions will always fall into this category, as do a majority of Problem Solving and Data Interpretation questions. You can usually plug your answer into the problem to check to see if it is correct. However, be careful not to use substitution as your primary strategy as it can cost you a lot of time. Once you have simplified the problem and eliminated incorrect answers, try plugging the remaining answer choices into the problem if you are not sure which answer is correct.

Multiple-Choice: Choose One or More Answer Choices

These questions have one or more answer choices that are correct. You will be told to select or choose all that apply. There is no partial credit for these questions; you must select all, and only, the correct answers in order to receive credit for your response. Assess each answer choice on its own to determine if it answers the question correctly. As with the previous question type, make sure you read all the answer choices.

Numeric Entry Questions

Numeric Entry questions present a unique challenge in that you do not have answer choices to choose from. Instead, you must complete the necessary calculation and key your answer in the designated box. A numeric entry question may look like this:

$$2^2 + 2^8 =$$

[   ]

Once you perform the calculation, you will enter your answer into the box. If your answer is an integer or a decimal, you will enter it into a single box. If your answer is a fraction, you will enter the numerator into the top box and the denominator in the bottom box. Be sure to enter the units in the box after the value, if required. You should enter the entire outcome of the calculation unless instructed not to do so. Let us look at some other considerations related to numeric entry questions:

- Because you do not have answers to choose from, it may not be as easy to realize when you have made a mistake in your calculations. Read the question carefully and ensure you are performing the correct calculations and reporting the answer in the correct units, if applicable.
- Round your number only after you have completed the entire calculation. Often, decimals can be entered as calculated. However, if the question asks you to round your number, make sure you do so, but not until after you arrive at your final answer.
- You have some flexibility in how you record your answer as all equivalent answers are credited responses. For example, if your answer is $\frac{8}{16}$, you do not need to further reduce your answer to $\frac{1}{2}$. Both are correct, so save some time by not further reducing the fraction and move on to the next question.

Using Testing Resources

Taking a math exam on a computer is less than ideal for a number of reasons. Probably the most notable reason is that you cannot actively annotate the problem and solve it by hand. So for the Quantitative Reasoning section, you are going to have to make the best use of the resources you have available to you: your scratch paper and the on-screen calculator.

Scratch Paper

You will be provided scratch paper for the exam that you can use on any (or all) of the sections. It is important to note that you are not permitted to bring your own scratch paper, and you must wait until the exam begins before writing anything on the scratch paper. Use the scratch paper to perform calculations, keep up with eliminated answers, and remind yourself of key formulas. Many of the calculations on the exam can be answered and transferred via the calculator function (below). But scratch paper is a useful tool and can help you avoid costly mistakes.

On-Screen Calculator

The on-screen calculator will only be displayed during the Quantitative Reasoning section. You may find the calculator useful for performing operations with larger numbers or finding square roots. While the calculator is a helpful tool, its functionality is only as useful as your knowledge of the concepts being tested. With its basic functionality, the calculator cannot replace core mathematical knowledge. You will also need a keen sense of when to use this tool: some problems can be solved more easily without the calculator, and some cannot be solved with a calculator at all. Using the calculator should not always be your first choice when attacking problems.

One of the most useful features of the calculator is the Transfer button. Once you have calculated your response, you can simply click the transfer button and your response will be entered into the numeric entry text box.

How to Prepare for the Quantitative Reasoning Section

In the two Quantitative Reasoning sections you will be asked to solve problems, analyze data, and compare quantities to determine their relationship. This assessment area is designed to test your ability to apply mathematical principles

to real-world situations and interpret data from visual presentations. In addition to the strategies we will explore in the subsequent chapters, there are several tools included in this text to help you hone your approach to the Quantitative Reasoning section.

Math Primer

Before launching into the Quantitative Reasoning chapters that discuss Quantitative Comparison and Problem Solving in more detail, you should ensure that you work through the Math Primer in the following chapter, followed by a problem practice set (chapter 12). The Math Primer will review key concepts in arithmetic, algebra, geometry, and data interpretation. In terms of structuring your study plan for this section of the exam, the Math Primer should be your first step, even if you have a strong math background. Many of the concepts tested on the GRE are high-school level, and most test-takers will not have seen the content for some time. It will best situate you to attack the section, avoid costly mistakes, and adopt critical time-saving strategies.

Problem Sets, Sample Tests, and Print/Online Explanations

After each subsequent chapter focused on a particular question type (chapters 13-14), you will have the opportunity to test out your understanding of the concepts with a problem set. Use these problem sets to apply the strategies discussed in the chapter. Review the answer explanations to help you gain a better understanding of how to arrive at the correct answer choices. Also plan to spend a good deal of time with the Practice Exam answer explanations, in both print and online video formats, especially if some of the covered math concepts are proving difficult for you.

Chapter Overview

Your performance on the Quantitative Reasoning section depends heavily on your understanding of the math concepts reviewed in the Math Primer. It is essential to have a solid understanding of the fundamentals of arithmetic, algebra, geometry, and problem solving when approaching this section.

Memorizing formulas is not enough. You must know how to apply various mathematical concepts to real-world situations and interpret data, find missing data points, and solve equations of varying complexities.

The subsequent chapters and the Math Primer will provide you with the tools to bolster your math proficiency, strengthen your problem solving skills, and develop a strategic approach to optimize your test performance. You should also review the extensive math information provided on the ETS website, as well as the detailed video explanations posted on the online version of this book's exams.

FAST FACTS: Section Breakdown

- Two **scored** Quantitative Reasoning sections per exam.
- Can occur in any order after the Analytical Writing section.
- **35 minutes** per section. You can only work on one section at a time.
- **20 questions** per section.
- Depending on your exam, you may have an additional unscored section of Quantitative Reasoning. Remember to approach all sections as if they are scored.

Question Breakdown

Question Type	Question Task	Approx. # of Questions
Quantitative Comparison	Quantitative Comparison questions require you to analyze the relationship between two given quantities and select the answer choice that best describes the relationship. These questions focus more on understanding mathematical relationships and less on actual mathematical calculations.	7–8 questions
Problem Solving	Problem Solving questions require you to use various mathematical formulas and processes to solve for the correct answer to the given problems. These are multiple-choice questions that can have either one or multiple correct answers. These questions may also require you to input your own answer without being provided any answer choices to select from.	9–10 questions
Data Interpretation	Data Interpretation questions require you to interpret data from charts and graphs in order to solve for the correct answer. These questions occur as part of a set where you will use one chart or graph to answer multiple questions.	2–3 questions

UP NEXT: The Math Primer provides an overview of the key concepts related to arithmetic, algebra, geometry, and data interpretation. Understanding the concepts discussed in the next chapter will play a pivotal role in your performance on the Quantitative Reasoning section.

II | MATH PRIMER

Math on the GRE

The Quantitative Reasoning section tests your understanding of basic mathematical principles in four subject areas: Arithmetic, Algebra, Geometry, and Data Interpretation. On the exam, you will need to be able to recognize and understand the basic principles associated with these subject areas and demonstrate your ability to reason mathematically in order to solve problems, identify quantitative relationships, and interpret data from visual displays. Problems are often presented as word problems that discuss math concepts in the context of real-world problems. Other problems require pure math calculations.

The Math Primer is a refresher of concepts you will encounter on the exam. It will cover key definitions, operations, theories, and approaches to problem solving to help you re-familiarize yourself with concepts you may not have seen since high school. The Math Primer is intended as an overview and is not an extensive exploration of the topics you may see on the exam. Not all topics on the exam are covered in the Primer. If you find certain concepts are still a challenge for you after reading through the Primer content and working through the practice problem set (chapter 12), you may benefit from a more in-depth exploration of these concepts using the appropriate texts and resources to help you focus on those particular areas.

Remember that you can use a calculator on the math section. However, the calculator cannot replace your understanding of how to apply mathematical concepts. As you prepare for the Quantitative Reasoning section, pay close attention to the application of the concepts you are studying. How do they apply to real-life situations? Can you recognize a concept in a word problem? Being able to step beyond the basic understanding of the concepts will help you optimize your Quantitative Reasoning score.

Let us explore the major concepts tested in each of the subject areas. Again, this is not a comprehensive list.

Arithmetic

- Real numbers including integers, prime numbers, rational numbers and irrational numbers
- Number sequences
- Factors and multiples
- Fractions and decimals
- Arithmetic operations
- Percentages, ratios, and rates
- Absolute value

Algebra

- Algebraic expressions
- Coordinate planes, slopes, and intercepts
- Functions and relations
- Linear equations
- Quadratic equations
- Inequalities
- Rules of exponents and Roots

Geometry

- Right, isosceles, and other special triangles
- Pythagorean theorem
- Properties and measurements of circles
- Polygons
- Perimeter, area, and volume
- Properties and measurements of three-dimensional figures

Data Interpretation

- Descriptive statistics
- Understanding data from charts and graphs
- Frequency distributions
- Probability
- Permutations
- Means and averages

Mathematical Conventions on the GRE

While math can be straightforward at times, there are many nuances that need to be considered when working with problems to determine how you interpret information. The test-writers have narrowed the focus of the problems in the Quantitative Reasoning section and outlined some standard characteristics true of all the questions on the exam. Here are some of the key conventions:

- All numbers on the exam are real numbers. There will be no questions relating to imaginary numbers.
- Geometric figures are **not** drawn to scale unless otherwise indicated.
- While you should not assume lengths based on how geometric figures look, you should assume that all lines in a figure are straight lines and that the figure lies on a plane unless otherwise indicated.
- Contrary to geometric figures, coordinate planes and numbers lines **are** drawn to scale.
- Graphs on the exam, including histograms, pie charts, and line graphs are drawn to scale and you can make assumptions based on the visual presentation of the data.
- π is assumed to represent the value 3.14.
- For geometry questions, the sum of the measure of the interior angles of a triangle equals 180°.
- For Data Interpretation questions, consider each question separately. No information except what is given in the display of data should be considered from one question to another.

> **Prep Tip:** For the full list of Mathematical Conventions for the Quantitative Reasoning section, visit the ETS website at: https://www.ets.org/s/gre/pdf/gre_math_conventions.pdf.

Arithmetic: The Basics

Arithmetic encompasses the fundamental building blocks of math. It includes basic concepts like the mathematical operations of addition, subtraction, multiplication and division. Almost all the questions you encounter on the exam will require you to apply principles of arithmetic in some capacity. You will need to understand the order of operations, real numbers, ratios, and fractions. The concepts discussed in this section will help you refresh your understanding of basic arithmetic and prepare you to navigate the more difficult exam concepts such as algebraic expressions and geometry.

Math Building Blocks

Before we dive into the specifics of arithmetic and the other concepts tested on the Quantitative Reasoning section of the exam, let us review the fundamental building blocks of math, especially common symbols and types of numbers. These concepts will appear in some form on the exam and a clear understanding of these fundamentals is key to your success in this section.

What's That Sign?

Most people taking the GRE have not studied basic math in quite some time. While some of the basics may have stuck with you, it does not hurt to do a quick check to test your current ability to identify what key symbols and operations on the exam are asking you to do. Below are some of the most common signs used in mathematics; you will encounter these in some capacity on the exam. Some of these will be addressed in more detail in subsequent sections of the Math Primer.

Math Symbol	Common Name	Description
<	Less than	Used to signify that the quantity to the left of the symbol is less than the quantity to the right.

Math Symbol	Common Name	Description
>	Greater than	Used to signify that the quantity to the left of the symbol is greater than the quantity to the right.
≤	Less than or equal to	Used to signify that the quantity to the left of the symbol is less than or equal to the quantity to the right.
≥	Greater than or equal to	Used to signify that the quantity to the left of the symbol is greater than or equal to the quantity to the right.
√	Square root	An irrational number that produces a specified quantity when multiplied by itself.
|x|	Absolute value	Reflects the positive distance of the expressed number from zero.
!	Factorial	The product of the whole numbers from 1 to a given number.
‖	Parallel Lines	Signifies that two lines are parallel to each other and do not intersect at any point.
⊥	Perpendicular Lines	Signifies that two lines separated by this symbol intersect to form a right angle.
π	Pi	The geometric ratio of a circle's circumference to its diameter; the value used on the GRE is 3.14.

Real Numbers

You will encounter only real numbers on the GRE, so you need not concern yourself with studying concepts related to imaginary numbers. Real numbers are numbers found on the number line and are, with the exception of zero, either positive or negative. Several classes of numbers are included in the real numbers category and will appear on the exam. Let's look at the various types of real numbers you can expect to see.

Whole Numbers

Whole numbers are positive counting numbers including zero that contain no decimal or fraction parts.

0, 1, 2, 3, 4, 5...

Integers

Integers are all positive and negative whole numbers, including zero. Integers that occur in a sequence like the ones below are called consecutive integers.

-2, -1, 0, 1, 2, 3...

Rational Numbers

Rational numbers are any numbers, positive or negative, that can be expressed as a ratio of two numbers. All integers and fractions are considered rational numbers.

$$\frac{1}{2} \quad \frac{3}{4} \quad \frac{1}{4}$$

Irrational Numbers

Irrational numbers are all numbers, positive or negative, that are not rational and cannot be expressed as a ratio.

$$\pi, \sqrt{5}$$

Prime Numbers

A prime number is a number that has only two positive divisors, 1 and itself. For example, 5 is a prime number because it is only divisible by 1 and itself. Prime numbers are tested often on the exam.

> It is best to familiarize yourself with the most common prime numbers, which are those that occur below 100:
> 2, 3, 5, 7, 11, 13, 17, 19, 23, 29, 31, 37, 41, 43, 47, 53, 59, 61, 67, 71, 73, 79, 83, 89, & 97

There are some other properties of prime numbers you should know:

- Neither 0 nor 1 is a prime number
- Only positive numbers can be prime numbers
- 2 is the only even prime number

Factors

A factor is an integer that divides into another integer evenly and has no remainder.

> Take the number 24 as an example:
>
> - 1, 2, 3, 4, 6, 8, 12, and 24 are all factors of 24 since they all divide evenly into the number and have no remainder. On the other hand, the number 5 is **not** a factor since when you divide 5 into 24, there **is** a remainder.

Greatest Common Factor

The greatest common factor of two numbers is the largest factor shared by both numbers.

Suppose you wanted to find the greater common factor of 48 and 60. You would first start by identifying the factors for each number:

- Factors of 48: 1, 2, 3, 4, 6, 8, **12**, 16, 24, 48
- Factors of 60: 1, 2, 3, 4, 5, 6, 10, **12**, 15, 20, 30, 60

The greatest common factor of 48 and 60 is 12. The least common factor—in this case, 1—is not likely to be tested on the exam.

Multiples

A multiple is essentially the opposite of a factor. Instead of division, multiples are determined by multiplication. A multiple of a number is the product of the number and any other whole number. Zero is a multiple of every number.

0, 8, 16, 24, 32, 40, 64, and 800 are all multiples of 8 because they are the product of multiplying 8 by another number. When any whole number is multiplied by 8, the product is a multiple.

Least Common Multiple

The least common multiple of two or more whole numbers greater than zero is the smallest whole number divisible by each of the numbers.

If you wanted to find the least common multiple of 5 and 6, for example, you would start by identifying the multiples of each.

- Multiples of 5: 10, 15, 20, 25, 30, 35, 40...
- Multiples of 6: 12, 18, 24, 30, 36, 42...

Since you are looking for the least common multiple, you want to select the smallest number that occurs in both lists. In the case, the least common multiple is 30. The greatest common multiple is not likely to be tested on the exam.

Numeric Operations

The GRE Quantitative Reasoning section includes problems that will require you to add, subtract, multiply, and divide real numbers, including fractions, decimals, roots, and algebraic expressions with non-numeric variables. There are key operations you should keep in mind when dealing with numbers in order to work more efficiently and minimize mistakes.

Laws of Operations

Commutative Property: Addition and multiplication are commutative operations; the order in which they are performed does not impact the answer.

$$a \cdot b = b \cdot a$$
$$a + b = b + a$$

Associative Property: Addition and multiplication are also associative; when written as an expression, they can be regrouped without impacting the final answer.

$$a + (b + c) = (a + b) + c$$
$$(a \cdot b) \cdot c = a \cdot (b \cdot c)$$

Distributive Property: The distributive property outlines how values in an expression should be distributed to the terms being added or subtracted. The distributive property can also be used in division.

$$a(b + c) = ab + ac$$
$$\frac{a + b}{2} = \frac{a}{2} + \frac{b}{2}$$

Order of Operations

The commutative, associative, and distributive properties outline some standard approaches to dealing with addition and multiplication. When other operations are involved, it is important to understand the proper order in which to solve each component of the problem.

The acronym **PEMDAS** outlines the correct order for mathematical operations. Performing operations out of order, specifically those dealing with more than addition and multiplication, will often lead you to the incorrect answer.

Parentheses: Complete anything in **parentheses** first.

Exponents: Next, calculate any **exponents.**

Multiplication/Division: Then attack **multiplication** and **division** elements from left to right.

Addition/Subtraction: Finally, attack **addition** and **subtraction** elements from left to right.

Not all equations will contain all these elements. However, be sure to still follow the order when attacking the elements that are present.

Let us look at an example:

$100 - 4(7 - 4)^3$	First, solve for the values in the parentheses
$100 - 4(3)^3$	Solve $(7 - 4)$ and replace the value in parentheses with 3
$100 - 4(3)^3 = 100 - 4(27)$	Solve the exponent
$100 - 4(27) = 100 - 108$	Multiply and divide
$100 - 108 = -8$	Solve addition and subtraction elements

The final answer is −8. Remember to work equations in the proper order and that multiplication, division, addition, and subtraction should be solved from left to right.

Absolute Value

Absolute value is the distance of a number from zero. The value is always expressed as a positive number. Absolute value is symbolized by a number being enclosed in two vertical bars.

$$|12|$$

The absolute value of a positive number is always just the number itself.

$$|12| = 12$$

The absolute value of a negative number is derived by dropping the negative sign in front of the number.

$$|-14| = 14$$

You may see absolute value appear in a number of ways on the exam, including as expressions where you must solve for a value. Here's an example:

$4 - 2 + |5 - 7| =$

$\quad\quad |5 - 7| = |-2| = 2$ Solve what is in the brackets

$\quad\quad 4 - 2 + 2 = 4$ Plug in the value to the rest of the expression and solve

Fractions

Now, let us look at a subset of rational numbers, namely fractions and ratios.

There is no shortage of fractions on the GRE. You will see them appear in word problems, as part of algebraic expressions, and in pure problem solving questions. The two main components of a fraction are the numerator and the denominator.

$$\frac{a}{b} \quad \begin{matrix} \longrightarrow \text{ numerator} \\ \longrightarrow \text{ denominator} \end{matrix}$$

You will need to know how to perform various operations with fractions, including addition, subtraction, multiplication, division, simplifying, and converting them to mixed numbers. Let us look at some of the key facts about fractions and operations related to them.

Reciprocals

The reciprocal of a fraction is found simply by reversing the numerator and the denominator. For example, the reciprocal of $\frac{2}{3}$ is $\frac{3}{2}$. The product of any fraction and its reciprocal is always 1. All whole numbers except zero have a reciprocal where the reciprocal of a is $\frac{1}{a}$.

Equivalent Fractions

Since fractions represent the part of a given whole, increasing the whole and the part by the same amount does not change the relationship. Consider the fraction $\frac{1}{2}$. If you multiplied the numerator and denominator by 3, for example, you would end up with the equivalent fraction $\frac{3}{6}$.

Reducing Fractions

There are a number of instances in which you will need to reduce fractions on the exam; in fact, whenever you are able to do so, you should. When you reduce a fraction, you simply express the fraction in its lowest terms.

Let us suppose you have the fraction $\frac{40}{80}$. To reduce the fraction, identify the greatest common factor shared by the numerator and denominator. In this case, 40 and 80 share several factors:

> Factors of 40: 1, 2, 4, 5, 8, 10, 20, **40**
> Factors of 80: 1, 2, 4, 5, 8, 10, 20, **40**

The greatest common factor of the numerator and the denominator is **40**. To reduce the fraction, determine how many times the greatest common factor divides into both the numerator and the denominator.

> Numerator: $\frac{40}{40} = 1$ Denominator: $\frac{80}{40} = 2$ Reduced fraction: $\frac{40}{80} = \frac{1}{2}$

Mixed Numbers

A mixed number is a fraction that is preceded by an integer. For example: $2\frac{3}{7}$.

It is often not possible to work with mixed numbers and perform operations like addition and subtraction. You must instead convert a mixed fraction into a standard fraction having just a numerator and a denominator. Converting a fraction is rather straightforward. First, you multiply the denominator and the integer, then add the product to the numerator. The denominator from the mixed fraction will remain the same.

$$2\frac{3}{7} = \frac{7 \cdot 2 + 3}{7} = \frac{17}{7}$$

Adding and Subtracting Fractions

Adding and subtracting fractions is a straightforward operation when the fractions have the same denominator. In these cases, you simply add or subtract the numerators; the denominator remains the same.

> *Examples:* $\frac{2}{4} - \frac{1}{4} = \frac{1}{4}$ $\frac{8}{13} + \frac{23}{13} = \frac{31}{13}$

Adding and subtracting fractions that do not have the same denominator involves a bit more calculation. The most efficient way to approach adding and subtracting fractions is cross-multiplying. Let us take $\frac{11}{21} + \frac{4}{11}$ as an example.

First, multiply the denominator of the second fraction by the numerator of the first fraction:

$$\frac{11}{21} \quad \frac{4}{11}$$
$$11 \cdot 11 = 121$$

Then, multiply the denominator of the first fraction by the numerator of the second fraction:

$$\frac{11}{12} \quad \frac{4}{11}$$
$$12 \cdot 4 = 48$$

The sum of these two operations is your new **numerator**: 48 + 121 = **169**. You are not done yet, however: to find your new denominator, multiply both denominators:

$$\frac{11}{12} + \frac{4}{11} = \frac{11(11) + 4(12)}{12(11)} = \frac{169}{132} \quad \text{The sum of the fractions}$$

The process is the same for subtracting fractions, except that instead of adding the products of the cross-multiplication to get the new numerator, you will subtract.

Multiplying Fractions

When multiplying fractions, the process is the same regardless of whether or not the denominators are the same.

$$\frac{8}{11} \cdot \frac{7}{13} = \frac{8 \cdot 7}{11 \cdot 13} = \frac{56}{143}$$

Dividing Fractions

Dividing fractions is similar to the process of multiplying fractions since multiplication and division are inverse operations. To divide fractions, multiply the first fraction by the reciprocal or inverse of the second fraction.

$$\frac{1}{5} \div \frac{3}{7} = \frac{1}{5} \cdot \frac{7}{3} = \frac{7}{15}$$

Ratios

Ratios are often written as fractions and compare two quantities. Ratios, like fractions, deal with parts of the whole, but also express the relationship between two quantities that may not be part of the same whole.

Ratios can be written as fractions or using the common notation $x : y$. For example, if a word problem tells you that the ratio of girls to boys in the class is four boys for every three girls, you can write that as: $\frac{4}{3}$ or $4 : 3$.

If a question asks you what the ratio of girls to boys is, whatever follows the term *of* is the numerator and whatever follows *to* is the denominator.

Ratios often appear on the exam in word problems. Be careful and make sure you understand what ratio the question is asking you to examine. Let us look at a few examples:

> Nathan has 7 sodas and 4 bottles of water in his cooler. What is the ratio of sodas to bottles of water in the cooler?

Since you are looking for the ratio of sodas to bottles of water, your ratio would look like this:

$\frac{soda}{bottles\ of\ water}$ **or** sodas : bottles of water

$\frac{7}{4}$ or $7:4$ Once we know what our ratio looks like, we plug in the numbers.

$7:4:2$ Ratios are not always expressed with just two variables. Suppose Nathan has 7 sodas, 4 bottles of water, and 2 juice boxes. To express the ratio of the drinks in the cooler, add the juice boxes to the original ratio.

This is a fixed ratio, meaning that each portion of the ratio directly corresponds to a particular item in the cooler. So, if you reordered the ratio so that it read $4:7:2$, you no longer have the ratio of sodas to bottled waters to juice boxes. Instead, you had the ratio of bottled waters to sodas to juice boxes.

> Tori's soccer team loses 10 games out of every 30 games that it plays. What is the ratio of Tori's soccer team's wins to losses?

$\frac{wins}{losses}$ or wins : losses   You are looking for the ratio of wins to losses.

Be careful not to assume the ratio of wins to losses is $10:30$. While that is the order the parts are listed in the problem, the order does not correspond to the question. Further, the question does not explicitly tell you the number of wins. 30 is the number of games played, so we need to calculate the number of wins before we can determine the ratio.

$30 - 10 = 20$ Subtract the number of losses from the total number of games

$\frac{wins}{losses} = \frac{20}{10} = \frac{2}{1} = 2:1$ Insert the number of wins into your ratio formula

Proportions

Proportions are an extension of ratios. Proportions are equations that set two ratios equal to one another and are helpful to determine ratios when quantities in a specific ratio relationship increase or decrease.

> If Nathan has 7 sodas and 4 bottles of water, proportions tell us that if Nathan has 14 sodas, he would have 8 bottles of water. This proportion can be expressed as:
>
> $$\frac{14}{8} = \frac{7}{4}$$

Decimals

A decimal, like a fraction, expresses a part of a whole. Decimals are tested often on the GRE and it is important to understand the fundamentals of a decimal, including how the specific digits of the decimal are described. Take the decimal 123.456, for example. Each digit has its own mathematical label:

1 2 3 . 4 5 6

1: Hundreds   3: Ones   5: Hundredths

2: Tens   4: Tenths   6: Thousandths

Fractions to Decimals

You may occasionally need to change either the expressions in the problem or your answer from fractions to decimals or decimals to factions. Remember that unless otherwise specified, a decimal or fraction that are equivalent are acceptable for numeric entry questions.

> To change a fraction to a decimal, simply divide the denominator into the numerator.
> $$\frac{7}{20} = 7 \div 20 = 0.35$$

Decimals to Fractions

Suppose you have the decimal 54.67. To convert a decimal to a fraction, first remove the decimal point and make the resulting whole number your numerator and, for right now, make 1 your denominator:

$$54.67 = \frac{5467}{1}$$

Then, count the number of digits after the decimal point. In this case, .67 follows the decimal point. So, two digits follow the decimal point. Place a 0 after the 1 in the denominator for each digit that occurs after the decimal point in order to determine the fractional equivalent to your decimal.

$$54.67 = \frac{5467}{100}$$

In order to verify that you have the correct fraction, simply divide the denominator into the numerator--you will end up right back at 54.67.

Percentages

Percentages, like fractions and decimals, represent a portion of the whole and are heavily tested on the exam in a number of ways. Percentages are based on the whole of 100. 20% of something is essentially 20 parts of 100. Percentages can be written a number of different ways. For example, we can write 20% as follows:

$$20\% \text{ or } \frac{20}{100} \text{ or } .20$$

On the exam, you may be asked to calculate what percentage an integer is of another integer. For example, a problem solving question may ask you: *5 is what percentage of 20?*

$5 = ?\%(20)$	Write the problem as an equation
$5 = \frac{x}{100}(20)$	Since percentages are always based on 100, you can add more information to the equation to help you solve and substitute an unknown variable for the value we are missing.
$5 = \frac{20x}{100} = \frac{2x}{10} = \frac{x}{5}$	Reduce the fraction
$5 = \frac{x}{5}$	Cross-multiply
$25 = x$	5 is **25**% of 20

You solved the problem and got the correct answer, but it took a lot of steps, which translates to a lot of time. There are some common formulas you can use on the exam to help approach percentage problems of various types. Let us look at these in more detail.

Part of the Whole Formula

Problems involving percentages on the exam will normally, like the previous problem, give you two of the values and ask you to calculate the third. In the previous example, you had 5, the part, and 20, the whole. You were looking for the percentage. You can solve the problem with fewer steps by using a formula:

Formula: $percent = \frac{part}{whole}$

$percent = \frac{5}{20} = .25 \ or \ 25\%$

Let us look at a few more examples:

Example 1:
What is 20% of 42?

$percent \cdot whole = part$ Percentage Formula

$.20 \cdot 42 = 8.4\%$ Solve

Example 2:
12 is 40% of what number?

$\frac{part}{percent} = whole$ Percentage Formula

$\frac{12}{.40} = 30$ Solve

Percent Increase and Decrease

The GRE commonly tests the percent of increase and decrease. While word problems are most common, questions are presented in a number of different ways and may ask you to determine, for example, a new price based on a price increase of a certain percentage, or the decreased percentage of revenue for one fiscal year compared to a previous year. Like the previous problems, you will be given some pieces of information and asked to find the missing element. Let us look at some common formulas to help you calculate percentage increase and decrease.

Example:
The staff at Salsa Kitchen was reduced from 40 to 29 employees. What is the percent decrease in staff?

To calculate the percentage decrease, use the following formula:

$percentage \ decrease = \frac{amount \ of \ decrease}{original \ whole} \cdot 100$

In order to calculate the *amount of decrease*, you must find the difference of the number of current employees and the number of original employees. In this case, Salsa Kitchen started with 40 employees and now has 29, for a difference of 11.

$percentage \ decrease = \frac{11}{40} \cdot 100$

$percentage \ decrease = .275 \cdot 100 = \textbf{27.5\%}.$

Example:
Ansley works in a bookstore for $12.00 per hour. If her pay is increased to $14.00, then what is her percent increase in pay?

To calculate percentage increase, use this formula:

$$percentage\ increase = \frac{amount\ of\ increase}{original\ whole}$$

In order to calculate the *amount of increase*, you must find the difference of Ansley's current hourly pay and her previous hourly pay. In this case, Ansley started off earning $12.00 an hour before her pay increased to $14.00 an hour. The amount of increase is $2.00.

percentage increase = $\frac{2}{12} \cdot 100$

percentage increase = $\frac{1}{6} \cdot 100 =$ **16.66%**

Combined Percentages

Sometimes questions on the exam will ask you to calculate more than one percentage. You may also be asked to find the percentage of a percentage. It is important to understand that you cannot compare percentages that are not part of the same whole. This is a common trap on the exam and you can count on an answer choice that matches the outcome of this mistake.

Example:
During the semi-annual sale, dresses were reduced by 20%. Then, the price was further reduced by 10%. If a dress was originally $200, what is the final price of the dress?

The dress was first reduced by 20% then by 10%. While it may be tempting to calculate the new final price by reducing the original price of $200 by 30%, that is not correct.

.20 · $200 = $40.00	First, calculate the first price reduction of 20%
$200.00 − $40.00 = $160.00	Subtract $40.00 from the original price

If the price of dress was reduced by 20%, there would be a $40.00 price difference from the original price. So, after the first reduction, the price of the dress would be $160.00.

.10 · $160 = $16.00	Calculate the second price reduction
$160.00 − $16.00 = $144.00	Reduce the dress by the new discount

If you had erroneously decreased the original price of $200 by 30%, you would have arrived at $140, which is incorrect.

Algebra: The Basics

Algebra involves many of the same concepts as arithmetic like absolute value, fractions, and numerical operations. Algebra often uses variables, which are letters used to represent an unknown quantity. Variables are incorporated into expressions and you will often be asked to solve equations to find their value. The concepts discussed in this chapter present themselves in various mathematical capacities on the exam. You will need to understand concepts like factoring, polynomials, algebraic expressions, exponents, roots, and inequalities. Let us start by reviewing some important vocabulary associated with algebra.

Essential Algebra Vocabulary

Coefficient: A multiplier in front of a variable that indicates how many of the variable there are. For example, for the term 5x, 5 is the coefficient. Whenever a term occurs without a coefficient in front of it, like *x*, the coefficient is 1.

Constant: A numerical quantity that does not change.

Equation: Equations are the building blocks of algebra. An equation is two expressions linked together with an equal sign where values of each expression can be solved or simplified. $2x + 1 = x - 10$ is an example of an equation.

Expression: An expression is made up of a single or multiple algebraic term(s), linked together by operations. $5x - 6$, $6xy$, and $x - 1$ are all expressions.

Term: A component of an algebraic equation that either represents the product or quotient of a constant and variable, or a specific value separated by arithmetic operations. In the expression $4x + 3b - 2$, $4x$, $3b$, and 2 are all terms.

Variable: A letter used to represent an unknown value. Any letter may be used for variables and you many not always need to or be able to find the specific value associated with the variable. In many cases on the exam, however, you will solve to find the value of variables.

Simplifying Algebraic Expressions

Before you dive into solving more complicated equations, you need to understand a few simplification tools that allow you to change algebraic expressions into simpler but equivalent forms.

Algebraic Laws of Operations

Like with arithmetic, algebra also has three basic properties for dealing with equations: commutative, additive, and distributive.

Commutative Property: Addition and multiplication are commutative operations; the order in which they are performed does not impact the answer. The commutative property does not hold for subtraction.

$$2a \cdot 3b = 3b \cdot 2a$$
$$2a + 3b = 3b + 2a$$

Associative Property: Addition and multiplication are also associative; when written as an expression, they can be regrouped, and like terms can be combined without impacting the final answer.

Addition:

$$= 2a - 3a + 5b + 2b$$
$$= (2a - 3a) + (5b + 2b)$$
$$= -a + 7b$$

Multiplication:

$$= (6a \cdot 5b) \cdot 4b$$
$$= 6a(5b \cdot 4b)$$
$$= 6a(20b^2)$$
$$= 120ab^2$$

Distributive Property: The distributive property outlines how values in an expression should be distributed when performing more than one operation (addition, subtraction, multiplication).

$$3a(4b - 6c) = (3a \cdot 4b) - (3a \cdot 6c)$$
$$= 12ab - 18ac$$

The associative, commutative, and distributive properties apply to many of the problems you will see on the exam. In some expressions and equations, you may need to combine the operations of the properties to arrive at your answer.

Combining Like Terms

Combining like terms is an effective approach to simplifying and solving algebraic expressions. As you work through the expression, using the appropriate law(s) of operation, look for terms that have the same characteristics and combine them into a single term. Any term that shares the same variable in the same form can be combined.

$x^3 + x^2 + 2x + 3x - 4$	In this case, $2x$ and $3x$ are like terms and can be combined.
$x^3 + x^2 + 5x - 4$	Notice that x^3 and x^2 cannot be combined. While they share the same base, the exponent x is different.

Substitution

Substitution is also another effective way to solve algebraic expressions or to express them in terms of other variables. Let us look at a sample question:

> Evaluate $4x^2 - 8x$ when $x = 3$.

Here, you would substitute the value 3 for every x in the expression. Remember the order of operations; solve the parentheses and exponents first:

$$4(3)^2 - 8(3) =$$
$$4(9) - 24 = 36 - 24$$
$$= 12$$

Substitution may sometimes require you to replace non-mathematical symbols with values or operations. For example, you may see a question that uses a non-mathematical symbol instead of an operation sign. In this case, the question will always outline what the symbol represents.

> Suppose $x \blacksquare \dfrac{8 - x}{x^2}$ where $x > 0$. Evaluate $3 \blacksquare$.

While it may appear confusing at first, this is simply a substitution question.

$\dfrac{8 - x}{x^2}$	x times $\blacksquare$ is equal to this expression
$3 \blacksquare = \dfrac{8 - 3}{3^2} = \dfrac{5}{9}$	$3 \blacksquare$ tells you that 3 is the value of x. You will need to substitute the value 3 wherever you see an x, then solve.

Factoring and Polynomials

Factoring is another approach to simplifying algebraic expressions and is essentially the opposite of distribution, though they are commonly used together. Factoring allows you to evaluate complex expressions by breaking it into simpler expressions, taking into consideration monomials, polynomials, binomials, and trinomials.

Monomials: A single term expression. For example, $3x$ or $4y$.

Polynomials: An expression with more than one term. For example, $3x^2 + 2y + 3$.

Binomials: A polynomial expression with exactly two terms. For example, $4x + 6$.

Trinomials: A polynomial expression with exactly three terms. For example, $4y^2 + 3x - 2$.

When there is a monomial factor common to all the terms in the polynomial expression, it can be factored out to create simpler expressions. Suppose you have the following expression:

$4x + 8xy$

$4x(1 + 2y)$ $\qquad$ $4x$ is the common factor and can be used to simplify the expression

Common Polynomial Equations

There are common polynomials that you may encounter on the exam. Knowing how to recognize and factor these can save you time on exam day.

The difference of squares can be factored out into the product of two simpler expressions.

$$a^2 - b^2 = (a - b)(a + b)$$

Some polynomials can be factored into two matching binomials.

$$a^2 - 2ab + b^2 = (a - b)(a - b)$$

Some polynomials are trinomials that are perfect squares.

$$a^2 + 2b^2 + b^2 = (a + b)^2$$

Since factoring is the opposite of distribution, these equations are all commutative.

Roots and Exponents

Exponents

You may have noticed that polynomials often involve exponents. While this is not always the case, exponents are an important component of algebra and have their own set of rules you should be familiar with going into the exam. An

exponent tells you how many times to multiply a number by itself to find a particular value. If we have the exponent 3^2, the number 3 is called the base while the number 2 is referred to as the exponent or power.

To solve an exponent, multiply the base by itself the number of times expressed by the exponent. Take 5^3, for example. If you were to rewrite the expression without exponents and solve, it would look like this:

$5 \cdot 5 \cdot 5 = 125$

Any base with an exponent of 2 is commonly referred to as *squared* and any base with an exponent of 3 is referred to as *cubed*. It is helpful to be familiar with some of the common exponents you may see on the exam. The following chart outlines common squares and cubes that commonly appear in arithmetic and algebra problems.

Common Squares	Common Cubes
$1^2 = 1$	$1^3 = 1$
$2^2 = 4$	$2^3 = 8$
$3^2 = 9$	$3^3 = 27$
$4^2 = 16$	$4^3 = 64$
$5^2 = 25$	$5^3 = 125$
$6^2 = 36$	$6^3 = 216$
$7^2 = 49$	$7^3 = 343$
$8^2 = 64$	$8^3 = 512$
$9^2 = 81$	$9^3 = 729$
$10^2 = 100$	$10^3 = 1000$

Rules of Exponents

Working with exponents is pretty straightforward when you only have a base and a positive exponent like 3^2. But you will see exponents on the exam that include negative numbers and involve mathematical operations like multiplication and division. The following chart is a helpful tool to familiarize yourself with the rules of exponents and how to deal with various presentations of exponents on the exam.

Exponent Rule	Example
$x^0 = 1$	Any nonzero number to the zero power is equal to 1. Note that 0^0 has no defined value. *Example:* $5^0 = 1$
$x^1 = x$	Any nonzero number raised to the power of 1 is equal to the number itself. *Example:* $6^1 = 6$
$(x^a)(x^b) = x^{a+b}$	When you multiply exponents with the same base, add the exponents to calculate the value of the expression. *Example:* $(4^2)(4^3) = 4^{2+3} = 4^5 = 1024$

Exponent Rule	Example
$\dfrac{x^a}{x^b} = x^{a-b}$	When you divide exponents with the same base, subtract the exponents to calculate the value of the expression. *Example:* $\dfrac{4^3}{4^2} = 4^{3-2} = 4^1 = 4$
$(xy)^a = (x^a)(y^a)$	The product of two bases raised to a power can be simplified and solved by raising each number in the expressions to the same power. *Example:* $(4^2)(2^2) = 8^2 = 64$
$(x/y)^a = \dfrac{x^a}{y^a}$	The quotient of two bases raised to a power can be simplified and solved raising each number in the expressions to the same power. *Example:* $(3/4)3 = \dfrac{3^3}{4^3} = \dfrac{9}{64}$
$x^{-a} = \dfrac{1}{x^a}$	Any nonzero number raised to a negative power is equivalent to its reciprocal raised to a positive power. *Example:* $3^{-2} = \dfrac{1}{3^2} = \dfrac{1}{9}$
$(x^a)^b = x^{ab}$	When a power is raised to another power, multiply the exponents. *Example:* $(3^2)^3 = 3^{2\cdot3} = 3^6 = 729$

Exponents in Expressions and Equations

The exponent rules cover the basics of dealing with exponents that primarily involve multiplication. It is important to note that it is not possible to add and subtract exponents in an expression if they do not have the same base and the same exponent. Consider the following expression:

$$2^9 + 2^7$$

This expression is in its simplest form. You cannot add the terms to get a new expression of 2^{16}. Each part of the expression should be solved separately to arrive at your answer: $2^9 = 512$ and $2^7 = 128$. When you add the two together, you get 640. When you calculate 2^{16} you get 65,536. That's a vast difference in answers!

Exponents in these cases **must** be computed separately. The same goes for subtraction. However, when working with terms that share the same base and have the same exponents, you can add and subtract to simply the expression. Suppose you have the algebraic expression $3x^4 + 6x^4$. Here your base and exponent, x and 4, respectively, are the same. You can add the two terms together, keeping the base and exponents intact. Your new expression will be $9x^4$.

You may or may not have the information needed to fully solve the expression, but you can put it in its simplest terms.

Negative Numbers and Exponents

There is another possible situation involving exponents to keep in mind when a negative number is raised to a positive power.

When you raise a negative number to a positive power, the same rules apply for multiplying negative and positive numbers together. The product of a negative and positive number is a negative number, while the product of two negative numbers is a positive number. How does that relate to exponents? Since an exponent represents the number of times you multiply a number by itself, when you have a negative number raised to an exponent, whether it is an odd or even exponent will impact whether your final answer is positive or negative.

> $-4^2 = (-4)(-4)$
>
> In this case, the value of the expression $(-4)(-4)$ is 16. However, the value of -4^3 is calculated $(-4)(-4)(-4)$, which is -64.

When you raise a negative number to an even exponent, the result will be a positive number. When you raise a negative number to an odd exponent, the result will be a negative number.

Roots

Exponents are closely linked to roots, another mathematical concept that deals with the number of times a number goes into another number. Like exponents, roots appear on the exam in various forms, and an understanding of the basic principles of roots will help you simplify expressions and solve equations.

Roots are the inverse function of exponents. The roots you will encounter on the exam are generally confined to square roots and cube roots. You will need to either solve or simplify them. A root is symbolized by a figure that looks like a check mark with a trailing bar which extends over the number whose root is being taken: $\sqrt{4}$.

The above example is the standard notation for a square root. In this case, the expression is translated as "the square root of 4." To solve, you are looking for a number that, when squared equals 4. If you look back at the common exponents table you will find that $2^2 = 4$. So the square root of 4 is 2.

You may sometimes see the root symbol with an exponent in front of it: $\sqrt[3]{27}$.

In this case, you must take the *cubed* root of 27. You need to identify the number that when cubed, equals 27. Again, if you refer back to the chart of common squares and cubes, you will see that $3^3 = 27$. So the cubed root of 27 is 3.

The GRE will only ask you to find the square root of positive numbers. However, the square root may be negative or positive, because any real number squared will always yield a positive number. If you are comparing quantities, for example, and have the equation: $\sqrt{100} = x$, it is easy to assume $x = 10$. Yet x could also be -10, and must be considered.

Simplifying Roots

You cannot add or subtract roots that appear in equations or expressions. You can, however, multiply or divide them in order to solve or simplify. In some cases, you may be able to solve for the value regardless of the operation being performed. For example:

$$\sqrt{4} + \sqrt{16}$$

Here, you can take the root of each of the terms separately, so 2 and 4, then find the sum, 6. You are not adding the roots; instead, you are adding values of the solved roots. Solving for $\sqrt{20}$ would be incorrect.

You can multiply the same roots in a given expression. You cannot, however, multiply a square root by a cubed root. Consider this example:

$$\sqrt{2} \cdot \sqrt{8} \cdot \sqrt[3]{27}$$

$$\sqrt{16} \cdot \sqrt[3]{27} \qquad \text{Simplify}$$

$$\sqrt{16} = \pm 4 \quad \sqrt[3]{27} = 3 \qquad \text{Solve for roots}$$

$$4 \cdot 3 = 12 \text{ OR } -4 \cdot 3 = -12$$

You can also divide roots of the same type. Here, you can complete the division as you would without the roots to simplify the expression. Then, solve the new simplified root to determine your answer.

$$\frac{\sqrt{16}}{\sqrt{4}} = \sqrt{\frac{16}{4}} = \sqrt{4} = \pm 2$$

Using these general principles, you can also reduce numbers under the root sign to create smaller but equivalent expressions. You can simplify the original root and create a new expression that includes simpler terms and solve:

$$\sqrt{81} = \sqrt{9} \cdot \sqrt{9} = \pm 3 \cdot \pm 3 = \pm 9$$

Fractional Exponents

You may have a number raised to a fractional exponent. To simplify and solve, convert the exponent to a root.

$$4^{\frac{1}{2}} = \sqrt{4^1} = \pm 2$$

In these instances, the denominator tells you the type of root, while the numerator tells you what power to raise the base number or variable.

Solving Algebraic Equations

Equations are algebraic functions that set two expressions equal to each other. Equations consist of numbers, operations, variables, or non-mathematical symbols. Your goal is usually to isolate the variables and solve or simplify as much as possible.

Since equations set two expressions equal to each other, when you manipulate the equation, you must ensure that you perform all operations to **both** sides of the equation. This is the most fundamental principle of working with algebraic equations.

Equations can have any number of variables. On the exam, you will see equations with one variable, on up to four or five unique variables. Equations that do not contain any exponents are the most common on the exam and are referred to as **linear equations**.

$x + 20 = 45$	The equation is telling you that the sum of x and 20 is equal to 45.
$x + 20 - 20 = 45 - 20$	You want to isolate x in order to solve for its value. Subtract 20 from each side of the equation. This keeps x positive and isolates it at the same time.
$x = 25$	

Equations with one variable on one side tend to be easier to solve than those with multiple variables or variables on both sides of the equation. Naturally, the latter requires more manipulation and computation. In a time crunch, seeking out one-variable equations may help you get to more questions in the time you have remaining.

Let us look at an equation with the same variable on both sides:

$5x - 7 = 3x + 10$	To solve for x, you still need to isolate the variable. Solve to get all the terms with the variable on one side of the equation. First, subtract $3x$ from both sides.
$5x - 3x - 7 = 10$	Next, finish isolating the variables by adding 7 to both sides. When you add 7 to the left side of the equation, it cancels out the -7 already there.
$5x - 3x = 17$	Calculate
$2x = 17$	Divide by 2
$x = 8.5$	

To make sure you have the right answer, you can plug the value you have for x into the original equation.

$$5(8.5) - 7 = 3(8.5) + 10$$
$$42.5 - 7 = 25.5 + 10$$
$$35.5 = 35.5$$

Absolute Value Equations

Solving equations with absolute value expressions involves a little more work than equations that do not. Remember that the absolute value of a number is the positive distance from zero to that number on a number line. When you take absolute value of algebraic equations, you will have two answers: one where the expression between the absolute value brackets is positive and one where the expression in the absolute value brackets is negative. Here's an example:

If $|x + 3| = 10$, then $x = ?$

Just like you would in any other equation, you want to isolate the variable. You can worry about the implications of the absolute value later. In fact, write the equation out, without the absolute value notation:

$$x + 3 = 10$$
$$x = 10 - 3 = 7$$

You have solved for x, but you are not done yet. Since the expression on the left side asks you to take the absolute value of the expression, and absolute value is always expressed as a positive number, you need to consider that instead of 10, the expression can also yield an answer of −10. To do so, adjust the right side of the equation to −10 and solve.

$$x + 3 = -10$$
$$x = -10 - 3 = -13$$

You can plug your answers back in to the original equations to see if they are correct. Both these values are correct. It is important to consider both possibilities when dealing with absolute value although the question may not specifically prompt you to so.

Variables in the Denominator

When variables are in the denominator, they warrant special attention. You still want to isolate the variable and solve or simplify. Consider this example:

$$9 = \frac{1}{x + 3} + 5$$

$$4 = \frac{1}{x + 3}$$ Subtract 5 from both sides to try to isolate the variable

$$4(x + 3) = (x + 3) \cdot \frac{1}{(x + 3)}$$ Multiply each side by the expression in the denominator

$$4(x + 3) = 1$$ The expression $x + 3$ on the right side cancels out

$$x + 3 = \frac{1}{4}$$ You could distribute the 4, but you are trying to isolate the variable. Divide each side by 4 to further isolate the variable.

$$x = \frac{1}{4} - 3 = \frac{1}{4} - \frac{12}{4}$$ Subtract 3 from both sides to solve for x by turning the integer into a fraction with the same denominator

$$= -\frac{11}{4} = -2.75 = -2\frac{3}{4}$$

Equations with More than One Variable

Of course, the test creators won't let you slide with solving for just one variable. Sometimes you will see equations with two variables. As with one variable expressions, your goal is to either solve or simplify. You can do so using many of the methods previously discussed. Equations with more than one variable, as you might imagine, can be more challenging than their one variable counterparts, and often require more steps to arrive at the answer. Usually, you are also given two separate equations to help you arrive at the answer.

Example:
Solve for x and y if $2x + 5y = 7$ and $x + 4y = 2$

$x + 4y = 2$	Solve for one of the variables in terms of the other variable
$x = 2 - 4y$	
$2(2 - 4y) + 5y = 7$	Now plug in the expression for x into the first equation and solve for y
$4 - 8y + 5y = 7$	
$4 - 3y = 7$	
$-3y = 3$	
$y = -1$	
$x = 2 - 4(-1)$	Now that you have the value for y, plug it in and solve for x
$x = 2 + 4 = 6$	

Remember, plug in the values you calculated to check your answers. To determine which variable to try to solve for first, look for the equation where one variable is easier to isolate and start there.

Quadratic Equations

The quadratic equation is a special equation where specific polynomials are set to equal zero.

$$ax^2 + bx + c = 0$$

For the quadratic equation, $a \neq 0$, and a, b, and c are constants representing the coefficients that precede the variable x.

Earlier in this section, we reviewed factoring and binomials, which are key components to finding values in a quadratic equation. Consider the example:

$x^2 - 5x + 6 = 0$	
$(x - 2)(x - 3) = 0$	To solve for x, first factor out the binomial terms:

Math Prep Tip: If you are unsure if you have factored properly and identified the correct binomials, check your work using distribution. As you multiply in order, write out the products; if you have factored correctly, your distribution should yield the original equation.

$(x - 2)x - (x - 2)3$	Distribute the first term in the first binomial into both terms in the second binomial
$((x)(x) - 2x) - (3x - 6)$	Next, do the same with the second term in the first binomial
$x^2 - 2x - 3x + 6 = x^2 - 5x + 6$	Now, combine the products to see if it matches your original equation

Everything looks good! Let us get back to solving the problem.

$x - 2 = 0$	$x - 3 = 0$	Quadratic equations **always** have two solutions. The two solutions may be the same number. To solve for the values of x, set each of the binomial factors to 0.
$x = 2$	$x = 3$	Both 2 and 3 are solutions to the equation. Plug in your answers to check if the values are correct.
$(2)^2 - 5(2) + 6 = 0$	$(3)^2 - 5(3) + 6 = 0$	
$4 - 10 + 6 = -6 + 6 = 0$	$9 - 15 + 6 = -6 + 6 = 0$	Solve

The values check out when plugged in. The solution for the quadratic equation is $x = 2$ **OR** $x = 3$.

Math Prep Tip: The quadratic equation may be rewritten to generate the quadratic formula:

$$x = \frac{-b \pm \sqrt{b} - 4ac}{2a}$$

The quadratic formula is not tested on the exam.

Inequalities

Inequalities are similar to equations. Instead of setting two expressions equal, however, inequalities describe their relative value. Inequalities express four quantity comparisons:

x greater than y: $x > y$
x less than y: $x < y$
x greater than or equal to y: $x \geq y$
x less than or equal to y: $x \leq y$

Solving Inequalities

Inequalities are approached using the same techniques as the equations in this section. Your goal is still to isolate the variables and solve for their value, if possible. As with equations, whatever function you perform on one side, you must perform on the other. Inequalities have one difference that can impact your answer choice if you are not careful. Whenever you divide or multiply both sides by a negative number, you must flip the inequality sign to ensure the inequality remains valid. Let's look at an inequality example:

$$3 - \frac{x}{4} \geq 2$$

$$-\frac{x}{4} \geq 2 - 3 = -\frac{x}{4} \geq -1 \qquad \text{First, isolate the variable}$$

$$(-4)\left(-\frac{x}{4}\right) \leq (-4)(-1)$$

$$x \leq 4 \qquad \text{Since we multiplied both sides by a negative number we changed the direction of the inequality sign. The negative signs cancel out.}$$

The expression reads *x* is less than or equal to 4. While you have solved for *x*, this is not your answer. The complete answer is all the values equal to or less than 4. Inequalities are sometimes represented on a number line. The above example on a number line would look like:

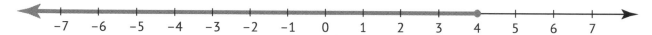

The filled-in point over the 4 indicates that 4 is included in the possible list of values. If the final answer was $x < 4$, the circle would **not** be filled in. The number line in that case would look like:

Coordinate Geometry

Coordinate geometry is the transition point from algebra to geometry and involves the use of algebraic expressions to create graphical displays on a coordinate plane. The coordinate plane is composed of a vertical and horizontal axis that run perpendicular to each other. All points on a coordinate plane can be plotted in reference to these axes, which intersect at zero. This meeting point is referred to as the **point of origin**.

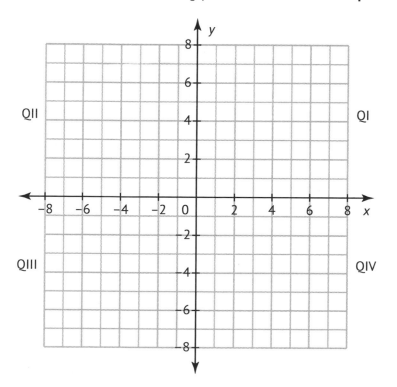

Quadrant	x-coordinate	y-coordinate
I	positive	positive
II	negative	positive
III	negative	negative
IV	positive	negative

The coordinate plane has four distinct quadrants when the origin is placed at the center. Quadrant I is in the upper right corner, quadrant II is in the upper left corner, quadrant III is in the lower left corner, and quadrant IV is in the lower right corner.

Points are plotted on a coordinate plane. Every point has two coordinates, one on the x-axis and one on the y-axis. The origin sits at the intersection of the two axes and has coordinates (0,0). The coordinates of points not at the center are determined by their positive or negative difference from the origin. Coordinates are always written with the x coordinate first: (x,y). You can determine whether the x and y coordinates are positive or negative based on the quadrant they fall in.

On the exam, it is helpful to know these quadrant locations for coordinates to save time and prevent you from having to plot the points on the coordinate plane each time.

Graphing Coordinates

Sometimes you need to either graph coordinates or determine the value of coordinates already on the graph. When given a set of coordinates, simply start at zero and plot the distance across (left or right) for the value of x, then up or down for the value of y.

Let us look at a set of coordinates and how to graph them on the coordinate plane. Suppose you are asked to identify a graph that has a point with the coordinates (3,2). Your graph would look like this:

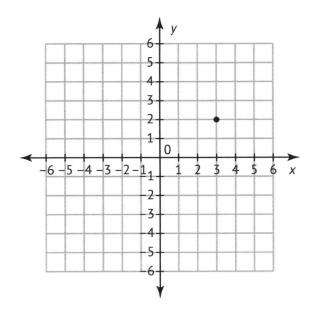

You can see the coordinates start at the point of origin, shift 3 spaces to the right, then shift 2 spaces up. If you refer back to the quadrant chart, you can see that it predicted our coordinates, which are both positive, would be in quadrant I.

Calculating Distance on the Coordinate Plane

You may be asked to calculate the distance between two points on a coordinate plane. If the points are in the same vertical or horizontal plane, you can simply count the spaces between the points. Distance is always positive.

You can also use the distance formula to plug in coordinates and calculate the distance between two points.

Distance Formula:

$$distance = \sqrt{(x_2 - x_1)^2 + (y_2 - y_1)^2}$$

To find the distance between two coordinates—let us say (5,–2) and (–4,9)—plug in the values in the equation and solve.

$$distance = \sqrt{(-4 - 5)^2 + (9 - (-2))^2}$$

$$distance = \sqrt{(-9)^2 + 11^2}$$

$$distance = \sqrt{202}$$

Midpoint

The midpoint is also a measure of distance between points on a coordinate plane. Instead of the distance from one point to another, the coordinates of the midpoint are the average of the endpoints. To find the midpoint of two points, take the average of your endpoints using the midpoint formula:

> **Midpoint Formula:**
>
> $$midpoint = \frac{x_1 + x_2}{2}, \frac{y_1 + y_2}{2}$$

Suppose you have the points (–1,2) and (3,–6). Plug in the coordinates to find the midpoint:

$$midpoint = \frac{-1 + 3}{2}, \frac{2 - 6}{2}$$

$$midpoint = (1,-2)$$

Slope

Points on a coordinate plane connect to form lines. The slope is the measure of how steep a line is in relation to the x-axis and y-axis. The equation of a line can be written as: **y = mx + b**, where *m* is the slope, *b* is the y-intercept, and *x* and *y* represent possible coordinate values. This equation is commonly referred to as **slope-intercept form**.

> **Slope-Intercept Form:**
>
> $$y = mx + b$$

The y-intercept is just another way of describing the point that falls directly on the y-axis. Likewise, the x-intercept describes the point that falls directly on the x-axis. All lines will have no more than one x and one y intercept.

The slope is the measure of *the rise over the run* of a line, or the change in the y-coordinate values (rise) and the change in x-coordinate values (run). You need two points to find the slope of a line.

Consider the coordinates (4,3) and (–2,–1). Calculate the change in x and y to find the slope, *m*.

$$m = \frac{\text{change in } y}{\text{change in } x} = \frac{3 - (-1)}{4 - (-2)} = \frac{4}{6} = \frac{2}{3}$$

You may sometimes be asked to find the slope of a line from an equation instead of coordinates. Suppose you have the equation 2x + y = 5. To find the slope, put the equation in slope-intercept form, y = mx + b:

$$2x + y = 5$$

$$y - 5 - 2x \text{ OR in slope-intercept form: } y = -2x + 5$$

The slope of this line is –2.

Properties of Slopes

Knowing some of the common properties of slopes and what they look like graphically can help save you time and calculation on the exam.

- The slope of a line can be either positive or negative.
- Slopes do not have to be whole integers, they can be fractions as well.
- Parallel lines on the same coordinate plane will always have the same slope. For example, if the slope of line a is 3, **all** lines parallel to that line will also have a slope of 3.
- The slope of a line on the same coordinate plane that is perpendicular to another line is the **negative reciprocal**. If a line has a slope of 2, **all** lines perpendicular to that line will have a slope of $-\frac{1}{2}$.

A **positive** slope rises from left to right.

A **negative** slope falls from left to right.

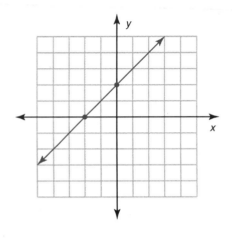

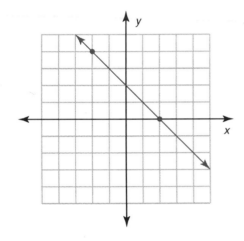

Any **horizontal** line has a slope of 0 since there is no change to the y value.

The slope of any **vertical** line cannot be defined because all of its points have the same x-coordinate.

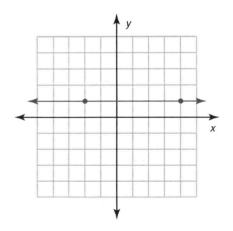

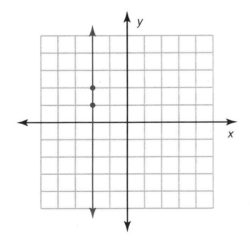

Functions

Algebraic functions can be expressed as a graph or as an equation and describe a relationship between corresponding inputs and outputs. Functions are typically represented by the notation $f(x)$ and indicates calculations to be performed.

For example, you may see something similar to the following:

$$f(x) = 2x + 4$$

For the function above, f is the name of the function. Any letter can be used in place of f to name a function.

A question may present you with the above equation and ask you to solve $f(3)$. To solve, replace each x in the equation with the input of 3. For $f(3)$:

$$f(3) = 2(3) + 4$$
$$f(3) = 10$$

Functions can also be graphed on a coordinate plane. Depending on the equation, the graph may not always be a straight line. Instead, functions can be parabolas.

$$f(x) = -x^2 - 8x - 15$$

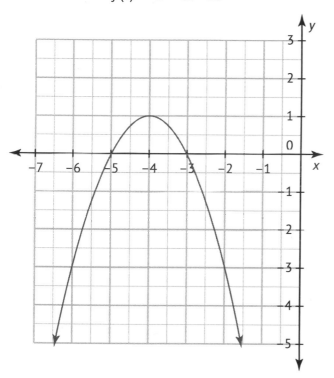

$$f(x) = -x^2 + 8x - 19$$

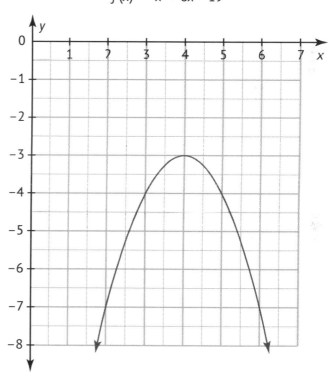

Geometry: The Basics

Geometry focuses primarily on the measurements of shapes, lines, angles, and planes. Several key areas of geometry are tested on the GRE. You will see problems that involve triangles, circles, and two-dimensional shapes of various sizes with different numbers of sides. This section will refresh your memory of the related formulas and concepts, outline key geometric concepts that occur frequently on the exam, and equip you with problem solving strategies to improve your accuracy.

Diagrams and Formulas

Most of the geometry questions on the exam will be accompanied by a diagram. In most cases, this works to your advantage. Often the diagrams contain useful information to help you answer the question. For example, if you have a diagram of a circle and the diameter is noted as 4 cm, you can calculate the radius of the circle, which is half the diameter.

It is important to note that geometry diagrams on the exam are typically **not** drawn to scale. You should not make assumptions based on how diagrams "look." Instead, you should use the information presented in the questions and any given measurements to calculate the information you are looking for to find a corresponding answer choice.

We will review key geometric formulas in this section. While the formulas are helpful to know, they are useless if you are unsure of how to use them. Questions on the exam, particularly those dealing with triangles, will require you to think beyond simply plugging numbers into a formula. Instead, you will have to critically analyze the given components to arrive at the correct answer.

Lines, Angles, Planes, and Shapes (L.A.P.S)

The building blocks of geometry are lines, angles, planes, and shapes. You will encounter one or more of these components in all the geometry questions on the exam. While geometry is a dense subject matter that includes some very complex principles, remember that the GRE is a test of your understanding of high-school level math and is primarily concerned with your basic math skills. As such, complex topics like differential geometry, model theory, and geometric proofs will not appear on the exam.

The exam will focus specifically on coordinate and plane geometry. Planes are two-dimensional flat surface areas that extend infinitely in all directions. The surfaces of geometric shapes like polygons, triangles, and hexagons all lie on planes; lines and points are also essential components of geometric planes. Using points, angles, and units of measurement, you can calculate critical information about a shape, plot coordinates on a plane, and draw conclusions about angle measurements. This section will cover the **L.A.P.S** fundamentals, including key definitions, formulas, and approaches to various problems.

Lines

A line is a one-dimensional figure on a plane. Lines are always straight and drawn with arrows at each end to indicate their infinite nature. Lines extend in both directions infinitely.

Lines are uniquely determined by two points. Points are found on all geometric shapes. They are not measurable units, although the distance between two points is a common calculation which you will be asked to perform. In the diagram below, **A** and **B** are points on the line. These points are unique and only one line runs through them. Remember that the line extends infinitely in both directions.

Instead of figures, you may see the common notation $\overleftrightarrow{AB}$ used. The notation indicates that you have a line, with no defined end, that crosses through points **A** and **B**.

Rays

A ray can be defined by two points where it begins at one of the points and passes through a second point while extending infinitely in one direction. The length of a ray cannot be determined and thus, neither can you find its mid-point.

In the diagram below, the ray begins at point **A**, passes through point **B**, and continues infinitely in one direction. As with a line, you can use a shorthand notation for this figure. The notation $\overrightarrow{AB}$ shows the points on the ray and that it continues infinitely in one direction.

Segments

A segment is a part of a line. However, segments have a measurable length. Unlike a line, segments do not continue infinitely. The annotation for a segment is written as $\overline{AB}$.

The key characteristics of a segment are its two end points and its midpoint. The end points mark finite ends of a segment while the midpoint is positioned at the center of a segment. Only segments have midpoints.

In the diagram below, **A** and **B** are the end points of the segment. **M** represents the midpoint or center of the segment.

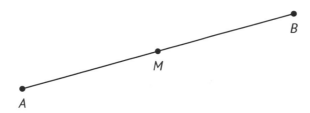

A and **B** are the same distance from the midpoint: $\overline{AM} = \overline{MB}$. If you have an exam question that tells you **M** is the midpoint of segment $\overline{AB}$ and that $\overline{MB} = 3$, you can deduce that $\overline{AM}$ is also 3.

Parallel Lines

Parallel lines are two lines which exist on the same plane but do not intersect each other. You should not assume that because two lines are not touching in a diagram that they are parallel lines, since it is possible they may intersect at some point. For exam questions addressing parallel lines, the question will explicitly state the lines are parallel or will use the common notation for parallel lines.

$\overleftrightarrow{AB}$ and $\overleftrightarrow{CD}$ are parallel lines. Their relationship can be annotated as $\overleftrightarrow{AB} \parallel \overleftrightarrow{CD}$.

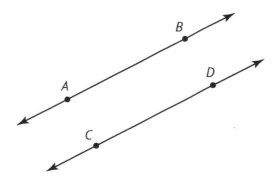

Perpendicular Lines

Perpendicular lines are two lines that intersect each other forming a 90° angle. We will discuss angles in more detail below. Just like with parallel lines, never assume you are dealing with perpendicular lines unless the instructions specifically tell you so or you can identify the 90° angle. The standard notation for two lines that are perpendicular is $\overleftrightarrow{AB} \perp \overleftrightarrow{CD}$.

Intersection

An intersection, as its name implies, refers to the point where two lines, segments, or rays intersects. Perpendicular lines have an intersection point, but not all lines that intersect are perpendicular since they do not all form 90° angles.

Angles

Angles are formed when two lines intersect. The point of intersection is referred to as the **vertex** of the angle. Angles are measured in degrees and can be either acute, obtuse, right or straight. The measure of the angle determines its classification.

Type of Angle	Degree Measurement	Visual Representation
Acute	Acute angles are angles that measure less than 90˚	
Right	Right angles measure **exactly** 90˚	
Obtuse	Obtuse angles are angles that measure between 91˚ and 180˚	
Straight	Straight angles are angles that measures **exactly** 180˚ and are equivalent to a straight line	

The typical naming convention for angles is to use the labels for the three points on the intersecting lines, segments, or rays, making sure to place the vertex in the middle. The common symbol to represent an angle is ∠.

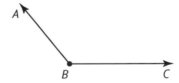

This angle can be written as ∠ABC or ∠CBA. This angle can also be simply named ∠B. However, only use this notation when there are no other angles that share B as the vertex.

Other Types of Angles

Any time a line intersects another line, at least one angle is formed. Questions will ask to you identify the measures of angles. Knowing a few fundamentals about different type of angles occurring on the same line and how they relate to each other will help you save a lot of time. Let us look at the key angle relationships.

Supplementary and Complementary Angles

Two angles with a sum of 180° are called **supplementary angles**.

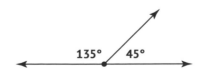

Two angles with a sum of 90° are called **complementary angles**.

Vertical Angles

Two lines or line segments that intersect form **vertical angles**. Vertical angles, or opposite angles, are congruent and have the same angle measurement.

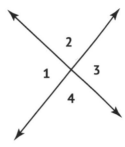

In the figure above, ∠2 and ∠4 are vertical angles. ∠1 and ∠3 are also vertical angles. If ∠4 = 50°, then ∠2 = 50° since they are vertical angles. Moreover, if ∠4 = 50°, then ∠1 = 130° because ∠4 and ∠1 are supplementary.

Adjacent Angles

Angles that share a common vertex and common side are called **adjacent angles**. Take a look at the following example.

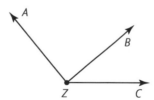

∠AZB and ∠BZC are adjacent angles because they share a common vertex, Z, and a common side, $\overrightarrow{ZB}$.

Transversals

A transversal is a line that intersects two or more lines at two or more points.

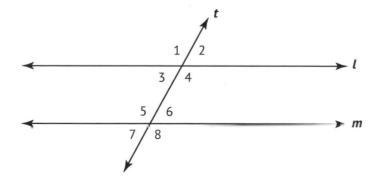

When a transversal intersects a pair of parallel lines, as in the above example, the resulting angles are related in some way:

- Angles 1, 4, 5, and 8 are equal.
- Angles 2, 3, 6, and 7 are equal.
- The sum of any two adjacent angles, such as 1 and 2 or 7 and 8, equals 180° since they form a straight angle on a line.
- The sum of any large angle + any small angle = 180° since the large and small angles in this figure combine into straight lines, all the large angles are equal, and all the small angles are equal.

You will see these concepts of angles appear again in the next sections where we will explore properties and measurements of polygons.

Shapes: Polygons

You will encounter a number of different types of polygons on the exam. A polygon is a two-dimensional enclosed figure with three or more straight sides. Polygons are named based on the number of sides they have.

Polygon Name	Number of Sides
Triangle	3
Quadrilateral	4
Pentagon	5
Hexagon	6
Heptagon	7
Octagon	8
Nonagon	9
Decagon	10
Dodecagon	12

Polygons can be either regular or irregular. Regular polygons have all sides of equal length and equal angles. Irregular polygons do not. It is important to understand the difference so that you do not make erroneous assumptions about the size of a figure that could lead you to an incorrect answer. The test questions will tell you if you are dealing with a regular or irregular polygon.

While all polygons are different in the number of sides they have, they do share some fundamental characteristics.

- The area of a polygon is the measure of the area of the region inside the polygon.
- A polygon with equal sides and equal interior angles is a regular polygon.
- The sum of the exterior angles of any polygon is 360°.
- The perimeter of a polygon is the sum of the lengths of its sides.

Geometry questions will focus primarily on finding various measurements, like volume, area, and circumference, of the polygons. A majority of the polygons on the exams will be triangle and four-sided polygons, also known as quadrilaterals.

This section will look at the basic properties of polygons, and the formulas used to calculate the measurement of the sides and angles. It will also discuss circles and how to approach figures that include more than one polygon or circle.

Triangles have many properties, rules, and calculations and merit a deeper review given their complexity and popularity on the exam. First, let us look at some general principles of quadrilaterals.

Quadrilaterals

Quadrilaterals are four-sided polygons. Quadrilaterals can be regular or irregular and the sum of their interior angles is 360°. The most common quadrilaterals tested on the exam are squares and rectangles, but there are also several others.

Rectangles

A rectangle is a quadrilateral where the opposite sides are parallel and the interior angles are all right angles. The opposite sides of a rectangle are of equal length. The diagonals of a rectangle are also of equal length.

> **Formula for the Area of a Rectangle**
>
> *area = base · height*

Diagonals of a Rectangle

The two diagonals of a rectangle are always equal to each other. Both diagonals divide the rectangle into two equal right triangles. Since the diagonals of the rectangle form right triangles that include the diagonal and two sides of the rectangle, if you know two of the values, you can calculate the third with the Pythagorean equation (discussed below).

Square

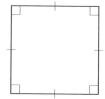

A square is a rectangle with four equal sides. All squares are rectangles but not all rectangles are squares.

> **Formula for the Area of a Square**
>
> *area = s²*
>
> In the formula, *s* is the length of a side.

Diagonals of a Square

The diagonals of a square bisect each other at right angles and have equal lengths. The diagonals also cut the square into two 45-45-90 triangles. If you know the length of one side of the square, you can calculate the length of the diagonal.

Parallelogram

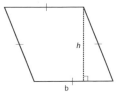

A parallelogram is a quadrilateral with two sets of parallel and equal sides. The length and width do not need to be the same in a parallelogram but the opposing sides will always be equal and the adjacent angles will be supplementary.

> **Formula for the Area of a Parallelogram**
>
> *area = base · height*

Diagonals of a Parallelogram

The diagonals of a parallelogram divide the figure into two congruent triangles.

Polygon Angles

The sum of the interior angles inside of a polygon is determined by the number of sides in the figure; this is true for both regular and irregular polygons. The figures you will see most often on the exam, triangles and quadrilaterals, both have set measures for their interior angles. Triangles will always total 180 degrees and quadrilaterals will total 360 degrees.

> You can always figure out the total measurement of the internal angles of a polygon by using the formula:
>
> $$(n - 2) \cdot 180$$
>
> In the formula, *n* equals the number of sides.

Triangles

Triangles are three-sided polygons. The sum of the interior angles is 180°. The height of the triangle is the perpendicular distance from the vertex to opposite leg and can be found inside or outside of the triangle.

> **Formula for the Area of a Triangle**
>
> *area = $\frac{1}{2}$ base · height*

Equilateral Triangles

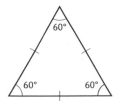

An equilateral triangle has three equal sides and three equal angles.

Once you know that you have two 60° angles, you can assume you are dealing with an equilateral triangle.

Isosceles Triangles

An isosceles triangle has two equal sides and two equal angles.

The two equal angles are opposite the two equal sides. The sides opposite equal angles are always equal, and the angles opposite equal sides are always equal.

Right Triangles

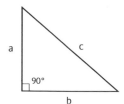

Right triangles are tested more than any other type of triangle on the exam. A right triangle is any triangle that contains a right angle. The side opposite the right angle is the hypotenuse. The other two sides are called legs. The remaining two angles add up to 90 degrees.

Right Triangles and the Pythagorean Theorem

The Pythagorean Theorem is one of the most tested theories on the exam, which makes sense as it applies to right triangles and right triangles are tested frequently. The theory establishes the relationship of a right triangle's legs to its hypotenuse.

Pythagorean Theorem

$$a^2 + b^2 = c^2$$

In this equation, **a** and **b** are the legs and **c** is the hypotenuse.

Since right triangles adhere to the Pythagorean Theorem, they rarely yield integers for the lengths of the legs. But a few integer triplets perfectly conform to the Theorem. These are referred to as **Pythagorean triples**. The ones you will see on the exam include:

- 3, 4, 5
- 5, 12, 13
- 7, 24, 25
- 8, 15, 17

Also note that any multiples of these triples conform. For example, 6, 8, 10 are multiples of the triples 3, 4, 5. Memorizing these will help you identify measurements and answer questions more quickly.

Shapes: Circles

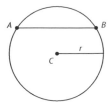

Circles are not polygons because they do not have straight sides. Circles are tested on the exam and you will mainly be asked to find some part of its measurements. Here are some quick facts about circles:

- All circles contain 360°
- The distance from the center to any point on the circle is called the radius. The radius of a circle is a critical piece: if you know a circle's radius, you can figure out all its other measurements.
- The diameter of a circle stretches between endpoints on the circle and passes through the center.
- A chord also extends from endpoint to endpoint on the circle, but it does not necessarily pass through the center.
- In the figure above, point C is the center of the circle, r is the radius, and $\overline{AB}$ is a chord.

Formula for the Circumference of a Circle

The circumference is the distance around the circle.

$$circumference = 2\pi r$$

The standard value for *pi* on the exam is 3.14.

Formula for the Area of a Circle

$$area = \pi r^2$$

In this formula, r is the radius. When you need to find the area of a circle, your real goal is to figure out the radius. For an added challenge, sometimes a question may give you the diameter or the circumference and you will need to calculate the radius (half the diameter) to solve for the area.

Shapes: Solids

Rectangular Solids

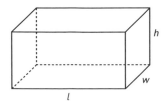

A rectangular solid is a prism with a rectangular base and edges that are perpendicular to its base.

A rectangular solid has three key dimensions: length, width, and height. If you know these three measurements, you can find the solid's volume and surface area.

Formula for the Surface Area

$$A = 2 \cdot w \cdot l + 2 \cdot l \cdot h + 2 \cdot h \cdot w$$

Formula for the Volume

$$volume = l \cdot w \cdot h$$

Cubes

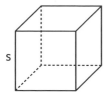

A cube is a rectangular solid with sides (*s*) that are all equal. Cubes have six faces, each of which is a square, meaning the length, width, and height of each are equal.

> **Formula for the Surface Area**
>
> *volume* = $6s^2$

> **Formula for the Volume**
>
> *volume* = s^3

Right Circular Cylinders

A right circular cylinder is a geometric solid that has two circular bases. A right circular cylinder has a lateral measurement, and its height forms a rectangle.

> **Formula for the Volume**
>
> The only measurement you will be asked to calculate for right cylinders is the volume.
>
> *volume* = $\pi r^2 h$

Data Interpretation: The Basics

Data interpretation questions test your ability to derive information from graphs, charts, and other visual displays. Data interpretation questions are more of an extension of problem solving questions than a unique question type or concept. For these questions, you will interpret data from charts, graphs, and other images and use this information to solve for the correct answer(s).

This section will provide a brief overview of central tendency, probability, and frequency distributions. See Chapter 14 for a more detailed guide to the Data Interpretation questions on the GRE.

Measures of Central Tendency

Measures of central tendency identify the distribution of certain values in an attempt to make data more understandable and allow for accurate interpretation. The three measures of central tendency are the mean, median, and mode.

Mean

The **mean** is commonly referred to as the average, and is the sum of all terms divided by the number of terms. To express the mean as an equation, set the mean equal to its relationship with the terms in the data set:

$$mean = \frac{sum\ of\ terms}{number\ of\ terms}$$

Suppose on your last four statistics exams, you received the following scores: 84, 92, 93, 87. If you wanted to find the mean of your scores, calculate using the equation for the mean:

$$mean = \frac{84 + 92 + 93 + 87}{4} = \frac{356}{4} = 89$$

Sometimes, instead of all the terms, a test question might provide you with the mean and ask you to identify the other values. You can rearrange, simplify, and substitute to arrive at your answer.

Median

The **median** of a set of data is the middle term when the numbers are written in ascending order. For example, to calculate the median of the group 7, 12, 14, 6, 4, 3, and 17, you would first list the numbers in order.

3, 4, 6, 7, 12, 14, 17

Then find the middle number, which is in this case is 7. If, however, the number 21 was added to this set, you would have **two** numbers in the middle: 7 and 12. In this case, you average the two numbers (7 + 12, divided by 2) to reach a median of 9.5.

Mode

The **mode** is simply the number that occurs the most. In the group 1, 2, 3, 3, 3, 3, 4, and 7, the mode is 3 since it appears the most frequently in the group.

Range

The **range** of a data set is the difference between the largest term and the smallest term. For example, the range of 12, −24, 13, 2, and 4 is 13 − (−24) = 37.

Probability

Probability is the measure of the number of specific outcomes compared to the number of possible outcomes:

$$p = \frac{\text{\# of specific outcomes}}{\text{\# of possible outcomes}}$$

If you have 10 cookies in a bag—3 chocolate chip, 2 oatmeal, 4 lemon, and 1 peanut butter—the probability of your reaching into the bag and selecting a lemon cookie is $\frac{4}{10}$ or $\frac{2}{5}$. Probability can be written as a fraction or a decimal.

You may be asked to determine multiple-event probability, such as the probability of reaching into the bag of cookies a second time and grabbing a lemon cookie. In these instances, you must find the probability for each event and then multiply them.

Frequency Distribution

A **frequency distribution** is a table used to describe a data set. It also lists intervals or ranges of data values—called **data classes**—together with the number of data values or **frequency** from the set that are in each class.

Suppose that the exam scores of 20 psychology students are as follows:

97, 92, 88, 75, 83, 67, 89, 55, 72, 78, 81, 91, 57, 63, 67, 74, 87, 84, 98, 46

You can construct a frequency table with classes 90−99, 80−89, 70−79 etc., by counting the number of grades in each grade range.

Class	Frequency (f)
90–99	4
80–89	6
70–79	4
60–69	3
50–59	2
40–49	1

Note that the sum of the frequency column is equal to 20, the total number of test scores that you were given.

12 | # PRACTICE
PROBLEM SET

The Math Primer walked you through key concepts in arithmetic, algebra, and geometry in order to prepare you to tackle questions that will appear in the Quantitative Reasoning sections of the exam. The following problems test your understanding of these concepts. The problems primarily ask you to perform calculations to obtain values like area and volume, or to simplify and solve equations. While some questions appear as they will on the exam, the primary purpose of this section is to reinforce the key concepts discussed in the Primer.

Evaluate each expression.

1. $(-1) + (-3)$

2. $(-6) + (-6)$

3. $1 - 2$

4. $(-2) + (-5)$

5. $\left(-\frac{3}{2}\right) + \left(-\frac{3}{2}\right)$

6. $\left(-3\frac{3}{8}\right) - 3\frac{7}{8}$

7. $6 - \frac{4}{5}$

8. $4\frac{7}{8} - \frac{5}{4}$

9. $2 - \frac{10}{-2}$

10. $(-2)\left(\frac{4}{2}\right)$

11. $(-3 + -6 - 3)(-3)$

12. $(2)(6 + -3 - 2)$

13. $3\frac{1}{4} + 1\frac{3}{5}$

15. $\frac{1}{2} + \frac{3}{4}$

14. $4\frac{2}{3} + 4\frac{5}{6}$

16. $3\frac{1}{3} + \frac{1}{4}$

Find each quotient.

17. $\frac{14}{9} \div \frac{-6}{7}$

18. $\frac{-3}{4} \div 2$

Find each product.

19. $-1\frac{8}{9} \cdot \frac{7}{10}$

20. $1\frac{2}{5} \cdot -\frac{7}{4}$

Simplify. Your answer should contain only positive exponents.

21. $4n^2 \cdot 8n$

23. $7m^2 \cdot 7m^4$

22. $8n \cdot 6n^2 \cdot 3n^2$

24. $4n^2 \cdot 2n^2$

25. $-8k^3 \cdot 4k^2$

27. $-6 \cdot (-6)^2 \cdot (-6)^3$

26. $6x \cdot -7x^4$

28. $-2 \cdot (-2)^3$

Find each square root.

29. $\sqrt{64}$

31. $\sqrt{49}$

30. $\sqrt{121}$

32. $\sqrt{144}$

Solve each equation.

33. $|-9x| = 36$

35. $\left|\frac{r}{8}\right| = 2$

34. $|-8a| = 48$

36. $|2k| = 12$

Solve each inequality and graph its solution.

37. $|9m| \leq 63$

<------+---+---+---+---+---+---+---+---+------>
    -8   -6   -4   -2   0   2   4   6   8

39. $|2 + n| \leq 10$

<------+---+---+---+---+---+---+------>
    -12   -8   -4   0   4   8

38. $\left|\dfrac{v}{9}\right| > 2$

<------+---+---+---+---+---+---+---+---+------>
  -20   -15   -10   -5   0   5   10   15   20

40. $|3x| \leq 3$

<------+---+---+---+---+---+---+---+---+---+---+---+---+------>
  -4 -3 -2 -1 0   1   2   3   4   5   6   7   8

Simplify each expression.

41. $4 - 2(a + 2)$

43. $5n + 5(1 - 4n)$

42. $6x - 2(7 - x)$

44. $-10(1 - 5k) - 8$

Solve.

45. $(36n^6 + 3n^5 + 27n^4) \div 9n$

46. $(36n^3 + 27n^2 + 5n) \div 9n^3$

47. $(2n^3 + 10n^2 + 50n) \div 10n$

48. $(5x^3 + 3x^2 + 6x) \div 6x^3$

Simplify.

49. $\dfrac{3}{3 + 2\sqrt{5}}$

50. $\dfrac{4}{-1 + 5\sqrt{2}}$

Solve each equation.

51. $-123 = -6 + 3(-8m - 7)$

53. $5(6 - 6x) = -120$

52. $6(7 - 7k) = 336$

54. $266 = 7(3 - 7a)$

Solve each equation by factoring.

55. $x^2 = 6x$

57. $p^2 = 10p - 16$

56. $n^2 + 10n = -21$

58. $x^2 + 2x = 8$

Factor each completely.

59. $7x^3 - 14x^2 + x - 2$

60. $15a^3 + 9a^2 + 10a + 6$

Find the slope of each line.

61.

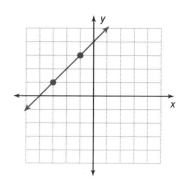

63.

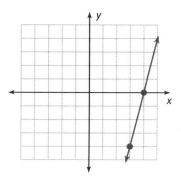

62.

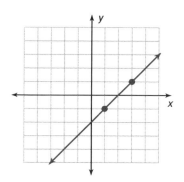

64.

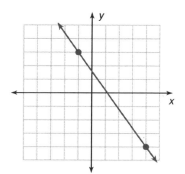

Find the slope of the line through each pair of points.

65. (−17, 13), (−18, 14)

66. (16, 5), (−7, −10)

Solve each question. Round your answer to the nearest hundredth.

67. Castel traveled to the ferry office and back. The trip there took five hours and the trip back took six hours. What was Castel's average speed on the trip there if he averaged 30 km/h on the return trip?

69. Ming can pick forty bushels of apples in 10 hours. Imani can pick the same amount in 13 hours. If they worked together how long would it take them to pick 40 bushels?

68. Lisa left the science museum and drove west. Willie left one hour later driving at 45 mph in an effort to catch up to Lisa. After driving for two hours Willie finally caught up. Find Lisa's average speed.

70. Working alone, Imani can pick forty bushels of apples in 8 hours. Nicole can pick the same amount in 13 hours. Find how long it would take them if they worked together.

Find the measure of angle b.

71.

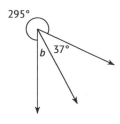

74.

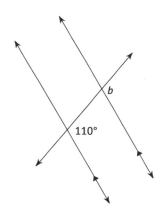

72.

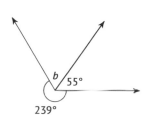

75.

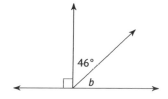

73.

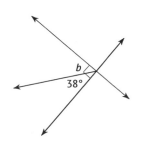

76.

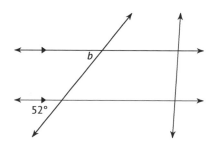

Find the measure of each missing angle.

77.

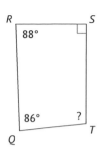

79.

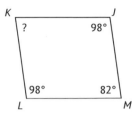

78.

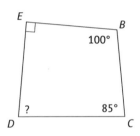

80.

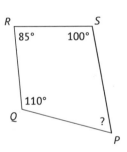

Find the area.

81. Given Trapezoid

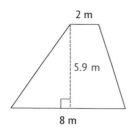

2 m

5.9 m

8 m

82.

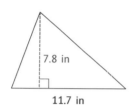

7.8 in

11.7 in

83. Given Paralellogram

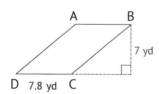

A   B

7 yd

D   7.8 yd   C

84. Given Trapezoid

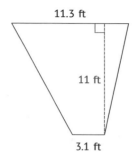

11.3 ft

11 ft

3.1 ft

85.

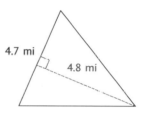

4.7 mi

4.8 mi

86.

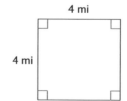

4 mi

4 mi

Find the measure of the arc or central angle indicated. Assume that lines which appear to be diameters are actual diameters.

87. $m\overset{\frown}{SU}$

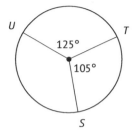

88. $m\angle TRU$

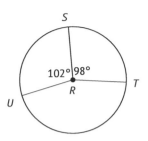

Find the circumference.

89.

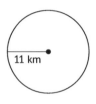

11 km

91.

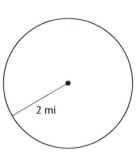

2 mi

90. area = 49π ft^2

92. area = 81π ft^2

Find the radius of each circle.

93. area = 36π km²

94. area = 100π m²

Find the diameter of each circle.

95. area = 25π yd²

96. area = 144π m²

Find the probability of each event.

97. A car dealership has nine cars in the lot. Unfortunately, the keys to the cars have been mixed up. The manager randomly grabs a key and tries to start a car. A salesman also randomly picks a key and tries to start another car. What is the probability that both cars start?

98. Jimmy and Heather each purchase one raffle ticket. If a total of fourteen raffle tickets are sold and two winners will be selected, what is the probability that both Jimmy and Heather win?

99. A basketball player has a 50% chance of making each free throw. What is the probability that the player makes at most four out of six free throws?

Ⓐ $\frac{29}{128} \approx 22.656\%$

Ⓑ $\frac{247}{256} \approx 96.484\%$

Ⓒ $\frac{57}{64} \approx 89.063\%$

Ⓓ $\frac{191}{256} \approx 74.609\%$

100. A gardener has thirteen identical-looking tulip bulbs, of which eight will produce yellow tulips and five will become pink. He randomly selects and plants five of them and then gives the rest away. When the flowers start to bloom, what is the probability that exactly three of them are yellow?

Ⓐ $\frac{175}{572} \approx 30.594\%$

Ⓑ $\frac{560}{1287} \approx 43.512\%$

Ⓒ $\frac{10}{21} \approx 47.619\%$

Ⓓ $\frac{25}{77} \approx 32.468\%$

Find the volume of each figure.

101.

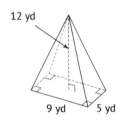

12 yd

9 yd   5 yd

103.

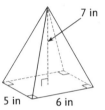

7 in

5 in   6 in

102.

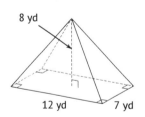

8 yd

12 yd   7 yd

104.

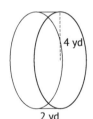

4 yd

2 yd

Find the distance between each pair of points.

105. $(7, -1), (7, 7)$

106. $(8, -2), (1, -3)$

Find the value of x.

107.

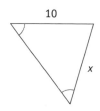

109.

108.

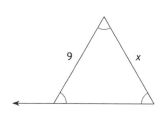

110.

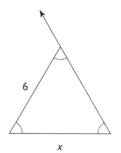

Find the midpoint of each line segment.

111.

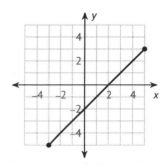

112.

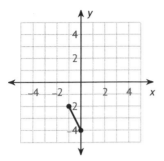

Find the missing side of each triangle.

113.

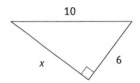

10

x 6

115.

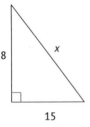

8   x

15

114.

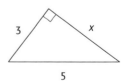

3   x

5

116.

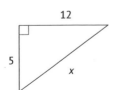

12

5   x

Find the area.

117.

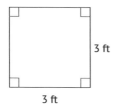

3 ft

3 ft

Find the missing side lengths. Leave your answers as radicals in simplest form.

118.

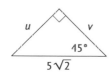

u

v

45°

$5\sqrt{2}$

120.

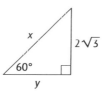

x

$2\sqrt{3}$

60°

y

119.

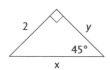

2

y

45°

x

1. −4

2. −12

3. −1

4. −7

5. −3

6. $-7\frac{1}{4}$

7. $5\frac{1}{5}$

8. $3\frac{5}{8}$

9. 7

10. −4

11. 36

12. 2

13. $4\frac{17}{20}$

14. $9\frac{1}{2}$

15. $1\frac{1}{4}$

16. $3\frac{7}{12}$

17. $-1\frac{22}{27}$

18. $-\frac{3}{8}$

19. $-1\frac{29}{90}$

20. $-2\frac{9}{20}$

21. $32n^3$

22. $144n^5$

23. $49m^6$

24. $8n^4$

25. $-32k^5$

26. $-42x^5$

27. $(-6)^6$

28. $(-2)^4$

29. 8

30. 11

31. 7

32. 12

33. {−4, 4}

34. {−6, 6}

35. {16, −16}

36. {6, −6}

37. $-7 \leq m \leq 7$:

38. $v > 18$ or $v < -18$:

39. $-12 \leq n \leq 8$:

40. $-1 \leq x \leq 1$:

41. $-2a$

42. $8x - 14$

43. $-15n + 5$

44. $-18 + 50k$

45. $4n^5 + \frac{n^4}{3} + 3n^3$

46. $4 + \frac{3}{n} + \frac{5}{9n^2}$

47. $\frac{n^2}{5} + n + 5$

48. $\frac{5}{6} + \frac{1}{2x} + \frac{1}{x^2}$

49. $\frac{-9 + 6\sqrt{5}}{11}$

50. $\frac{4 + 20\sqrt{2}}{49}$

51. {4}

52. {−7}

53. {5}

54. {−5}

55. {6, 0}

56. {−3, −7}

57. {8, 2}

58. {2, −4}

59. $(7x^2 + 1)(x - 2)$

60. $(3a^2 + 2)(5a + 3)$

61. 1

62. 1

63. 4

64. $-\frac{7}{5}$

65. −1

66. $\frac{15}{23}$

67. 36 km/h

164

68. 30 mph

69. 5.65 hours

70. 4.95 hours

71. 28°

72. 66°

73. 52°

74. 110°

75. 44°

76. 52°

77. 96°

78. 85°

79. 82°

80. 65°

81. 29.5 m²

82. 45.63 in²

83. 54.6 yd²

84. 79.2 ft²

85. 11.28 mi²

86. 16 mi²

87. 130°

88. 160°

89. 22π km

90. 4π mi

91. 14π ft

92. 18π ft

93. 6 km

94. 10 m

95. 10 yd

96. 24 m

97. $\frac{1}{72} \approx 1.389\%$

98. $\frac{1}{91} \approx 1.099\%$

99. C

100. B

101. 180 yd³

102. 224 yd³

103. 70 in³

104. 100.53 yd³

105. 8

106. 5√2

107. 10

108. 9

109. 12

110. 6

111. (1, −1)

112. (−0.5, −3)

113. 8

114. 4

115. 17

116. 13

117. 9 ft²

118. $u = 5, v = 5$

119. $x = 2\sqrt{2}, y = 2$

120. $x = 4, y = 2$

13 | QUANTITATIVE COMPARISON

Quantitative Comparison: The Basics

Quantitative Reasoning questions require you to compare two quantities and assess their relationship to each other if there is enough information to do so. Each section of Quantitative Reasoning has seven or eight Quantitative Comparison questions that typically occur near the beginning of the section.

The presentation of Quantitative Comparison questions and their answer choices will always be the same. You will be given two columns, each with the given quantity or expression, and you will choose one answer from the same four standard answer choices. Some questions will provide you with additional information to consider; this information should be applied to the quantities or expressions in both columns before you select an answer choice. Often, the questions have variables but do not include sufficient information to solve for those variables. Remember in these cases that you are not solving for a value in Quantitative Comparison question. Instead, you are looking to determine how the quantities in the two columns **relate**.

This chapter will help you understand Quantitative Comparisons and discuss strategies to attack the questions quickly and accurately.

> **Prep Tip:** Quantitative Reasoning questions are the only questions on the exam that present you with the same four answer choices each time. Memorize these to save time!

Sample Quantitative Comparison Problem

$$\frac{x}{y} = \frac{3}{4}$$

Quantity A	Quantity B
$\frac{2x - y}{y}$	$\frac{x}{x + y}$

As you can see, Quantity A and Quantity B are listed in separate columns. You are also given additional information to consider when analyzing the relationship between Quantity A and Quantity B: $\frac{x}{y} = \frac{3}{4}$. This information should be applied to both quantities before you make a comparison. All Quantitative Comparison questions will mirror this sample, though some of them may not have the given information at the top.

The answer choices for Quantitative Comparison questions will **always** be the same and will appear in the same order.

> (A) Quantity A is greater
> (B) Quantity B is greater
> (C) The two quantities are equal
> (D) The relationship cannot be determined from the information given

Let us examine these choices a bit more closely.

Quantity A is greater: (A) is the correct answer when the quantities or expressions are compared after any additional information is applied and the value of column A is greater.

Quantity B is greater: (B) is the correct answer when the quantities or expressions are compared after any additional information is applied and the value of column B is greater.

Quantities are Equal: (C) is the correct answer when the quantities or expressions are compared after any additional information is applied and the values of both columns are equal.

Not enough information: (D) is the correct answer when it is not possible to determine how the two expressions relate to each other. (D) is **never** the answer when both columns are values. For example, if Quantity A = 10 and Quantity B = 25, (D) will not be the answer since we can solve it in its entirety and determine that 10 is less than 32 (25 solved). The answer would instead be (B).

In our sample problem, answer choice (B) is correct.

Quantitative Comparison Strategies

We already discussed how knowing the answer choices ahead of time can help you quickly navigate through the questions. Let us look at some other time-saving strategies to help you navigate the questions.

Substitute

If one or both of the quantities are algebraic expressions, substitute a variety of numbers in place of the variables and then compare the quantities. To confirm the comparison, be sure that the substitute numbers will create a variety of outcomes. Zero is also a number and warrants consideration when comparing quantities. Consider all kinds of appropriate numbers before you give an answer: e.g., zero, positive and negative numbers, small and large numbers, fractions and decimals.

> **Prep Tip:** When plugging in a variety of numbers (negatives, positives, large, small, etc.), if you discover that Quantity A is greater than Quantity B in one instance and Quantity B is greater than Quantity A in another case, it is not possible to determine the relationship between the quantities. Choose answer choice D and move on.

Size Up the Figures

You can expect to see geometric figures in Quantitative Comparison questions. One thing to keep in mind is that the shapes are not typically drawn to scale, and you should assume the figures are this way unless the instructions tell you so. When working with geometric figures, do not make presumptions based on how a figure "looks." Instead, be sure to use the given information and/or measurements to make your comparison.

Simplify

Many of the Quantitative Comparison questions will have expressions that can be simplified. You generally will not have to perform all of the calculations necessary to reach a definitive answer. Simplify or estimate one or both of the expressions only as much as is necessary to compare them. Once you establish that one is always greater or that the values must always be equal, you can stop and make your answer choice selection. Again, the goal is not to solve but to understand how the quantities compare.

Simplify by Elimination

Sometimes, quantities share similar terms that can help you simplify the equation in order to assess the comparison of the quantities. For example, if both columns feature $2x$, you can simply simply subtract it from the equations and evaluate the remainder of the expression.

Understand the Centered Information

Remember that sometimes a question will provide you with additional information to consider when comparing the quantities. This information will always be centered and positioned atop the two columns. You must consider this information and apply it to **both** quantities.

Let us revisit the sample problem we saw earlier to better understand how to work with this information.

$$\frac{x}{y} = \frac{3}{4}$$

Quantity A	Quantity B
$\frac{2x - y}{y}$	$\frac{x}{x + y}$

- Ⓔ Quantity A is greater
- Ⓕ Quantity B is greater
- Ⓖ The two quantities are equal
- Ⓗ The relationship cannot be determined from the information given

In this example, you are given additional information to consider when analyzing the relationship of Quantity A and Quantity B: $\frac{x}{y} = \frac{3}{4}$. These instructions should be applied to both quantities before you make a comparison. Here, we can take the centered information and substitute it into the expressions in both columns. Since we know $\frac{x}{y} = \frac{3}{4}$ we can go ahead and plug in the values for x and y and solve:

Quantity A: $\frac{2(3) - 4}{4} = \frac{6 - 4}{4} = \frac{2}{4} = \frac{1}{2}$ Quantity B: $\frac{3}{3 + 4} = \frac{3}{7}$

$\frac{1}{2}$ is greater than $\frac{3}{7}$, or (A). Remember, however, that we need to test more than just one type of number in order to accurately compare the quantities. Let us try a negative number.

If we think back to the Math Primer and our review of fractions, we know that when we have a negative denominator and negative numerator it simplifies to a positive numerator and denominator: $\frac{-3}{-4} = \frac{3}{4}$. Any multiples that would simplify to $\frac{3}{4}$ can be used. Let us try −6 and −8.

Quantity A: $\frac{2(-6) - (-8)}{-8} = \frac{-4}{-8} = \frac{1}{2}$ Quantity B: $\frac{-6}{-6 + (-8)} = \frac{-6}{-14} = \frac{3}{7}$

After plugging in a negative number, the quantity of Column A is still and will always be greater. The correct answer is (A).

Understand the Fundamentals

Quantitative Comparison questions rely heavily on your knowledge of the fundamental principles covered in the Math Primer. Think back to the last question. That one question alone required you to demonstrate your understanding of fraction rules, order of operations, and simple algebraic expressions. Not all questions will include so many different concepts. Some questions may include more.

This chapter's problem set will present you with Quantitative Comparison questions that incorporate skills from arithmetic, algebra, and geometry. Remember that figures in this section are not drawn to scale and that you must consider the outcome of a variety of numbers, including negative numbers and zero, where appropriate to compare the column quantities. As you work through the problem set, refer back to the Math Primer to refresh your understanding of concepts that may still be confusing for you.

Chapter Overview

Quantitative Comparison questions ask you to compare quantities in two columns and determine whether one is greater than or equal to one another, or if there is not enough information to determine a relationship between the two quantities.

Quantitative Comparison questions are uniform in both presentation and answers choices. Occasionally, you will be given additional information above the columns; be sure to apply the information to both columns before making a comparison.

The answer questions will always look the same. Become familiar with the answer choices to help you to save time when on the exam.

Quantitative Comparison Strategies

- Because Quantitative Comparison questions ask only for a comparison, do not get hung up on trying to find exact values for every question. Simplify until you have the information you need to determine how the quantities compare.
- You can often plug in numbers to determine how columns compare. Be sure to use a variety of numbers, including positive and negative numbers and zero when appropriate.
- Use substitution and simplification to make the two columns look as similar as possible. Find the connection between the columns and use that in addition to any center information as the building block for your approach.

UP NEXT: We will look at Problem Solving questions and their subset Data Interpretation questions. Together, these make up a majority of the Quantitative Reasoning questions and test the full range of concepts found in the Math Primer.

Quantitative Comparison Practice Set

1.
$$3a - 10 = b$$
$$3b - 10 = a$$

<table>
<tr><td>Quantity A</td><td>Quantity B</td></tr>
<tr><td>a</td><td>b</td></tr>
</table>

   Ⓐ Quantity A is greater
   Ⓑ Quantity B is greater
   Ⓒ The two quantities are equal
   Ⓓ The relationship cannot be determined from the information given

2.
$$a < 0 < b$$

<table>
<tr><td>Quantity A</td><td>Quantity B</td></tr>
<tr><td>$-2(a + b)$</td><td>$-ab$</td></tr>
</table>

   Ⓐ Quantity A is greater
   Ⓑ Quantity B is greater
   Ⓒ The two quantities are equal
   Ⓓ The relationship cannot be determined from the information given

3.
DEF is a triangle such that the measure of angle D is 45°.
The measure of angle F is twice the measure of angle E.

<table>
<tr><td>Quantity A</td><td>Quantity B</td></tr>
<tr><td>Measure of Angle D</td><td>Measure of Angle E</td></tr>
</table>

   Ⓐ Quantity A is greater
   Ⓑ Quantity B is greater
   Ⓒ The two quantities are equal
   Ⓓ The relationship cannot be determined from the information given

4.

B

$x°$

$y°$ $x°$

A   C

Use the figure above to answer the question.

<u>Quantity A</u>   <u>Quantity B</u>
    AB   BC

Ⓐ Quantity A is greater
Ⓑ Quantity B is greater
Ⓒ The two quantities are equal
Ⓓ The relationship cannot be determined from the information given

5.

A bag contains green, blue and yellow glass marbles.
The ratio of green to blue glass marbles is 2 : 7.
The ratio of green to yellow glass marbles is 3 : 5.

<u>Quantity A</u>   <u>Quantity B</u>
Number of blue glass marbles   Number of yellow glass marbles

Ⓐ Quantity A is greater
Ⓑ Quantity B is greater
Ⓒ The two quantities are equal
Ⓓ The relationship cannot be determined from the information given

6.

$$\sqrt{a^2 + 39} = 8$$

<u>Quantity A</u>   <u>Quantity B</u>
    a 4

Ⓐ Quantity A is greater
Ⓑ Quantity B is greater
Ⓒ The two quantities are equal
Ⓓ The relationship cannot be determined from the information given

7.

$$\blacksquare x = -x + \frac{1}{x}$$

Quantity A	Quantity B
Value of $\blacksquare x$ if $x = 4$	Value of $\blacksquare x$ if $x = 3$

- (A) Quantity A is greater
- (B) Quantity B is greater
- (C) The two quantities are equal
- (D) The relationship cannot be determined from the information given

8.

Line q on a coordinate plane is defined by the equation $-2x + 3y = 6$.

Quantity A	Quantity B
Slope of a line perpendicular to line q	The slope of a line parallel to line q

- (A) Quantity A is greater
- (B) Quantity B is greater
- (C) The two quantities are equal
- (D) The relationship cannot be determined from the information given

9.

Quantity A	Quantity B
3^3	2^7

- (A) Quantity A is greater
- (B) Quantity B is greater
- (C) The two quantities are equal
- (D) The relationship cannot be determined from the information given

10.

A set has exactly five consecutive positive integers.

Quantity A	Quantity B
The percentage change in the average of the numbers when one of the numbers is dropped from the set	20%

- (A) Quantity A is greater
- (B) Quantity B is greater
- (C) The two quantities are equal
- (D) The relationship cannot be determined from the information given

Quantitative Comparison Practice Set Answers

1. **C.**

   Substitute $3b - 10$ for a in the first equation and solve for b. Then, plug your resulting value into the equation to find a. Your calculations will yield a value of 5 for both a and b, so C is correct.

2. **D.**

   The given tells you that a is negative and b is positive since a is less than 0 and b is greater than 0. Since b is always positive and a is always negative, their product will be a negative number. The expression in column B, then, will always be positive since the result will always be a negative product with a negative sign in front of it ($-ab$). Plug in values to try to determine how the quantities relate. If you plug in -1 for a and 2 for b and solve, column B is greater. But if you plug in a large enough negative number, say -49, column A will be greater. Because of these different outcomes, we cannot determine the relationship.

3. **C.**

   You are given the quantity of column A. Using your understanding of triangles, calculate the value of column B.

   $$A + B + C = 180$$
   $$45 + B + 2B = 180$$
   $$45 + 3B = 180$$
   $$3B = 135$$
   $$B = 45$$

4. **D.**

   In a triangle, equal angles have equal opposite sides. So, AB = AC. You have no information about angle y, so you cannot determine any information about side BC.

5. **A.**

   Calculate the problem this way:

$\frac{2}{7}$ and $\frac{3}{5}$	The ratios of green marbles to blue marbles and green marbles to yellow marbles
$\frac{7}{2}$	The ratio of blue marbles to green marbles
$\frac{9}{y} \cdot \frac{b}{9} = \frac{3}{5} \cdot \frac{7}{2} = \frac{21}{10}$	Multiply the ratios of green to yellow and blue to green together
$\frac{9}{y} \cdot \frac{b}{9} = \frac{b}{y} = \frac{21}{10}$	Simplify

   $$b = 21 \text{ and } y = 10$$

6. **D.**

   Square both sides of the equation to get rid of the square root. Solve for a. Be careful not to pull the plug too early on this one. You end up with 5 as the value for a, but the value could also be -5. When you plug in both possible answers, the results favor column A in one instance and column B in the other. The quantities cannot be compared.

7. **B.**

   Plug in 3 from column A and 4 from column B for x into the equation $\blacksquare x = -x + \frac{1}{x}$. Solve, then simplify the mixed fraction. The quantity of B is greater.

8. **B.**

   Determine the slope of both a parallel and a perpendicular line. Solve using $y = mx + b$.

$2x + 3y = 6$	Given
$y = \frac{2}{3}x + 2$	Solve for y

You now have the slope intercept. Remember that perpendicular lines are negative reciprocals of each other and parallel lines have identical slopes. So, Quantity A = $-\frac{3}{2}$ and Quantity B = $\frac{2}{3}$. (B) is the answer.

9. B.

Solve the exponents: $3^3 = 27$ and $2^7 = 128$.

10. B.

$$= \frac{x + (x+1) + (x+2) + (x+3) + (x+4)}{5}$$
The **previous average** of the five consecutive positive integers

$$= \frac{5x + 10}{5} = x + 2$$
Solve

$$= \frac{x + (x+1) + (x+2) + (x+3)}{4}$$
Then, calculate the **new average** by dropping the largest term

$$= \frac{4x + 6}{4} = x + \frac{3}{2}$$
Solve

$$\frac{previous\ average\ -\ new\ average}{previous\ average}$$
Now calculate the percentage decrease using the formula

$$= \frac{(x+2) - \left(x + \frac{3}{2}\right)}{x + 2} \cdot 100 = \frac{\frac{1}{2}}{x + 2} \cdot 100$$
Substitute your values

To find the maximum percentage, set x at its minimum. The given tells you x is a positive integer, so its lowest possible value is 1. Plug in 1 for x and solve.

$$\frac{\frac{1}{2}}{1 + 2} \cdot 100 = \frac{\frac{1}{2}}{3} \cdot 100 = \frac{100}{6} = 16.666\%$$
Solve

This is the value for column A. So column B is greater.

14 | PROBLEM SOLVING
AND DATA INTERPRETATION

Problem Solving and Data Interpretation: The Basics

Problem Solving in the Quantitative Reasoning section, it is pretty straightforward. Quite simply, the questions ask you to solve the problem you are presented and select the correct answer choice. Problem Solving questions are the catch-all questions on the GRE. They draw from all the math content areas and are presented as word problems, geometric figures, or algebraic expressions. Some Problem Solving questions might ask you to interpret data from a graph or chart; these are a sub-set of questions we call Data Interpretation questions.

All of the necessary calculations for these questions can be done using scratch paper or the on-screen calculator. Some will require no calculations at all, but rather an understanding of fundamental mathematics concepts. You will encounter 9–10 Problem Solving questions per section of Quantitative Reasoning.

This chapter will outline the common types of Problem Solving and Data Interpretation questions and provide you with strategies to address them efficiently and appropriately.

Sample Problem Solving Question

> If Erica can complete a project in four hours and Corey can complete the same project in six hours, how many hours will it take Erica and Corey to complete the project if they work on the project?
>
> (A) 3
> (B) $2\frac{2}{5}$
> (C) 2
> (D) $2\frac{3}{4}$
> (E) $5\frac{1}{2}$

Word problems are common in the Quantitative Reasoning section. This is a classic rate of work problem where you need to determine how long it would take to complete a project with two people working together at different rates.

$$\frac{(4)(6)}{(4 + 6)} = \frac{24}{10} = 2\frac{2}{5}$$

To calculate the rate of work, find the product of the time it takes both Corey and Erica to complete the project individually, then divide by the sum of the time it takes them.

Since your answer choices are written as fractions, you do not need to reduce further.

This question is a word problem that has only one correct answer. This problem also could have asked you to write your answer into a provided text box, instead of choosing via lettered answer choice. Remember that still other kinds of questions in this section may ask you to select all that apply.

> **Prep Tip:** Questions that have more than one response are usually preceded by a square instead of an oval. This is true for all sections on the exam. The practice exams included in this book and online also use this demarcation to let you know when you need to select more than one answer.

Characteristics of the Problems

The problems you will be asked to solve run the gamut in terms of difficulty. Sometimes you will be able to answer quickly with calculations while others may take a little longer and require more computation. The difficulty of the questions often increases when multiple concepts are tested. The less difficult questions often require the application of just a single concept.

As we discussed, all the mathematical concepts in the Math Primer are fair game when it comes to Problem Solving questions. Make sure you are familiar with these not only in theory, but also in application. You can then be equipped to approach the questions regardless of the number of concepts tested.

Developing a Strategy

All Problem Solving questions can be approached with the same general strategy. The critical pieces to the approach are to identify the question task, determine your plan of attack, then select and check your answer. Let us explore these steps in more detail.

Understand the Problem

The first step is figuring out what your question task is. What math concepts are being tested in this question? Does the problem have more than one calculation that needs to be made? Make sure you are clear on the final value you are trying to find.

Scan the Answer Choices and Determine Your Approach

With some questions you are asked explicitly which of the choices has a particular property. In this case, scan the answers and eliminate those that do not meet the requirement. Then determine your approach to the problem. Depending on the question, you might decide to substitute the answer choice into the original given expression. In other questions, it may be helpful to work backward from the choices. You may also need to apply various theories, formulas, and principles—with triangles for example—to solve the problem.

Use the Calculator Smartly

Using the calculator should not always be your first choice when attacking problems. Some problems can be solved more easily without the calculator, and some cannot be solved with a calculator at all. One of the most useful features of the calculator, aside from its ability to quickly solve complex operations for you, is the Transfer button for numeric entry questions. Once you have calculated your response, you can simply click the transfer button and your response will be entered into the numeric entry text box.

Data Interpretation Problems

Data Interpretation questions are an extension of Problem Solving questions, rather than a unique question type. For these questions, you will interpret data from charts, graphs, and other images and use this information to solve for the correct answer. Like Problem Solving questions, these questions have a variety of answer choice options and can have more than one correct answer. You may also have more than one question that corresponds to the graph or chart.

Like the rest of the questions in the Quantitative Reasoning section, you do not need an advance level of knowledge to approach these questions. You will, however, need to understand the basics of reading graphs and charts and deriving meaning from the data. You can expect to see 2–3 of these questions on the exam.

Data Representations

For Data Interpretation questions, you will see data represented in a number of different ways, including:

- Bar graphs, including stacked bar graphs
- Pie Charts
- Line Graphs, often with multiple variables charted on the axes

> **Prep Tip:** On the computer-adaptive exam, working with graphs can be a challenge. If necessary, use your scratch paper to sketch out a general replica of the draft that provides you with the essential information and jot down notes and explore relationships in the data.

Developing a Strategy

Data Interpretation questions can be approached with the same general strategy as Problem Solving questions, though there are some particular things you should be on the lookout for when you encounter these question types.

Understand the Graph

What data is being represented? What are the variables? Before moving on to the questions, make sure you have a clear understanding of what the graph or chart is representing. Read all the information on the graph or chart and try to determine how they relate to each other.

Be Careful with the Data

Some of the charts and graphs can be confusing since they can have many variables. When you have pinpointed what the question is asking you to analyze, double-check the graph to make sure you are analyzing the proper data.

Numbers and Percentages

Perhaps one of the most common mistakes in Data Interpretation is the conflation of numbers and percentages. It is important to note that the two are quite different and will yield different results in your analysis. In some cases you may have both in a single graph. So double-check your calculations and the question to make sure you are using and analyzing the correct terms.

Chapter Overview

Problem Solving questions are the catch-all questions on the GRE. They draw from all the math content areas and are presented as either word problems, geometric figures, or algebraic expressions. Some Problem Solving questions might ask you to interpret data from a graph or chart; these are sub-set of questions we call Data Interpretation questions.

Problem Solving questions have a variety of options when it comes to answer choices; there may be more than one response to the question or you may have to input your answer into a text box.

Approaching the Problems

Understand the Problem

The first step is figuring out what your question task is. What math concepts are being tested in this question? Does the problem have more than one calculation that needs to be made? Make sure you are clear on the final value you are trying to find.

Scan the Answer Choices and Determine Your Approach

With some questions you are asked explicitly which of the choices has a particular property. In this case, scan the answers and eliminate those that do not meet the requirement. Then determine your approach to the problem.

Use the Calculator Smartly

Using the calculator should not always be your first choice when attacking problems. Some problems can be solved more easily without the calculator, and some cannot be solved with a calculator at all.

Data Interpretation

Data Interpretation questions are more of an extension of Problem Solving questions than a unique question type. For these questions, you will interpret data from charts, graphs, and other images and use this information to solve for the correct answer. These problems will be accompanied by a number of visual representations including:

- Bar graphs, including stacked bar graphs
- Pie Charts
- Line Graphs, often with multiple variables charted on the axes

Approaching the Problems

These questions follow the same general principles as Problem Solving questions but have some unique considerations you should keep in mind.

Understand the Graph

- What data is being represented?
- What are the variables?
- Read all the information on the graph or chart and try to determine how they relate to each other.

Be Careful with the Data

- Some of the charts and graphs can be confusing since they can have many variables.
- Double-check the graph to make sure you are analyzing the proper data.

Numbers and Percentages

- Confusing numbers and percentages are one of the most common mistakes in this section.
- Understand that the two are different and yield different results in your analysis.
- Double-check calculations and the question to make sure you are using and analyzing the correct terms.

Problem Solving and Data Interpretation Practice Set

1. The average of all consecutive integers from *x* to *y* inclusive is 39. Which of the following could be *x* and *y*? Select all that apply.

   A   33 and 45
   B   21 and 35
   C   25 and 53
   D   29 and 61
   E   33 and 45

2. Circle K has a total area of 9π. Circle M has a total area of 49π. Suppose the circles intersect at exactly one point. Which of the following could be the distance from the center for Circle K to the center of Circle M?

   Ⓐ   8
   Ⓑ   21
   Ⓒ   10
   Ⓓ   29
   Ⓔ   58

3. For her upcoming vacation, Jade packed three shirts, two pair of shoes, and four skirts. How many different outfits consisting of one skirt, one pair of shoes, and one shirt can Jade make with the clothes she packs? Enter you answer in the box below.

4. Which of the following is less than the sum of all the prime factors of 330? Select all that apply.

   A   17
   B   15
   C   19
   D   21
   E   23

5. What is the area of a triangle that has two sides that are 10 units in length and has a perimeter equal to that of a square that has an area of 81?

   Ⓐ   36
   Ⓑ   28
   Ⓒ   48
   Ⓓ   60
   Ⓔ   24

6. Suppose $f(x) = (x - 4)^2$ and $g(x) = x^2 - 5$. What is the value of $f(2) - g(2)$?

- (A) 5
- (B) 9
- (C) −1
- (D) 0
- (E) 3

7. Find the value of b in the figure below. Write your answer in the text box.

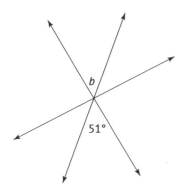

51°

8. The chart details the age at which several U.S. Presidents were took office. What is the median age of inauguration for the Presidents listed?

Age At Inauguration

President	Age	President	Age	President	Age	President	Age
Richard Nixon	56	Grover Cleveland	47	Ulysses S Grant	46	George Washington	57
James Buchanan	65	George W Bush	54	William McKinley	54	William H Harrison	68
Franklin Pierce	48	James A Garfield	49	Milllard Fillmore	50	Barack Obama	47
Thomas Jefferson	57	Franklin D Roosevelt	51	James K Polk	49	Chester A Arthur	51

- (A) 51
- (B) 47
- (C) 53
- (D) 56
- (E) 50

9. Find the area of the trapezoid below.

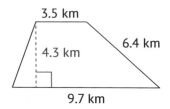

Ⓐ 28.38
Ⓑ 33.78
Ⓒ 31.25
Ⓓ 56.76
Ⓔ 50.25

10. Find the slope of the line on the coordinate plane below.

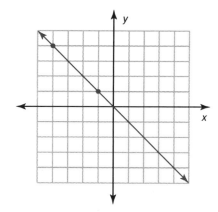

Ⓐ 1
Ⓑ −1
Ⓒ Undefined
Ⓓ 0
Ⓔ 2

Practice Set Answers

1. **C, E.**
   To find the average of a set of consecutive integers, take the average of the largest and smallest integers. Since you know the average you are looking for is 39, any answer choices with an average of 39 is correct.

2. **C.**
   You have two circles and you know the area for each circle. Since the circles only intersect at one point, find the radius of each circle so you can measure the distance from the center of one circle to the center of the other. If the area of Circle K is 9p and the equation for the area of a circle is A = pr2, for Circle K, r = 3. If the area for Circle M is 49p, for Circle M, r = 7. So, if the circles are next to each other, which they will need to be in order to share one point, the total distance from the the the center of Circle K to the center of Circle M simply adds the distance of each radius for a distance of 10.

3. **24.**
   Jade can create 3 · 2 · 4 outfits based on her packing to create 24 different outfits.

4. **A, B, C.**
   The prime factors of 33 are 2, 3, 5, and 11. The sum of the factors is 21. So, 17, 15, and 19 are all less than 21.

5. **C.**
   This question tests your knowledge of triangles and squares. To find the perimeter of the given square, take the square root of 81 to obtain a side length of 9. Multiply by 4 to calculate the perimeter of 36. Therefore, the missing side of the triangle must be 16. If we call the side with length 16 the base of the triangle (*b*), we can obtain the height using the following formula:

   $$h = \sqrt{a^2 - \frac{b^2}{4}} = \sqrt{10^2 - \frac{16^2}{4}} = \sqrt{100 - 64} = 6$$

   Solve the area equation by plugging in 6 for *h* in the following: $a = \frac{1}{2}b \cdot h$.

6. **A.**
   Plug in values for *x* in each function, then solve.

7. **51.**
   These are vertical angles and have the same measurements.

8. **A.**
   The median is the center number or sum of the two center numbers when all the terms are listed in order.

9. **A.**

   $$A = \frac{a + b(h)}{2}$$ Area formula of a trapezoid

   $$A = \frac{3.5 + 9.7(4.3)}{2}$$ Substitute in your values

   $$A = 28.38$$ Solve

10. **B.**
    Line trends downward from left to right.

15 | WRITING PRIMER

Writing on the GRE

The Analytical Writing section tests your ability to create cogent and well-supported arguments. The section is of particular importance to graduate and business schools, and was introduced specifically to ascertain the writing skills of candidates and their ability to meet the often writing-intensive curriculum characteristic of a majority of graduate school programs.

Though content is the most important factor essay reviewers consider when scoring your essay, it is important to ensure your essay is grammatically sound. It must demonstrate a strong command of written English. For the computerized exam, you will not have access to the typical word processing functions like grammar and spell check that you are likely accustomed to using. You will need to be diligent and ensure you leave a few minutes at the end of each essay to proofread and correct mistakes. While minor issues may not count against you, major issues or a lack of variety and complexity in your writing may significantly impact your cumulative score.

Reviewers want to see that you understand proper syntax and grammar, and that you can use a variety of complex sentence structures and vocabulary words. Use vocabulary that is appropriate and makes sense in context. Remember that there are ample opportunities in the Verbal Reasoning section for you to demonstrate your vocabulary prowess. In review, let us look at the characteristics of a top-scoring essay.

Follow Directions

In order to make your essay stand out and increase your chances of earning a top score, your essay needs to not only be well-written, but also fully address the prompt and align with the essay task. If the essay task asks you to choose a side and you write a well-developed essay that argues the merits of both sides and how both options are a good idea, then you are not going to score well, even with a well-written essay. The key to scoring well on the Analytical Writing section is more than writing well; you need to follow instructions, use the provided evidence, and adequately support your claims.

Organization and Clarity

Essay reviewers have lots of essays to review and do not have time to re-read your essays in order to grasp your point. Thus, it is critical that your essay is well-organized and that it clearly articulates your argument and your analysis of the prompt. Essay reviewers should not have to guess your position or search for your supporting evidence. Your position should be clearly stated and supported by both the provided evidence and the relevant evidence you choose to introduce. The flow of the essay should be logical and easy to follow. Make sure you divide your essay into paragraphs, grouping together ideas that are directly related to each other and ensuring that your transitions make sense. We will discuss some strategies to organize your essay logically, aligning with the key elements that essay reviewers are looking for when deriving your score.

Appropriate Use of Evidence

Creating a well-organized, logically sound, and clear essay largely depends on how you use evidence to support your argument. A well-written essay will marshal not only the provided evidence in support of your position, but will also include relevant evidence introduced by you to further strengthen your argument and support your position. The use of examples, real-world occurrences, and logical assumptions can all be helpful in constructing a well-supported, logical essay.

Critical Analysis and Logical Reasoning

Having an essay that is logically sound and provides a critical analysis of the issues and evidence is important. Your goal is to convince your reader of your point of view by providing a well-supported and logically sound case. Having a logically sound argument also means that you have avoided common logic pitfalls and interpreted the issue and evidence without the use of fallacious reasoning.

About the Writing Primer

The Analytical Writing chapters of this book address essay organization, use of evidence, and critical analysis and logical reasoning. This Writing Primer will walk you through common writing mistakes, discuss key characteristics of good, logically sound writing that essay graders are looking for in your essays, and provide a review of grammar, mechanics, and punctuation. After you review this Primer, you should know if further study outside this guidebook is necessary to provide the understanding needed to master areas that still present a challenge for you.

Grammar Review

Grammar plays a key role in the development of strong essays for the Analytical Writing section. Your writing must be clear, and your ideas must flow in a logical way that does not confuse the essay reviewers. Essay reviewers are looking for how well you respond to the prompt using concise but varied sentences that exhibit a clear understanding of grammar and an ability to clearly communicate your ideas. ETS asserts that essays receiving high scores "will demonstrate facility with the conventions (i.e., grammar, usage and mechanics) of standard written English." Let us look at some key grammatical conventions that can help you draft a high-scoring essay.

Subject-Verb Agreement

Basic Premise: The subject and verb of a sentence must agree in person and number. Singular subjects must be paired with singular verbs and plural subjects must be paired with plural verbs.

Person refers to whether the subject is the author (first person), the reader (second person), or someone/something else (third person).

First Person:	I will bake the cake for you. *The author is the subject who is causing the action.*
Second Person:	You should tell me what type of icing you want before I begin. You *is the subject who is causing the action.*
Third Person:	My mom will pick up the ingredients for the icing from the grocery store. *Here, the author's mom is the subject causing the action.*

Number refers to whether the subject is about one person, place, or thing (singular), or multiple persons, places, or things (plural).

Singular:	James Bailey was honored as one of the top philanthropists in Atlanta. *The subject is one person, James Bailey, so the verb* was *is singular.*
Plural:	The new playgrounds have seesaws and swing sets to accommodates lots of kids. *The subject is multiple playgrounds, so the verb* have *is plural.*

Some words and word groups are governed by special rules to ensure proper subject-verb agreement. The following table summarizes these special cases, and should be familiar to you by test-taking day.

Subject-Verb Agreement Rules	Example	Example
Two or more subjects joined by "and" require a plural verb.	The players *and* the coach are going to celebrate their win.	Jenny *and* Peter are going to the basketball game together later tonight.
Collective nouns require a singular verb.	The *group* was unable to come to a consensus.	The *committee* is unsure of how to move forward.
The pronoun "you" requires a plural verb.	*You are* not going to the dance dressed like that, are you?	*You know* that I abhor chocolate as a rule.
Two or more subjects joined by "or" or "nor" require that the verb agrees with the subject closest to it.	Neither the manager *nor* the the *employees agree* with the new policy change.	Neither the employees *nor* the *manager agrees* with the new policy change.
Some indefinite pronouns are singular (e.g., anything, everyone, either, no one, each, etc.) and others are plural (e.g., few, many, several, etc.).	*Everyone was* excited about the upcoming reunion since they had not seen each other in years.	*Many* of the new recruits *were* nervous about playing in their first game.
Occasionally indefinite pronouns can be singular OR plural, depending on their context.	Jim turned in the *project* and indicated that *some was* completed by him and the rest by his lab partner.	Jim turned in the lab *reports* and indicated that *some were* completed by him and some by his lab partner.
When a verb or gerund is used as a subject, it requires a singular verb.	*Shopping is* a good way to de-stress after a long week.	*Shopping* online *minimizes* the time you spend waiting in line.
The subject and verb must agree regardless of their proximity to each other.	*Each* of the articles *suggests* that stress is a precursor to cardiovascular disease.	The *goal* of the campaign *was* to raise awareness about heart disease.
In statements that begin with "there is" or "there are," the verb must match the subject that follows.	There *are* many *options* for font colors.	There *is* only one appropriate *option* that meets the required criteria.

Subject-Pronoun Agreement

Basic Premise: Pronouns must match the nouns they replace in person, number, and gender. Sentences that contain pronouns without a clear antecedent are not grammatically correct.

Person indicates whether the noun is the author (first person), the reader (second person), or someone/something else (third person).

Number indicates whether the noun is about one person, place, or thing (singular), or multiple persons, places, or things (plural).

First Person Singular: I am creating a new line of fashion items for my partner's boutique.
The pronoun I *references the author (singular) of the statement.*

Second Person: You should be able to pick them up soon.
The pronoun You *references the reader of the statement.*

Third Person Plural: They will be packed securely so you can transport them.
The pronoun They *references something other than the author/reader, in this case, the fashion items (plural) of the previous sentences.*

Gender indicates whether the noun is masculine, feminine, or a neutral object.

Masculine: Send an email to Peter. He will confirm your attendance at the conference.
The pronoun He *references the masculine noun* Peter.

Feminine: Send an email to Cynae. She will confirm your attendance at the conference.
The pronoun She *references the feminine noun* Cynae.

Object: Send an email to Peter. He will confirm that he received it.
The pronoun it *references the direct object of the* email.

Some words and word groupings have specific rules that apply to them to ensure agreement:

The pronoun *who* always refers to a person or people. The pronoun *that* always refers to objects.

Incorrect: I will never understand people *that* travel so much.

Correct: I will never understand people *who* travel so much.

Incorrect: Countries *who* limit free speech suppress the free flow of ideas.

Correct: Countries *that* limit free speech suppress the free flow of ideas.

A pronoun should agree with the noun closest to it if in a sentence with numerous nouns separated by *or* or *nor*.

Incorrect: Either the students or the *teacher* will represent *their* class at the carnival.

Correct: Either the students or the *teacher* will represent *her* class at the carnival.

Parallelism

In order to have proper parallel constructions, the items or phrases in any list must be in the same form. Parallelism errors are often awkward for readers because they do not follow the anticipated pattern the reader expects.

> **Incorrect:**   I need an assistant who is able to answer calls, book travel, and record keeping.
>
> **Correct:**   I need an assistant who is able to answer calls, book travel, and keep records.
>
> In this example, the parallelism error is fixed by converting record keeping to an infinitive verb form to match how the other job requirements are listed.

Modifiers

Misplaced or dangling modifiers can cause confusion for your reader. It is important to make sure that your sentences are structured properly and that phrases are modifying the proper subjects or objects of your sentence.

> **Incorrect:**   The public received some important information to protect their homes this summer from the fire chief.
>
> **Correct:**   The public received some important information from the fire chief to protect their homes this summer.
>
> The first sentence is ambiguous in that it appears that the public received information on how to protect their homes from the fire chief, as if she was the threat. The correction makes it clear that the fire chief disseminated the information to the public.

Similar to misplaced modifiers, dangling modifiers modify part of a statement, but there is key information missing that is needed to allow the reader to fully connect all the pieces of the sentence. Essentially, a dangling modifier is a word or phrase that modifies a word or words not explicitly articulated in the sentence. Most dangling modifiers are the result of an author omitting a subject of the sentence.

> **Incorrect:**   With a great deal of disappointment, the deal fell through.
>
> **Correct:**   With a great deal of disappointment, Jack announced that the deal fell through.
>
> Since the deal cannot be disappointed, the first example needs more information in order to make sense. By adding a subject to the sentence capable of experiencing the disappointment, the sentence more clearly expresses the point.

Punctuation and Capitalization

Proper capitalization and punctuation are critical aspects of writing and communicating clearly and concisely with your reader. Improper punctuation can change the intended meaning of your writing and confuse readers. Let us look at a brief overview of proper punctuation and capitalization.

Punctuation	Proper Usage	Examples
Period [.]	To end a complete thought.	This long day is finally over.
Question Mark [?]	To signify a question or statement of doubt.	How many years did he have to wait before he could re-apply?
Exclamation Point [!]	To show extreme excitement or surprise. Your use of exclamation points should be limited on the GRE.	I can't believe you just did that!
Comma [,]	To separate items in a series.	There are bagels, coffee, and donuts in the lounge.
	To separate a string of adjectives.	The paper was clear, concise, and well-researched.
	To separate two independent clauses joined by a coordinating conjunction.	I was going to go to the beach, but I decided to go to the mountains instead.
	To signify the end of an introductory or prepositional phrase.	In order for the team to be successful, they needed to complete the requisite training program.
	To introduce a quotation.	He said, "No, please don't do that."
	Between day of the month and year in dates.	July 13, 1982
	Between a city and state.	Somerville, Massachusetts
	After conjunctive adverbs.	She failed her theses defense; therefore, she will not graduate.
Semicolon [;]	To separate two closely related independent clauses.	She was devastated after the loss; we all expected she would be.
	To separate clauses joined by a conjunctive adverb.	She took more than a year to complete the project; however, she was still able to graduate with her class.
	To separate a series of equal elements that includes commas.	The world tour will include Budapest; Sofia, Varna, and Burgas; and Tbilisi.
Apostrophe [']	To indicate possessives.	It is hard to determine the mothers' motives since they all refuse to talk to the press.
	To make contractions. Your use of contractions on the exam should be minimal since the essays are considered formal writing tasks.	The dog couldn't figure out how to use the automatic food dispenser.
Quotations [" "]	To signify information quoted directly from an outside source.	She said that the professor told her that her argument was "loosely constructed."

ARGOPREP.COM/GRE

Requires Capitalization	Example
First person singular pronoun "I"	*I* will serve as the marshal for this year's parade.
Proper nouns	*Greg Whitmore* is the new director of *Housing Operations* at the *University of Chicago* located in *Cook County, Illinois*.
Days of the week and months	Our office is open *Monday* through *Friday*.
Proper names of historical periods or events and formally organized groups	The *Supreme Court* is the highest court in the *United States* justice system.
Proper names of ethnicities, nationalities, and languages	The school now offers *Spanish* and *Thai*.
Names of businesses, trademarks, and brand names	*Nike* and *Adidas* are fierce competitors in the sports apparel market.

Using Active Voice

Voice simply describes the structure of the action in your sentence. The structure is based on who or what receives the action. When using active voice, the subject of the sentence performs the action. When using passive voice, the subject of the sentence is the recipient of the action. Let us look at some examples.

Active Voice: The young musician composed his first original score this year.

Passive Voice: The first original score was written by the young musician this year.

Passive voice is not grammatically incorrect. However, passive voice is often not concise and can cause confusion for your readers. Active voice is much more clear and direct and often eliminates confusion about who is performing or receiving an action. It is also more interesting to read. You should endeavor to complete your essays in active voice to ensure you are clearly addressing the prompts and providing a clear road map of your logic for the essay reviewer to follow.

Vocabulary

One of the best ways to clearly articulate your point is to be strategic about your vocabulary use. Be consistent in how you describe things and avoid using "big" words for the sake of using big words. Use words that are appropriate for the context. Ensure you use words correctly and avoid terms that are commonly confused. The remainder of this guide is a refresher of commonly misspelled words and commonly confused and misused words.

Commonly Misspelled Words

a lot	definitely	harass	occasionally	seize
acceptable	describe	humorous	occurred	separate
accidentally	desperate	hypocrisy	paid	sergeant
accommodate	despise	immediately	parallel	similar
acquaintance	develop	incidentally	pastime	simile
acquitted	disappearance	independent	permissible	sophomore

196

advice	disappoint	irresistible	perseverance	succeed
affect	discipline	jewelry	precedence	supersede
attendance	dissatisfied	judgment	preceding	tragedy
beginning	duel	knowledge	prejudice	tries
believe	ecstasy	laboratory	principal	undoubtedly
benefit	effect	latter	privilege	
business	embarrassment	led	pursue	
calendar	environment	liaison	questionnaire	
cemetery	existence	loneliness	receive	
challenge	familiar	lose	recommend	
changeable	fascinate	marriage	reference	
commission	February	medieval	relevant	
committee	fiery	millennium	repetition	
conscience	formerly	miniature	rhyme	
conscientious	gauge	mischief	rhythm	
conscious	government	misspell	ridiculous	
criticize	grammar	murmur	sacrilegious	
deceive	grateful	necessary	shepherd	
definite	guarantee	noticeable	siege	

Commonly Confused and Misused Words

a/an
A is used ahead of consonants.
An is used ahead of vowels.

accept/except
Accept means to receive or take something or someone.
Except means to leave something out.

advice/advise
Advice is a noun that means suggestions or guidance.
Advise is a verb that means to direct or give advice.

affect/effect
Affect means to impact or influence something or someone.
Effect is a consequence or outcome of something.

among / between
Between references a relationship consisting of two things.
Among references a relationship of two or more things.

assure / ensure / insure
Assure means to provide comfort to someone.
Ensure means to guarantee that something will happen or be completed.
Insure means to protect against loss or damages from unexpected occurrences.

beside / besides
Beside means close to or next to.
Besides means in addition to.

compliment / complement
Compliment means to offer praise or express admiration.
Complement means two or more things or people that work well together.

choose / chose
Choose is used to express making a choice in the present or future tense.
Chose is used to express a choice already made and is in the past tense.

compare / contrast
Compare means to highlight similarities.
Contrast means to highlight differences.

continual / continuous
Continual means frequent or repeated recurrence.
Continuous means occurring without interruptions all of the time.

disinterested / uninterested:
Disinterested means to be impartial or unbiased.
Uninterested means having no interest at all.

e.g. / i.e.
The *e.g.* abbreviation means "for example." It is used to list some examples after a general statement. The list is usually considered incomplete.
The *i.e.* abbreviation means "that is" or "in other words." It is used to clarify something previously stated. When the clarification is a list of items, using i.e. indicates that the list is complete.

equal / equitable
Equal means the same.
Equitable means fair.

farther / further
Farther is used in reference to distance.
Further refers to additional numbers: further evidence. It can also mean a greater degree or extent of something: further guilt.

fewer / less
Fewer is used to refer to things that can be counted.
Less is used to refer to quantities that cannot be counted, usually percentages, volume, etc.

imply / infer
Imply refers to something that is expressed indirectly.
Infer refers to an assumption that is made based on given facts.

irregardless / regardless / irrespective

Irregardless is **not** a word despite its frequent use.
Regardless and *irrespective* mean despite or without consideration.

of / have

Of is often misused when *have* should be used instead: He should have left (correct) versus He should of left (incorrect).

their / there / they're

Their is a pronoun and shows possession of something by several people or things.
There refers to a location.
They're is the contraction of they are.

who / whom

Who always refers to the person performing whatever action in the sentence.
Whom always refers to the person receiving the action in a sentence.

your / you're

Your refers to something that you possess.
You're is the contraction of you are.

16 | ANALYZE AN ISSUE:
MODEL ESSAY

Prompt

If a goal is worthy, it is justifiable to approach achieving it by any means necessary.

Discuss the extent to which you agree or disagree with the statement and explain your position. Also discuss instances when the statement may or may not be true and how these instances impact your viewpoint.

Essay

Goals are the foundation of personal growth and are often harbingers for many of our achievements and contributions to society. People go to extraordinary lengths to reach their goals. But while a stanch commitment to achieving one's goals is typically admirable, it is a mistake to assert that a "by any means necessary" approach is justifiable in all circumstances.

Goals provide a roadmap for an individual's life and endow one with a sense of purpose, a feeling that one is working towards something meaningful. While usually beneficial to the individual, personal goals can also contribute to the betterment of society. For example, when individuals set goals to obtain education, to pursue medical careers, or to earn a leadership role in the military, their efforts and achievements impact more than just themselves; the results positively impact their communities and add value to society. If those individuals make extreme personal sacrifices for those goals, then the means are most likely justified, assuming they do not irreparably harm others or stand opposed to what is morally acceptable.

Not all goals belong to an individual, however. Nations, businesses, and communities, like individuals, have goals that prioritize their own interests. Here, regardless of the contribution made to society or the interests being protected, if the means by which the goal is achieved deviates from what is morally right or unjustifiably brings harm upon others, the goal loses its value and the novelty of achieving that goal is diminished.

That is not to say that extreme, morally questionable measures are not sometimes justifiable. There have been many instances in history that demonstrate this. During the Third Reich, Nazi Germany had as a goal the extermination of Jews and the proliferation of the Aryan race. Their extreme measures to achieve their goal were met by the extreme measures of the Allied Powers to prevent them from doing so. Some may argue that war is an unjustifiable means to an end. In this instance, the means by which the Allied Powers opted to achieve their goal was justified because, while it may have been morally questionable and caused harm to others, the alternative of not intervening would have had far greater consequences.

Goals are important for the growth of individuals and society as a whole. We should encourage the steadfast pursuit of goals with the understanding that in order for a goal to maintain its worth, the means by which that goal is achieved must be carefully considered. An achievement tainted by moral ineptitude or the unjustifiable sacrifice of others is in essence not an achievement at all.

Analysis

The essay takes a clear stance on the issue in the first paragraph, asserting that it is a mistake to assume that a "by any means necessary" approach is justifiable in all circumstances. The essay provides relevant examples for when "by any means necessary" is acceptable and lays out the groundwork for determining the extent of acceptable cases.

The body paragraphs provide an analysis of individual goals and the goals of larger entities like nations, businesses and communities. The author also reasserts that means to achieving goals that deviate from what is morally right or cause harm to others are not justifiable. The essay sufficiently addresses the question task by providing examples of when the taken position may not be true, with the fourth paragraph addressing the Allied Powers' goal to stop the extermination of Jews by the Third Reich.

The examples used are appropriate, persuasive, and align with the position the essay takes. There are minimal spelling and grammar errors, and the essay demonstrates a solid understanding of written English and critical reasoning. The essay receives a score of 6.

17 | ANALYZE AN ARGUMENT: MODEL ESSAY

Prompt

The following is an excerpt from a letter drafted by the Nimman Homeowners Association and sent to the current homeowners in Nimman:

"Eight years ago, the nearby neighborhood, Old City, experienced a significant increase in property values after implementing rigid standards that standardized the exterior home colors and landscaping requirements for all homes in the neighborhood. Given their success, Nimman is implementing similar standards for landscaping and exterior paint colors in order to raise the property value of homes in the neighborhood."

Discuss the evidence needed to fully assess the argument. Include examples and an explanation of how the evidence provided strengthens or weakens the argument.

Essay

The letter to homeowners sets forth recommendations to increase property values for Nimman based on the outcomes of similar changes implemented in Old City several years prior. Closer inspection of the letter's evidence challenges the assumptions made by the Homeowners Association. The argument is flawed in a number of ways.

First, the only evidence offered for the author's claim is that a nearby neighborhood implemented similar guidelines eight years ago and experienced an increase in property values. A lot can change in eight years that might impact the likelihood of a similar outcome. For example, people may have different priorities now than they did eight years ago or the area could have changed considerably in that time. Without more information about the full circumstances that led to the previous increase in property value, and by using an example so far in the past, the author is at best making a logical leap.

Second, the Homeowners Association contends that simply tightening the restrictions on landscaping and standardizing exterior paint colors of the homes will produce the same results in Nimman as they did in Old City. This assumption also fails to consider other factors that may have accounted for the increase in property value Old City experienced; it attributes the increase solely to the policy changes. Any number of confounding factors could have contributed to the increase, like an influx of businesses or greenspace that made the neighborhood more attractive and sought after, thereby driving up the property value.

The Homeowner Association's assertion is further questionable in its failing to establish that Old City and Nimman are comparable enough in all other aspects that making similar aesthetic changes would yield the same increase in property value. While the areas may be near each other, the communities could vary substantially enough that, even if the changes were the sole factor that accounted for Old City's property value, more would need to be done in Nimman in addition to those changes to make the areas equally desirable. The premises the Homeowners Association uses to support its conclusion are limited in scope and do not follow logically.

The Homeowners Association would have a more compelling argument had they gather evidence directly from homeowners in Old City that ascertained the factors that influenced their willingness to purchase a home in the area and the reasons they believe the property value experienced such an increase eight years ago. In addition, the Homeowners Association could have conducted surveys of residents near and in Nimman and Old City to gain an understanding of what qualities homeowners and potential homeowners value in a home and location presently. These two points of inquiry would have equipped the Homeowners Association with an understanding of past trends and present-day values, and provided them with more relevant and complete data to make more appropriate recommendations than those offered in the letter.

Analysis

The essay examines the provided evidence and its assumptions and clearly articulates the weakness of the argument. Paragraphs 2, 3 and 4 deconstruct the faulty logic of the Homeowners Association's argument, demonstrating why the

argument as a whole is weak. The analysis of the evidence sufficiently satisfies the question task to include and discuss the strength or weakness of the evidence presented.

The last paragraph offers clear and appropriate examples of information that could be used to formulate more accurate and data-driven recommendations. The essay contains no minor errors. There is appropriate sentence variation and a strong grasp of grammar and vocabulary. The response overall is cogent, properly addresses the question task, and demonstrates a clear mastery of written English and critical reasoning. The essay receives a score of 6.

GRE®

PRACTICE TESTS

PRACTICE TEST 1

GRE ®

Graduate Record Examinations

- This exam is 3 hours and 45 minutes long. Try to take this full exam in one sitting to simulate real test conditions.

- While taking this exam, refrain from listening to music or watching TV.

- When writing your responses for the Analyze an Issue and Analyze an Argument prompts, please use a computer, and turn off the spell-check feature to simulate real testing conditions.

- If **circles** mark a question's answer choices, choose one answer. If **squares** mark a question's answer choices, choose more than one answer.

- Use a basic calculator. Do not use a graphic or scientific calculator. On the real exam, you will have an on-screen calculator with only basic operation functions and a square root key.

- Concentrate and GOOD LUCK!

ANALYTICAL WRITING
ANALYZE AN ISSUE

ESSAY 1
30 MINUTES

The government has a responsibility to closely regulate herbal supplements that are made available for sale to ensure their safety and to validate their claims about health outcomes.

Discuss how much you agree or disagree with the claim and the support offered in defense of the claim.

GO TO THE NEXT PAGE

ANALYTICAL WRITING | ESSAY 2
ANALYZE AN ARGUMENT | 30 MINUTES

The following memo was issued by the sales manager of Wappy Waffle restaurants.

We recently made the decision to replace all of our syrups with a sugar-free substitute. We have been soliciting customer feedback and have determined that the change has had little impact on our customers. To date, only about 4 percent of customers have complained, indicating that an average of 96 people out of 100 have happily greeted the change. Additionally, many servers have reported that a number of customers who ask for syrup do not complain when they are given the sugar-free variety instead. Clearly, these customers cannot distinguish between the two.

After reviewing the author's argument, examine any alternate explanations that could reasonably compete with the proposed explanation. In your response, discuss how your alternate explanations challenge the assertions provided in the argument.

GO TO THE NEXT PAGE

For questions 1 to 6, you are to choose <u>one</u> answer for each blank from the corresponding column of choices.

1. Alana blamed her emotional distress on those around her. As a result, she _____ herself, causing her friends to believe that she wanted to be left alone.

   Ⓐ chastised
   Ⓑ sequestered
   Ⓒ admonished
   Ⓓ derided
   Ⓔ excused

2. Although the start-up had the potential for long-term (i)_____ and thriving business, it failed to capture the attention of venture capitalists due to its (ii)_____ published materials, which favored extremely detailed statistics that non-industry audiences had trouble following.

Blank i	Blank ii
Ⓐ viability	Ⓓ querulous
Ⓑ temerity	Ⓔ convoluted
Ⓒ fecklessness	Ⓕ disparate

3. Bobby stood in the winding (i)_____ for what seemed like hours. He was determined to (ii)_____ tickets to the newly announced Garth concert since it had long been his dream to see the band perform live.

Blank i	Blank ii
Ⓐ imbroglio	Ⓓ procure
Ⓑ stanchion	Ⓔ mulct
Ⓒ queue	Ⓕ extricate

4. The (i)_____ of available financial resources have made it difficult for the Hope Charter School to satisfy its (ii)_____ responsibilities. Bills have fallen behind and teachers lack classroom supplies. If the school is to survive, analyzing its finances and making a plan to ameliorate its dearth of resources is (iii)_____.

Blank i	Blank ii
Ⓐ concomitant	Ⓓ intractable
Ⓑ preponderance	Ⓔ pecuniary
Ⓒ paucity	Ⓕ mercurial

Blank iii
Ⓖ imperative
Ⓗ advisable
Ⓘ desultory

5. The careful examination of the stability of banks in the U.S. is to reassure (i)_____ investors by affirming that the banks they trust with their money are secure. The thorough process identifies both the most stable and the most (ii)_____ institutions and reports back to investors. Since the banks are reviewed by individuals with no vested interest in the banks or the investors, the recommendations are viewed as (iii)_____ and are highly regarded.

Blank i	Blank ii
Ⓐ timorous	Ⓓ tenuous
Ⓑ parsimonious	Ⓔ myopic
Ⓒ tawdry	Ⓕ duplicitous

Blank iii
Ⓖ unprejudiced
Ⓗ vacillating
Ⓘ veritable

GO TO THE NEXT PAGE

6. From the early 1880s onward, author Oscar Wilde found it hard to escape the (i)_____ belief that he happily (ii)_____ other people's ideas. By far the most controversial conflict in Wilde's career arose from criticisms that the painter James McNeill Whistler made about Wilde's unacknowledged (iii)_____ of his witticisms.

Blank i	Blank ii
Ⓐ histrionic	Ⓓ expunged
Ⓑ deterrent	Ⓔ espoused
Ⓒ delusive	Ⓕ filched

Blank iii
Ⓖ infraction
Ⓗ approbation
Ⓘ appropriation

GO TO THE NEXT PAGE

Questions 7 and 8 are based on the following bulletin issued by the U.S. Department of Agriculture in 1948. Select one answer unless otherwise indicated.

The place for a farmer to start grasshopper control is on his own land, and the time to start is before the hoppers hatch. Plowing and harrowing are effective in destroying eggs or in burying them so deeply that
5 most of the baby hoppers cannot climb to the surface. 5 In areas where grasshoppers are a menace, only fall-plowed, spring-plowed, or summer-fallowed land should be seeded. Though the practice of "stubbling-in" crops may deter soil erosion, it also boosts the hopper
10 birth rate. Where soil erosion is likely to be a serious 10 factor, county agents, agronomists, soil conservationists, and entomologists should be consulted in developing a tillage and seeding program that will provide as much grasshopper control as is consistent with approved
15 local farming methods. 15

When farmers practice grasshopper control on their own fields, their protected crops have more time to develop enough to survive attack, their control cost is reduced, and they can apply more of their control
20 efforts on hoppers coming in from outside. 20

7. The author gives all but which of the following premises to support his argument that farmers should first practice grasshopper control on their own land? Select <u>all</u> that apply.

    A Methods for controlling soil erosion can boost grasshopper populations

    B Plants will have more time to mature, increasing their likelihood of surviving an attack

    C Grasshoppers form local populations and do not move around

    D Once their own grasshopper populations are controlled, farmers can spend more time on control efforts against outside infestations

    E Farmers will save money on overall control costs

8. Which of the following, if true, would MOST weaken the author's argument?

    Ⓐ Outside grasshopper populations are even more devastating than those of one's own fields

    Ⓑ Soil erosion prevention tactics also control grasshopper birth rates

    Ⓒ A farmer's pest control on his own lands usually only succeeds in moving the population to his neighbor's

    Ⓓ Fall-plowed lands are a grasshopper's favorite breeding ground

GO TO THE NEXT PAGE

Questions 9 to 12 are based on the following passage. Select one answer unless otherwise indicated.

What makes vaccine access and administration such a complicated issue? The short answer is that vaccines require the coordination of many critical moving pieces in order to ensure the safe delivery of a viable
5 product from laboratory to recipient. In fact, the steps are so complex that even developed countries have a hard time managing them. The general idea of what a vaccine is—a syringe filled with liquid—is largely incomplete and prevents many from understanding
10 the full complexity of vaccine issues.

Originally, vaccines were developed as a powder (usually derived from the carcass of an infected animal) that contained a form of a specified disease and were administered to breed immunity. As science evolved, so
15 did the manufacture of vaccines and similar powders were created in a sterile environment and mass-produced. Vaccines that are manufactured as powders must be reconstituted with diluent. The diluent is a major complicating factor and threatens the sterility of
20 vaccines. The World Health Organization has outlined some of the issues related to the diluent, including a strict time window for administering the vaccine after it is reconstituted. Administering the vaccine after this time frame carries the risk of potentially fatal
25 staphylococcus.

Diluents are also not universal; each one is specific to the vaccine it accompanies. The diluent modulates the vaccine's pH and directly impacts the final chemical composition of the vaccine. When diluents are mixed
30 up and used with the wrong vaccine, the recipient is vulnerable to unpleasant side events that can be as severe as toxic shock. The mix-up can also render the vaccine useless. Other modalities for vaccine administration include freeze-dried vaccines that
35 require strict temperature controls, conditions that also present challenges for developing countries. The administration of the vaccine itself also creates challenges, as it requires knowledge of how to use sterile needles with the diluent, among other critical
40 considerations.

9. What is the primary purpose of the passage?

(A) To discuss the dangers of vaccines when administered to children at too young of an age
(B) To discuss some of the factors that contribute to the disparity in vaccine availability, especially in the developing world
(C) To analyze the World Health Organization's response to challenges associated with vaccine administration
(D) To discuss new technology available to make diluents less confusing
(E) To advocate for clearer instructions on the labels of vaccine

10. The passage mentions which of the following possible problems that can arise when dealing with vaccines? Select all that apply.

[A] Diluents can be mixed up and create an adverse reaction or render the vaccine ineffective
[B] The mass-production process of vaccines occurs in uncontrolled environments
[C] Vaccines not stored at the proper temperatures can be deadly
[D] Lack of sterile needles can present various dangers
[E] Labels can include incorrect directions

11. The author would most likely agree with which **one** of the following efforts to make vaccines more accessible in developing countries?

(A) Clear and large-print labeling of diluents that correspond to a particular vaccine
(B) The creation of a streamlined vaccine that is temperature stable and does not require a diluent
(C) A non-profit dedicated to providing sterile needles to developing countries
(D) A multi-level vaccine refrigeration unit that allows different vaccines to be kept in the same space but at different temperatures
(E) A non-toxic color solution that turns the vaccine pink when it has expired

GO TO THE NEXT PAGE

VERBAL REASONING
SECTION 3

12. "Diluent" introduced in Line 18 means:

Ⓐ an extender
Ⓑ an aggravating substance
Ⓒ a thickener
Ⓓ a thinning substance
Ⓔ a strengthener

Question 13 is based on the passage below. Select one answer unless otherwise indicated.

Drinking too much coffee can have long-term effects on the brain. Caffeine directly impacts serotonin receptors by over-stimulating them to produce too much serotonin. Frequent over-production of
5 serotonin causes structural damage to the brain in areas responsible for controlling speech and vision. Thus, if college students do not want to go blind or lose their speech prematurely, they should avoid caffeine.

13. Which of the following, if true, would weaken the author's claims? Select <u>all</u> that apply.

Ⓐ Serotonin controls the emotional center of the brain
Ⓑ Scientists establish a link between high serotonin levels and deafness
Ⓒ High levels of serotonin cause other systems to over-produce various hormones
Ⓓ College students have extremely low levels of blindness and speech impairment

Questions 14 to 16 are based on the following speech given by then-Senator Barack Obama in Philadelphia on 18 March 2008. Select one answer unless otherwise indicated.

"We the people, in order to form a more perfect union."

Two hundred and twenty-one years ago, in a hall that still stands across the street, a group of men gathered and, with these simple words, launched America's
5 improbable experiment in democracy. Farmers and scholars; statesmen and patriots who had traveled across an ocean to escape tyranny and persecution finally made real their declaration of independence at a Philadelphia convention that lasted through the
10 spring of 1787.

The document they produced was eventually signed but ultimately unfinished. It was stained by this nation's original sin of slavery, a question that divided the colonies and brought the convention to a stalemate
15 until the founders chose to allow the slave trade to continue for at least twenty more years, and to leave any final resolution to future generations.

Of course, the answer to the slavery question was already embedded within our Constitution—a
20 Constitution that had at its very core the ideal of equal citizenship under the law; a Constitution that promised its people liberty, and justice, and a union that could be and should be perfected over time.

And yet words on a parchment would not be enough
25 to deliver slaves from bondage, or provide men and women of every color and creed their full rights and obligations as citizens of the United States. What would be needed were Americans in successive generations who were willing to do their part—through protests
30 and struggle, on the streets and in the courts, through a civil war and civil disobedience and always at great risk—to narrow that gap between the promise of our ideals and the reality of their time.

14. The author introduces his speech with a quotation in order to do what? Select <u>all</u> that apply.

- [A] Draw a connection between the past and the present
- [B] Demonstrate his knowledge of America's founding documents
- [C] Discuss teamwork
- [D] Cite legal precedence
- [E] Set up terms later defined

15. What sentence best articulates the main idea of the passage? (Please circle or highlight the sentence directly in the passage)

16. In the passage, Obama argues that the role of the U.S. Constitution is:

- (A) to narrow the gap between ideals and reality
- (B) made vivid when standing in Philadelphia
- (C) fully realized
- (D) ambivalent to citizen action
- (E) to guarantee equal citizenship for all under the law

For questions 17 to 20, select two answers that best complete the blank and produce two sentences that are alike in meaning.

17. The Third Lemon Company _____ the exhibition as a collegial gathering to discuss the latest innovations in 3-D technology. It quickly digressed into a series of quarrels among the participants.

- [A] touted
- [B] wangled
- [C] induced
- [D] heralded
- [E] insinuated
- [F] habituated

GO TO THE NEXT PAGE

18. To the untrained eye that may only see random and chaotic paint strokes, abstract expressionist works of art may seem _____ .

    [A] whimsical
    [B] imperturbable
    [C] arbitrary
    [D] guileless
    [E] superfluous
    [F] eclectic

19. Sonjia underestimated the _____ conditions the group would encounter on their trip to Bolivia, due to the high altitude.

    [A] soporific
    [B] vertiginous
    [C] placid
    [D] dizzying
    [E] haphazard
    [F] fulsome

20. Doctors tell many Americans every year that they need to better manage their hypertension and lose weight to lower their risk of a heart attack. As a result, many decide to give up eating meat and make more _____ choices overall when planning their meals.

    [A] austere
    [B] cavalier
    [C] abstemious
    [D] garrulous
    [E] voracious
    [F] truculent

QUANTITATIVE REASONING
SECTION 4

| 20 QUESTIONS
| 35 MINUTES

1. Gabe is 5 years older than Paul. Gabe was twice as old as Paul three years ago.

Quantity A	Quantity B
5	Paul's current age

Ⓐ Quantity A is greater.
Ⓑ Quantity B is greater.
Ⓒ The two quantities are equal.
Ⓓ The relationship cannot be determined from the information given.

2.

Quantity A	Quantity B
The sum of integers from 21 to 51 inclusive	The sum of integers from 24 to 49 inclusive

Ⓐ Quantity A is greater.
Ⓑ Quantity B is greater.
Ⓒ The two quantities are equal.
Ⓓ The relationship cannot be determined from the information given.

3. A task is completed by x workers in 36 hours. The same task is completed by $(x + 2)$ workers in y hours.

Quantity A	Quantity B
36	y

Ⓐ Quantity A is greater.
Ⓑ Quantity B is greater.
Ⓒ The two quantities are equal.
Ⓓ The relationship cannot be determined from the information given.

4.

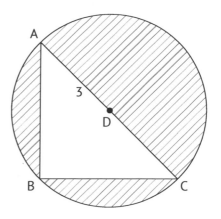

Triangle ABC is a right triangle.

Quantity A	Quantity B
The Shaded Area	$9\pi - 9$

Ⓐ Quantity A is greater.
Ⓑ Quantity B is greater.
Ⓒ The two quantities are equal.
Ⓓ The relationship cannot be determined from the information given.

5.

Water weighs 8.34 pounds per gallon. There are 7.48 gallons per cubic foot.

Quantity A	Quantity B
Volume of 15 tons of water	Half the volume of a tank 8' in diameter and 15' tall

Ⓐ Quantity A is greater.
Ⓑ Quantity B is greater.
Ⓒ The two quantities are equal.
Ⓓ The relationship cannot be determined from the information given.

GO TO THE NEXT PAGE

QUANTITATIVE REASONING
SECTION 4

6.
$$4x^2 - 17x + 4 = 0$$

Quantity A	Quantity B
x	$\sqrt{\dfrac{1}{16}}$

(A) Quantity A is greater.
(B) Quantity B is greater.
(C) The two quantities are equal.
(D) The relationship cannot be determined from the information given.

---

7. Solve the equation: $\dfrac{n+4}{10} = \dfrac{n-8}{2}$

(A) 7.3
(B) – 11
(C) 11
(D) 6.2
(E) – 10

---

8. Which one of the following is equivalent to the expression

$$\frac{(xy)^3(z^0)}{x^3y^4}$$

when $xyz \neq 0$?

(A) xyz

(B) xz

(C) $\dfrac{1}{y}$

(D) 1

(E) $\dfrac{z}{xy}$

---

9. Given the pentagon below, the value of h is 3. Find h_2.

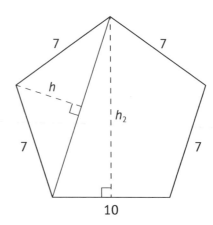

(A) $3\sqrt{15}$
(B) $\sqrt{55}$
(C) $\sqrt{15}$
(D) $2\sqrt{15}$
(E) 13

---

10. The new video game console was priced at $400 when it was released last year. This year, the price decreased by 15% during the holiday sale period. The game manufacturer recently announced that the same console will be re-released with new updates and expanded functionality. The retail price will be 25% greater than the previous sale price. When the game console is re-released, what will be the retail price?

(A) $360
(B) $425
(C) $380
(D) $415
(E) $395

GO TO THE NEXT PAGE

11. Working alone, it takes Randy 11 hours to inventory the instrument shop. Liz can complete the same inventory in 10 hours. If they worked together, how long would it take them to complete the inventory of the instrument shop?

    Ⓐ 5.24 hours
    Ⓑ 5.59 hours
    Ⓒ 5.77 hours
    Ⓓ 5.6 hours
    Ⓔ 5 hours

12. Wanda leaves the office and travels north at 30 MPH for 2 hours, then stops for 2 hours. Jeff leaves the office and travels east at 36 MPH for 4 hours, then stops. At this point they both turn and travel directly towards one another at their previous rates of speed. Once they meet, what is the average combined speed of Jeff and Wanda? Enter your answer in the text box below.

    [   ]

Use the following frequency chart to answer Questions 13 to 14.

Item	Cost	Number
Oatmeal Cookies	$1.76	4
Whole Milk	$3.99	2
Sugar Cured Ham	$4.54	2
7 Grain Bread	$3.27	3
CFL Light bulbs	$2.00	5
Ginger Soda	$0.67	6
Chocolate Candy Bar	$1.15	?

13. Given that the average price per item was $2.09, how many Chocolate Candy Bars did Cindy purchase?

    Ⓐ 1
    Ⓑ 2
    Ⓒ 3
    Ⓓ 4
    Ⓕ 0

14. How many Chocolate Candy Bars must Cindy purchase in order to end up with a median price of $1.88?

    Ⓐ 1
    Ⓑ 2
    Ⓒ 3
    Ⓓ 4
    Ⓔ 0

15. If $y \neq 0$, select all the terms that must be positive:

    Ⓐ $(y^2)^3$
    Ⓑ y^{-2}
    Ⓒ $y^2 \cdot y^{-4}$
    Ⓓ y^0
    Ⓔ $\frac{1}{y^{-5}}$

16. Given the line $4x - 7y = 17$, find the point of intersection with a line passing through points $(0, 4)$ and $(12, -2)$.

    Ⓐ $(\frac{1}{2}, 5)$
    Ⓑ $(13, 5)$
    Ⓒ $(6, 1)$
    Ⓓ $(\frac{3}{4}, 2)$
    Ⓔ The answer cannot be determined from the information given.

17. If $A, B, C, D,$ and E are points on a plane such that line CD bisects $\angle ACB$ and line CB bisects right angle $\angle ACE$, then $\angle DCE =$

    Ⓐ 22.5°
    Ⓑ 45°
    Ⓒ 57.5°
    Ⓓ 67.5°
    Ⓔ 72.5°

18. Jimmy stands at the window of an apartment which is 40 feet above the ground. He releases a glider which flies a straight path to his friend, who catches the glider 10 feet above the ground in the neighboring building. If the buildings are 40 feet apart, what is the distance traveled by the glider?

(A) $10\sqrt{17}$ feet

(B) $10\sqrt{41}$ feet

(C) $40\sqrt{2}$ feet

(D) 50 feet

(E) 70 feet

19. Emily has 12 cups of lemonade that is a solution of 15% lemon juice. She makes her lemonade from juice concentrate, which is 47% lemon juice. How much concentrate must she add to her lemonade in order to increase the solution to 23% lemon juice?

(A) 3.5 cups
(B) 4 cups
(C) 1.6 cups
(D) 2 cups
(E) 6.3 cups

20. The continental USA is 2,802 miles across. How many days will it take to cross the USA if you are traveling at 65 MPH, but stop 8 hours each day to sleep and 3 hours each day to eat? Enter your answer in the text box below.

For questions 1 to 6, you are to choose one answer for each blank from the corresponding column of choices.

1. The object's _____ lies in its sleek and ergonomic design.

   Ⓐ provenance
   Ⓑ quintessence
   Ⓒ quietude
   Ⓓ decrepitude
   Ⓔ residue

2. When (i)_____, the program did not measure up to the rigors of present-day banking standards, its executives having (ii)_____ as to the program's current state of disrepute.

Blank i	Blank ii
Ⓐ augmented	Ⓓ equivocated
Ⓑ assayed	Ⓔ mustered
Ⓒ expiated	Ⓕ predetermined

3. Toby's writing style did not match that desired by the tabloid. His pieces were often (i)_____ and lacked any sort of sensationalism or (ii)_____.

Blank i	Blank ii
Ⓐ terse	Ⓓ pugnacity
Ⓑ academic	Ⓔ torridity
Ⓒ scintillating	Ⓕ insight

4. To (i)_____ his advisors' fears, the king promised (ii)_____ for refugees from foreign lands, a decision that (iii)_____ his kingdom's current policy toward foreigners.

Blank i	Blank ii
Ⓐ stint	Ⓓ vigilance
Ⓑ allay	Ⓔ retaliation
Ⓒ incite	Ⓕ sanctuary

Blank iii
Ⓖ defrayed
Ⓗ transmuted
Ⓘ transfigured

5. In the seventeenth century the two royal houses ceased the (i)_____ practice of wearing the (ii)_____ crown jewels of their (iii)_____ to public events.

Blank i	Blank ii
Ⓐ panoramic	Ⓓ rapacious
Ⓑ ostentatious	Ⓔ opulent
Ⓒ palpable	Ⓕ viable

Blank iii
Ⓖ hierarchy
Ⓗ oligarchy
Ⓘ progenitors

GO TO THE NEXT PAGE

VERBAL REASONING
SECTION 5

6. While the will (i)_____ the deceased man's many wrongdoings, its (ii)_____ did not (iii)_____ the sorrow of his children.

Blank i
Ⓐ extolled
Ⓑ concocted
Ⓒ enumerated

Blank ii
Ⓓ veracity
Ⓔ ingenuity
Ⓕ turpitude

Blank iii
Ⓖ mitigate
Ⓗ mollify
Ⓘ inure

Questions 7 to 8 are based on the following passage. Select one answer unless otherwise indicated.

The only safe basis of psychotherapy is a thorough psychological knowledge of the human personality. Yet such a claim has no value until it is entirely clear what is meant by psychological knowledge. We can
5 know man in many ways. Not every study of man's inner life is psychology and the careless mixing of different ways of dealing with man's inner life is largely responsible for the vagueness which characterizes the popular literature of psychotherapy. It is not enough
10 to say that a statement is true or not true. It may be true under one aspect and entirely meaningless under another.

7. What best describes the author's main point?

Ⓐ One must base psychotherapy on psychology
Ⓑ Today's psychology is ill-defined, leading to poor understandings of psychotherapy
Ⓒ Psychology can be both true and not true
Ⓓ Not every study of a human's inner life is psychology

8. Which of the following, if true, MOST weakens the author's argument?

Ⓐ Every study of man's inner life is psychology
Ⓑ The popular literature of psychotherapy is not vague
Ⓒ We can know man in only one way
Ⓓ Psychological knowledge is well-defined and clear to most practitioners

GO TO THE NEXT PAGE

Questions 9 to 11 are based on the following excerpt from Eleanor Roosevelt's speech to members of the American Civil Liberties Union in Chicago in 1940. Select one answer unless otherwise indicated.

Now I listened to the broadcast this afternoon with a great deal of interest. I almost forgot what a fight had been made to assure the rights of the working man. I know there was a time when hours were longer and wages lower, but I had forgotten just how long that fight for freedom, to bargain collectively, and to have freedom of assembly, had taken.

Sometimes, until some particular thing comes to your notice, you think something has been won for every working man, and then you come across, as I did the other day, a case where someone had taken the law into his own hands and beaten up a labor organizer. I didn't think we did those things any more in this country, but it appears that we do. Therefore, someone must be always on the lookout to see that someone is ready to take up the cudgels to defend those who can't defend themselves. That is the only way we are going to keep this country a law-abiding country, where law is looked upon with respect and where it is not considered necessary for anybody to take the law into his own hands. The minute you allow that, then you have acknowledged that you are no longer able to trust in your courts and in your law-enforcing machinery, and civil liberties are not very well off when anything like that happens. So I think that after listening to the broadcast today, I would like to remind you that behind all those who fight for the Constitution as it was written, for the rights of the weak and for the preservation of civil liberties, we have a long line of courageous people, which is something to be proud of and something to hold on to. Its only value lies, however, in the fact that we profit by example and continue the tradition in the future.

9. Select the sentence in the text that expresses Roosevelt's thoughts on the consequences of citizens disregarding the confines of the law and handling issues as they see fit.

---

10. What is the value that the author places on the "long line of courageous people" mentioned in line 29?

Ⓐ An example for citizens today
Ⓑ A source of pride
Ⓒ A fact to remember
Ⓓ The precursor to today's continued civil liberties work

---

11. One can infer which of the following about the youth of the country, based on Roosevelt's speech?

Ⓐ They can be trusted to continue to fight for civil liberties
Ⓑ They will influence the furthering of democracy in the country
Ⓒ They will be subjected to similar struggles encountered by those who came before them

---

GO TO THE NEXT PAGE

Questions 12 and 13 are based on the following passage on cancer in adolescents and young adults. Select one answer unless otherwise indicated.

There are currently over 70,000 Adolescent and Young Adult (AYA) individuals (ages 15–39) diagnosed with cancer in the United States annually, making cancer the leading disease-related cause of death in this age
5   group and the fourth overall cause of death behind homicide, suicide and unintentional injury for the AYA population. Despite medical advances and increased rates of survival among all other groups of cancer patients and survivors, adolescent and young adult
10 cancer patients have shown no such increase over the course of the past 25 years. These disparities arise from many factors, including the lack of age-specific care guidelines that take into consideration the unique psychosocial and supportive care needs of the AYA
15 population, the dearth of clinical trials, and the near-total absence of clinics and treatment facilities devoted to the AYA cancer population.

AYA cancer patients have a distinct and involved process of dealing with and treatment for cancer that includes
20 such considerations as maturation and development, transitions in autonomy, educational pursuits, and the onset of adult responsibilities and life events including marriage and childbirth. Cancer in AYA patients is unique in that it complicates the life of a person at an age when
25 their lives are in a constant state of change. This ever-changing state is unique to the AYA population, and the issues related to such change and phenomena are not typically addressed when AYA patients are placed in pediatric or older adult care facilities where they are
30 in the minority patient population.

While the psychosocial differences in the AYA population have been mentioned in the literature of the last three decades, little has been done to mobilize and research solutions to address the disparity of treatment and the
35 specific programming needs and therapy for the AYA cancer population.

12. According to the author, what are the factors leading to the disparity in cancer treatment success and survival rates of the AYA population? Select <u>all</u> that apply.

    [A] Age differentials
    [B] Distinct psychosocial needs
    [C] Absence of clinical trials
    [D] Lack of devoted care facilities for AYA cancer patients
    [E] Minimal to no age-specific care guidelines

13. Which of the following projects would the author be MOST likely to support?

    Ⓐ A medical school program to specifically train pediatric oncologists
    Ⓑ Hospital beds in pediatric wards reserved for AYA cancer patients
    Ⓒ A study on AYA cancer patients' television viewing and Internet habits
    Ⓓ A documentary film that follows AYA and non-AYA cancer patients over the course of a year

GO TO THE NEXT PAGE

Questions 14 to 16 are based on the following letter written by author, feminist, and activist Mary Wollstonecraft in the 1760s. Select one answer unless otherwise indicated.

The bishops have not large revenues, and the priests are appointed by the king before they come to them to be ordained. There is commonly some little farm annexed to the parsonage, and the inhabitants

5 subscribe voluntarily, three times a year, in addition 5 to the church fees, for the support of the clergyman. The church lands were seized when Lutheranism was introduced, the desire of obtaining them being probably the real stimulus of reformation. The tithes,

10 which are never required in kind, are divided into three 10 parts—one to the king, another to the incumbent, and the third to repair the dilapidations of the parsonage. They do not amount to much. And the stipend allowed to the different civil officers is also too small,

15 scarcely deserving to be termed an independence; 15 that of the custom-house officers is not sufficient to procure the necessaries of life—no wonder, then, if necessity leads them to knavery. Much public virtue cannot be expected till every employment, putting

20 perquisites out of the question, has a salary sufficient 20 to reward industry;—whilst none are so great as to permit the possessor to remain idle. It is this want of proportion between profit and labour which debases men, producing the sycophantic appellations of

25 patron and client, and that pernicious *esprit du corps*, 25 proverbially vicious.

14. The author discusses which of the following to support her notion that village workers earn too little? Select all that apply.

- [A] church revenues
- [B] a small farm
- [C] unproductive fisheries
- [D] tithes
- [E] civil officer stipends

15. "Sycophantic appellations" in Line 23 refers to:

- (A) pedantic ghosts
- (B) flattering titles
- (C) tacit knowledge
- (D) musical performances
- (E) voracious appetites

16. The author would most likely agree with which of the following? Select all that apply.

- [A] An ideal society returns lands unjustly taken
- [B] An ideal society would pay everyone enough so that they do not have to work
- [C] An ideal society does not have patrons and clients
- [D] An ideal society needs its members to earn money in proportion to their labor
- [E] An ideal society needs more farm laborers

For questions 17 to 20, select two answers that best complete the blank and produce two sentences that are alike in meaning.

17. The fire at the homeless shelter left several hundred _____ residents without a home and critical necessities.

- [A] indigent
- [B] copious
- [C] nascent
- [D] impecunious
- [E] reticent
- [F] staid

18. The candidate for office _____ on political issues at every public function, distancing his supporters and losing voters.

    Ⓐ pontificated
    Ⓑ castigated
    Ⓒ inveighed
    Ⓓ maligned
    Ⓔ demurred
    Ⓕ acceded

19. The hired defamation team was ordered to _____ their target's reputation through fictional internet stories, thereby decreasing her chances of career success.

    Ⓐ exsiccate
    Ⓑ impair
    Ⓒ delineate
    Ⓓ desiccate
    Ⓔ aggrieve
    Ⓕ aggregate

20. Theologians have spent much time and ink in pondering whether or not the _____ characteristics of the divine are still subject to the whims of human will and conduct.

    Ⓐ iconoclastic
    Ⓑ immutable
    Ⓒ obtuse
    Ⓓ monotonous
    Ⓔ imperceptive
    Ⓕ sacrosanct

STOP

QUANTITATIVE REASONING
SECTION 6

20 QUESTIONS
35 MINUTES

1. A bag contains 3 orange, 6 red, and 5 blue marbles.

Quantity A	Quantity B
Chance of drawing marbles in the order: blue, blue, red, orange	Chance of drawing marbles in the order: red, orange, red, red

Ⓐ Quantity A is greater.
Ⓑ Quantity B is greater.
Ⓒ The two quantities are equal.
Ⓓ The relationship cannot be determined from the information given.

2. The area of the trapezoid is twice that of the rectangle.

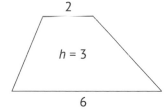

Quantity A	Quantity B
x	2

Ⓐ Quantity A is greater.
Ⓑ Quantity B is greater.
Ⓒ The two quantities are equal.
Ⓓ The relationship cannot be determined from the information given.

3. A flagpole stands perpendicular to the ground. At 1:45PM, the flagpole casts a shadow on the ground that is 144 inches long. Mary, who is also standing perpendicular to the ground casts a shadow that is 1.5 yards long at 1:45PM. Mary is a 6 foot tall woman. Assume that the triangles created in both instances are similar.

Quantity A	Quantity B
the height of the flagpole	192.5 inches

Ⓐ Quantity A is greater.
Ⓑ Quantity B is greater.
Ⓒ The two quantities are equal.
Ⓓ The relationship cannot be determined from the information given.

4. A pizza box requires a 16" × 30" piece of cardboard.
A pizza separator is 14" in diameter.
A sheet of cardboard is 46" × 64".
A pizza container consists of one box and one separator.

Quantity A	Quantity B
Number of boxes that can be cut from a single sheet of cardboard	Number of sheets of cardboard required to create 24 pizza containers

Ⓐ Quantity A is greater.
Ⓑ Quantity B is greater.
Ⓒ The two quantities are equal.
Ⓓ The relationship cannot be determined from the information given.

QUANTITATIVE REASONING
SECTION 6

5. $3x^3 + 5x^2 + 6x + 9 = 305$

Quantity A	Quantity B
4	Real solutions for x

Ⓐ Quantity A is greater.
Ⓑ Quantity B is greater.
Ⓒ The two quantities are equal.
Ⓓ The relationship cannot be determined from the information given.

6.

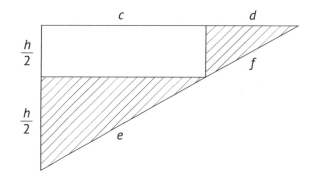

Quantity A	Quantity B
Area of the rectangle	Shaded area

Ⓐ Quantity A is greater.
Ⓑ Quantity B is greater.
Ⓒ The two quantities are equal.
Ⓓ The relationship cannot be determined from the information given.

7.

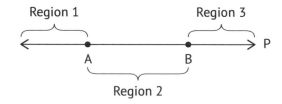

Point X is placed on line P such that distance AX is twice the distance BX.

Quantity A	Quantity B
Probability of point X being in region 2	Probability of point X being in region 3

8. If $\overset{\frown}{BC} = 45°$, find the measure of $\angle ABD$.

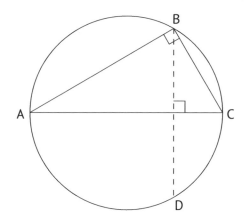

Ⓐ 22.5°
Ⓑ 45.0°
Ⓒ 120.0°
Ⓓ 67.5°
Ⓔ The angle cannot be determined.

GO TO THE NEXT PAGE

9. An office manager is charged with staffing. His first hire costs $15/hr, and generates revenue of $20/hr. This employee can work at 100% efficiency. Each additional employee hired can only work at 90% of the efficiency of the previous hire. What is the maximum number of employees he can hire before the employee costs more than the revenue he generates?

   (A) 2
   (B) 3
   (C) 4
   (D) 5
   (E) The answer cannot be determined from the information given.

10. If $5x = 4y = 2z$ and whole numbers $xyz \neq 0$, what is the least possible value of $x^2 + 2y + z$?

   (A) 22
   (B) 26
   (C) 36
   (D) 44
   (E) 72

11. Suppose a is a three-digit number that has 3 prime factors and b is a two-digit number that has 3 prime factors. What is the smallest integer ab that has 4 prime factors?

   (A) 360
   (B) 420
   (C) 1360
   (D) 3060
   (E) There is not enough information to determine the answer.

Use the Chart below to answer problems 12 and 13.

This chart is a plot of the error rate for 20 assembly teams which measures the rate of errors against the experience, in months, of the team at the task given.

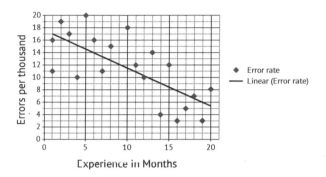

Experience in Months

12. Which equation best describes the trend line?

   (A) $y = \dfrac{2}{3}x + 16$

   (B) $3y - 2x = 46$

   (C) $x + y = 16$

   (D) $y = -\dfrac{1}{2}x + 16$

   (E) $x = 2y + 4$

13. With the scores sorted by variance from the trend line, what is the average variance of the middle quartiles?

   (A) 2.5
   (B) 1.0
   (C) 0.5
   (D) 0.0
   (E) −1

QUANTITATIVE REASONING
SECTION 6

14. The equation for line L is $3x - 4y = 10$. Find the point of intersection with the perpendicular line which passes through (3, 4).

Ⓐ $(5\frac{1}{25}, 1\frac{7}{25})$

Ⓑ $(3, -\frac{1}{4})$

Ⓒ $(2, -\frac{1}{2})$

Ⓓ $(\frac{11}{3}, \frac{1}{4})$

Ⓔ   The answer cannot be determined from the information given.

---

15. Gretchen works as a transcriptionist. She types 120 words per minute, but only has 70% accuracy. Fortunately her word processor has an auto-correct function that corrects 90% of her typos. However, it misses 5% of her typos and replaces the remaining 5% of typos with incorrect words. After all this she has to correct the remaining mistakes. It takes her 30 seconds to find and fix each typo and 1 minute to find and fix each wrong word. How long will it take her to transcribe and correct a 6,000-word document? Enter your answer in the text box provided.

16.

Number Guessed	Number of Students
13 Blocks	1
14 Blocks	3
15 Blocks	2
17 Blocks	7
18 Blocks	1
20 Blocks	5
21 Blocks	1
25 Blocks	1

In a class survey a Professor asked his students to guess how many irregular blocks could be fit into a jar. The chart above is the numbers guessed and the frequency of each guessed number. What is the standard deviation in the guesses?

Ⓐ   2.7
Ⓑ   2.9
Ⓒ   4
Ⓓ   7.45
Ⓔ   18

---

17. Sally is starting a crafting business. According to her business plan each crafting station generates $1,000 / week in revenue, with 70% of that spent on employees and supplies. If her initial investment is $250,000 to start her business and she spends $4,500 per month on building costs, what is the minimum number of crafting stations she must have in order to recoup her initial investment in 2 years?

Ⓐ   6
Ⓑ   12
Ⓒ   13
Ⓓ   20
Ⓔ   41

GO TO THE NEXT PAGE

18. 20! has how many distinct integer factors? Enter your answer in the text box below.

19. You have a rectangular plot that is *a* units by *b* units where *b* > *a*. Given that there is some value *c* for which *a* + *c* = *b*, which of the following expressions are true? Choose <u>all</u> that apply.

[A] $a^2 + 2ac + c^2 = b^2$
[B] $bc - c^2 = ac$
[C] $b^2 - bc = a^2 + ac$
[D] $2ac = ab + bc - c^2 - a^2$
[E] There are no true expressions.

20. Michael received an oil change for his car. The shop charged him the base price of the oil change plus a 4.5% sales tax and a 3.5% convenience fee, each of which were applied to the base price of the oil change. Michael gave the cashier $30 dollars and received the exact change back, which was less than $6.00. Which of the following statements below must be true?

Indicate <u>all</u> statements that are true.

[A] The base price of the oil change was more than $23.50
[B] The base price of the oil change was less than $28.20
[C] The sum of the sales tax and convenience fee was less than $2.46

VERBAL REASONING
ANSWER KEY: SECTION 3

1. **B.**
   The context given in the last sentence suggests that a separation occurred between Alana and her friends. *Sequestered* means to close oneself off from contact.

2. **A, E.**
   Viability means workability or feasibility. *Temerity* means recklessness, which a start-up might have but which does not often translate into *thriving*. *Fecklessness* or ineffectiveness is the opposite of what you want here. The presentation was built on information that was too intricately presented or argued, remaining *convoluted* to its non-specialist audiences. There is no evidence to tell us that the information was *disparate* or unrelated, only that it was difficult to access and understand.

3. **C, D.**
   While one might call a winding line an *imbroglio*, or confused situation, the context only lets us know that the line was long. While one might *mulct* or defraud someone with scalped tickets, Bobby wanted to *procure* or obtain tickets.

4. **C, E, G.**
   Paucity means shortage, which fits the context of the school's described situation of a lack of funds. *Pecuniary* relates to finances or budgets and matches this monetary context. While *advisable* and *imperative* both fit the last blank, *imperative* brings with it an urgency that matches the given context.

5. **A, D, G.**
   The investors needing to be reassured indicates that they may be nervous or *timorous*. Blank (ii) calls for the opposite of secure; *tenous* is the most appropriate choice. Answer choice I is a distraction. Just because the individuals have no vested interest does not mean their findings will be true or *veritable*. They will, however, be unbiased or *unprejudiced*.

6. **A, F, I.**
   The sentences paint Wilde as a pilferer of others' work, but without proof. *Delusive* means deceptive and suggests the claims are not true. *Filched* is to take without permission. Be careful not to confuse *approbation* (approval) with *appropriation* (taking).

7. **A, C.**
   The question asks for those answer choices that do not appear in the passage in support of the author's argument that farmers should first practice hopper control on their own land. C is the only answer choice that does not appear anywhere in the passage. A appears in the passage, but in the context of a soil erosion tactic known as "stubbling-in"—not in support of the author's argument. The other three answer choices—B, D, and E—are all explicitly mentioned by the author in connection to his argument in the passage's second paragraph.

8. **C.**
   Here, you want to locate the statement that most strongly contradicts the author's argument. Since you identified for the previous question that the author is arguing for the primacy of a farmer's pest control practice on his own lands as the most powerful deterrent in controlling grasshopper populations, the notion that this would only move the grasshoppers next door, leaving them room to return, most strongly weakens this argument. The author's argument is not dependent on the possibilities provided in A, B, or D, so they are irrelevant in contradicting the presented argument.

9. **B.**
   The first sentence alerts you to the fact that the issues to be discussed center around access to vaccines, so B is an immediate choice. The passage does not discuss children (A) or new technologies to lessen confusions (D), so these answer choices can be eliminated. The World Health Organization is mentioned, but in relation to their

guidelines on vaccines—the Organization is not the subject of the passage, ruling out answer choice C. The passage also outlines the challenges of vaccines and their administration—it does not advocate for any specific response, so E would be incorrect.

10. A, C, D.

Here, you want to identify what is specifically mentioned in the passage with regard to problems connected to vaccines. The author specifically says that the mass-production of vaccines occurs in sterile environments, so B is incorrect, while the passage never mentions vaccine directions (E). A, C, and D are all mentioned in the last paragraph in relation to the administration of vaccines.

11. B.

With this question, the directions are very important: you need to pick a single answer, and it needs to be the one the author would most agree with. All of the answer choices correspond with problems mentioned in the passage. To narrow down your list, find the common element behind many of the passage's mentioned problems: the diluent. Only B removes the diluent altogether, and thus eliminates multiple problems at once. The remaining answer choices only tackle one problem at a time, and thus are incorrect.

12. D.

Based on the context, you know that diluents make powder vaccines thinner (D), resulting in a substance that can be injected. There is nothing in the passage that suggests or confirms that a diluent can extend (A), aggravate (B), thicken (C), or strengthen (E) the original vaccine powder. Your choice of any of these would only be implied, not based on any direct evidence of the passage.

13. B, C.

When you need to identify what weakens an author's claims, the first step is to identify what the author's claims are as well as the premises on which the claims are based. In this short passage, the author argues that college students should avoid caffeine to retain their sight and speech. The author rests this claim on the fact that serotonin over-production damages the parts of the brain that control speech and vision. Thus, to most weaken the author's claims, look for the statements that contradict this. Here, deafness (B) with a proven link to high serotonin levels suggests that serotonin over-production might be responsible for more damage or other mechanisms than the author has claimed. Answer choice C also confuses the author's claim by suggesting that other hormones are also over-produced by high levels of serotonin – meaning that they could be directly responsible for the symptoms, rather than the serotonin itself.

14. A, B.

This is a contextual question, asking you to identify the purpose of a particular element of a passage. Here, if you did not recognize the quotation, the first paragraph tells you where, when, and why it was written. Its date of 1787 and its identification as the Declaration of Independence tells you that it was a founding American document (B). The rest of the passage discusses how later generations strove to perfect the founders' original unfinished vision, so the quotation and its invocation of this original vision also serve to link the past to the present (A). The remaining three choices of C, D, and E are not mentioned in the passage. Do not get caught by D: yes, founding documents serve as legal documents in U.S. courts, but that purpose is not invoked in this passage.

15. *The document they produced was eventually signed but ultimately unfinished.* Speeches like this one often progress through their ideas one by one (sometimes with one idea per paragraph), so look for the sentence that best connects the big themes of the various paragraphs. Here, after the first paragraph describes the creation of the Declaration of Independence, the remaining paragraphs all discuss its imperfections and the need for citizens to finish the work over time. These two topics meet in the first sentence of the 2nd paragraph, which serves to bind the two themes of the passage together.

VERBAL REASONING
ANSWER KEY: SECTION 3

16. E.

This is a straight content question, but requires careful reading. In Line 20, Obama specifically names "the ideal of equal citizenship under the law" as the core of the Constitution. Don't be fooled by A, which appears in the last sentence, or the mention of Philadelphia in the passage's introduction and Line 9 (B). Careful reading of the last paragraph tells you that Answers C and D do not match the passage, in which Obama states that the Constitution alone has not realized its own goals, and that citizen action is essential to the process.

17. A, D.

The exhibition, based on the context clue of *digressed*, was not as expected. *Quarrels* have a negative connotation; the opposite expectation would be positive. *Touted* and *heralded* both mean to promote and praise. *Wangled* (faked), *insinuated* (implied), and *habituated* (addicted to) all have negative connotations. *Induced* (brought about) might fit rather awkwardly but does not have a paired word to go with it.

18. A, C.

Whimsical and *arbitrary* match the sense given by the words *random* and *chaotic*. *Eclectic* connotes a selective and deliberate process that combines elements from varied sources, not at all in line with the provided context.

19. B, D.

High altitude gives you clues for how to fill in the blank. *Vertiginous* and *dizzying* are synonyms for symptoms that can result from altitude changes. Watch out for *haphazard*: it means random, distinct from its related term *hazardous*, meaning dangerous.

20. A, C.

Both *austere* and *abstemious* reflect a sense of spareness or lack of luxury, suggesting a scaling back on or simplicity to patients' diet choices. *Truculent* means aggressive, while *cavalier* suggests a carefree attitude. Neither fit the context.

QUANTITATIVE REASONING
ANSWER KEY: SECTION 4

1. B.

This problem tests your ability to translate a word problem into algebraic equations. First, you are given the fact that Gabe is 5 years older than Paul. This can be written as G = P + 5. Next, you are told that Gabe was twice as old as Paul 3 years ago. You can write Gabe's age 3 years ago as G − 3, and Paul's age at the time as P − 3. Remembering that Gabe's age was twice Paul's, you would write your equation as G − 3 = 2(P − 3). Now you are ready to solve for Paul's current age. You do this by substituting the first equation of P + 5 for G in the second equation.

(P + 5) − 3 = 2(P − 3)	substitution
P + 2 = 2P − 6	simplify
2 + 6 = 2P − P	add 6 − P to both sides
8 = P	

8 is greater than 5, so the correct answer choice is **B**.

2. A.

There is no need to add all the integers up in each set to see which sum is larger. Quantity A contains more terms and includes higher integers in the same range as Quantity B. Therefore, the Quantity A is greater.

3. A.

This is a twist on the classic algebraic rate-of-work problem. The problem asks you to compare the amount of time the given task takes to complete for different workers. It can be solved with a bit of logical reasoning. Intuitively, any given task will take fewer hours when more workers are present. In order to evaluate this mathematically, you need to set up the two work-rate equations:

1) $36x = T$ and 2) $y(x + 2) = T$

T is the task, x is the number of workers, and y is the value you are comparing to 36. Solving the first equation, we get $36 = \frac{T}{x}$. For the second equation, solving for y, we get $y = \frac{T}{x+2}$. You are now ready to evaluate the inequality. When working with inequalities of an unknown relationship be sure to use the ? between expressions. Once you know the relationship you can then insert the proper symbol:

36 ? y	initial inequality
$\frac{T}{x}$? $\frac{T}{x+2}$	substitute equation 1 from Quantity A on the left and equation 2 from Quantity B on the right
$T(x + 2)$? Tx	cross multiply (you can do this because you know that x and $x + 2$ will always be positive)
$x + 2$? x	divide both sides by T
2 > 0	Subtract x from both sides

2 is greater than 0 so **Quantity A** is greater than **Quantity B**. The correct answer choice is **A**.

4. D.

This problem tests your reasoning ability using geometry. The first thing to remember when answering a geometry question is that there is **no** guarantee that the drawing is either to scale or accurate. You must rely **ONLY** on the given information. While the diagram may lead you to believe that ABC must be an isosceles triangle, you are only given that the radius of the circle is 3 and ∠ABC = 90°. The best approach in this case is to create another diagram using the same givens and see what it might tell you. First, inscribe a rectangle in the circle, then draw the diagonal.

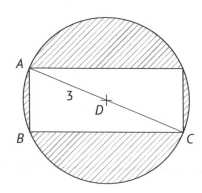

Triangle ABC is a right triangle and the radius is still 3. From this diagram it is clear that **any** rectangle or square thus inscribed will create triangle ABC as a right triangle with a hypotenuse that is the circle's diameter. From this you know that $\overline{AB}$ and $\overline{BC}$ are not always the same length. So now the task is to determine the range of possible areas of ABC. If we set $\overline{AB} = \overline{BC}$ we can determine a value for the area thus:

$a = \overline{AB}$ set up for substitution into the Pythagorean Theorem

Recall that $A_{\text{triangle}} = \frac{bh}{2}$, but we have set $\overline{AB} = \overline{BC}$ so both the base and the height are a. The formula becomes:

$A_{\text{triangle}} = \frac{bh}{2} = \frac{a^2}{2}$

You are ready now to use the Pythagorean Theorem.

$a^2 + b^2 = c^2$ Pythagorean Theorem

$a^2 + a^2 = 6^2$ substitute the length of $\overline{AB}$ (above) for a

$2a^2 = 36$ simplify

$a^2 = 18$ divide both sides by 2

$\frac{a^2}{2} = 9$ divide by 2 in order to match the Area formula above

You have shown that the area of the triangle is 9. Now compare this to the Area of the circle:

$shaded\ area = A_{\text{circle}} - A_{\text{triangle}}$

$= \pi r^2 - \frac{a^2}{2}$ substitute in the Area formulas

$= \pi 3^2 - 9$ substitute your given for r, value for Area

$= 9\pi - 9$ simplify

You will notice that this is equal to the value in **Quantity A**. However, remember that the triangle can be of **any** configuration as long as the hypotenuse is 6 (twice the circle's radius). So next, try setting a different relationship between the base and height. Trying $2 \cdot \overline{AB} = \overline{BC}$, we get the following solution for a^2:

Set $a = \overline{AB}$ and $b = \overline{BC} = 2a$ assign the variables

$a^2 + b^2 = c^2$ Pythagorean Theorem

$a^2 + (2a)^2 = 6^2$ substitute in your assignments

$$a^2 + 4a^2 = 36 \qquad \text{simplify the exponents}$$

$$5a^2 = 36 \qquad \text{simplify}$$

$$a^2 = \frac{36}{5} \qquad \text{divide both sides by 5}$$

$$a = \frac{6}{\sqrt{5}} \qquad \text{find the square root}$$

Now solve for *b* using the variable assignment from above:

$$b = 2a \qquad \text{substitute from given}$$

$$= 2 \cdot \frac{6}{\sqrt{5}} = \frac{12}{\sqrt{5}} \qquad \text{substitute known values and calculate } b$$

$$\frac{ab}{2} = \frac{6}{\sqrt{5}} \cdot \frac{12}{\sqrt{5}} \cdot \frac{1}{2} \qquad \text{substitute known values into Area of Triangle Formula}$$

$$= \frac{72}{10} = 7.2 \qquad \text{calculate}$$

At this point, it should be clear that the area of the triangle will not always equal 9, and therefore the relationship between **Quantity A** and **Quantity B** cannot be determined. The correct answer choice is **D**.

5. **A.**

    This problem tests your ability to work with unit conversions. Note that in this problem, your final answer will be expressed in cubic feet. The first thing to do is set up the equation:

    Volume of Empty Space = Volume of the Cylinder – Volume of Water

    Recall the formula for volume of a cylinder:

    Volume of a Cylinder = $h = \pi r^2$

    Next, convert the water units into a volume. We are given lb/gal and gal/ft³ while the amount of water in **Quantity A** is given in tons. Write out the units as fractions to see how to convert them:

    $$\frac{lbs}{gal} \cdot \frac{gal}{ft^3} = \frac{lbs}{ft^3}$$

    Now substitute in the given values according to the units in the formula:

    $$8.34\frac{lbs}{gal} \cdot 7.48\frac{gal}{ft^3} = 62.3832\frac{lbs}{ft^3}$$

    Next, you need to calculate the values of each quantity. For quantity A, recall that 1 *ton* = 2,000 *lbs*. Thus, 15 *tons* = 30,000 *lbs*. You can use the results of the water volume calculation above in order to convert weight into volume. Expressing your units as fractions or ratios makes it clear how to obtain the units you want.

    $$\text{water volume} = 30,000 \; lbs \div 62.3832\frac{lbs}{ft^3} = 480.8987 \; ft^3$$

    Note how dividing water volume serves to cancel the *lbs* unit and bring *ft³* to the numerator. Next use the data from **Quantity B** to find the volume of the cylinder:

    $$V = 15ft \cdot \pi\left(\frac{8ft}{2}\right)^2 \qquad \text{substitute values into the cylinder formula}$$

    $$V = 15ft \cdot \pi \cdot 16ft^2$$

    $$= 754ft^3 \qquad \text{calculate the exponent and simplify.}$$

Remember that the comparison is **Quantity A** against **half** the volume of the cylinder:

$754ft^3 \div 2 = 377ft^3$ calculate

Quantity A (481 ft³) is greater than **Quantity B** (377 ft³). The correct answer choice is **A**.

6. **D.**

This problem tests both your ability to factor a polynomial and your understanding of roots. There are two approaches to use in a problem like this. Because you are given a value to calculate in Quantity B, it is possible to calculate this value and then substitute it into the equation to determine the relationship. The second method is to factor the polynomial given in the center in order to determine the solutions for x. In either method, the first step should be to determine the value of Quantity B.

$\sqrt{\frac{1}{16}}$ given

$\frac{\sqrt{1}}{\sqrt{16}}$ apply the Quotient Rule (separate the numerator and denominator)

$\pm\frac{1}{4}$ calculate

Trying substitution first, you get the following results:

$$4x^2 - 17x + 4 = 0$$

$4 \cdot (\frac{1}{4})^2 - 17 \cdot (\frac{1}{4}) + 4 = 0$ $4 \cdot (-\frac{1}{4})2 - 17 \cdot (-\frac{1}{4}) + 4 = 0$

$4 \cdot (\frac{1}{16}) - 17 \cdot (\frac{1}{4}) + 4 = 0$ $4 \cdot (\frac{1}{16}) - 17 \cdot (-\frac{1}{4}) + 4 = 0$

$\frac{1}{4} - \frac{17}{4} + \frac{16}{4} = 0$ $\frac{4}{16} + \frac{17}{4} + \frac{16}{4} = 0$

$0 = 0$ $\frac{37}{4} \neq 0$

Therefore, the correct answer choice is **D**. If you factor the polynomial, you get the following:

$4x^2 - 17x + 4 = 0$

$(4x - 1)(x - 4) = 0$

$x = \frac{1}{4} \ or \ x = 4$

Again, the correct answer is **D**.

7. **C.**

This problem asks you to solve the given equation for the value of n.

$\frac{n+4}{10} = \frac{n-8}{2}$ given

$n + 4 = 5(n - 8)$ multiply both sides by 10

$n + 4 = 5n - 40$ distribute

$44 = 4n$ simplify by adding $40 - n$ to both sides

$11 = n$

The correct answer choice is **C**.

8. **C.**

This problem tests your ability to perform algebraic simplification. The given information means that x and y and z are not equal to zero. This is important, because if any of them were zero the expression would be undefined. To simplify the expression:

$\dfrac{(xy)^3 z^0}{x^3 y^4}$	given
$\dfrac{x^3 y^3}{x^3 y^4}$	$z^0 = 1$, so remove; distribute the exponent
$\dfrac{y^3}{y^4}$	$\dfrac{x^3}{x^3} = 1$, so it can be factored out
$\dfrac{1}{y}$	$\dfrac{y^3}{y^3} = 1$, so it can be factored out

The answer choice is **C**.

9. **A.**

This problem is testing your knowledge of geometry and the Pythagorean Theorem. First, you will use the Theorem to calculate the length of the base of the triangles with height h. Following that, you have the information to reapply the Theorem and calculate h_2. First we assign the variable a to the unknown triangle base. That gives us:

$a^2 = 7^2 - h^2$	Pythagorean Theorem
$a^2 = 7^2 - 3^2$	substitute for h
$a^2 = 49 - 9 = 40$	calculate

Because you are going to re-use the Theorem you do not need to solve completely for a. It is important here to remember that the length of the hypotenuse of the larger triangle is $2a$ and not simply a. Next, because lengths of the sides of the pentagon are symmetrical, the triangle with the base of 10 will be isosceles, so the line h_2 will bisect the base. Now substitute back into the Theorem:

$h_2{}^2 = (2a)^2 - \left(\dfrac{10}{2}\right)^2$	Pythagorean Theorem rearranged
$h_2{}^2 = 4a^2 - 25$	simplify
$h_2{}^2 = 4(40) - 25$	
$\quad = 160 - 25 = 135$	calculate
$h_2 = 3\sqrt{15}$	find the square root

The correct answer choice is **A**.

10. **B.**

This problem tests your understanding of increasing and decreasing percentages. You are given an initial value of $400, followed by a decrease of 15%, which is then followed by an increase of 25%. You need to provide the final value. To calculate a change by percentage, use the formula *initial value · (1 + percentage change)*. Your two changes are −15% and +25%, respectively, so you can write out the entire expression as:

$$\$400 \times (1 - 15\%) \times (1 + 25\%) = \$400(.85)(1.25) = \$425$$

The correct answer choice is **B**. REMINDER: For pure calculation problems like this, make use of the onscreen calculator.

QUANTITATIVE REASONING
ANSWER KEY: SECTION 4

11. A.

This is a rate-of-work problem that asks you to find the combined rate of work of two given workers. First, express the rate of work for both Randy and Liz, where R is Randy, L is Liz, and V is the inventory:

$$11R = V \qquad\qquad 10L = V$$
$$R = \frac{V}{11} \qquad\qquad L = \frac{V}{10}$$

You are trying to find out how many hours it will take them working together. First, write that equation:

$$x(R + L) = V \qquad\qquad \text{equation for work rate of both Randy and Liz}$$

Then substitute in the work rates for Randy and Liz:

$$x\left(\frac{V}{11} + \frac{V}{10}\right) = V \qquad\qquad \text{substitution}$$

$$\frac{xV}{11} + \frac{xV}{10} = V \qquad\qquad \text{distributive}$$

$$\frac{x}{11} + \frac{x}{10} = 1 \qquad\qquad \text{divide both sides by } V$$

$$11x + 10x = 110 \qquad\qquad \text{multiply both sides by the least common multiple of 110}$$

$$21x = 110 \qquad\qquad \text{simplify}$$

$$x = \frac{110}{21} = 5.24 \qquad\qquad \text{perform the calculation by dividing both sides by 21}$$

The correct answer choice is **A**.

12. 56.6 MPH

This is a classic traveling rate problem combined with solving a triangle. The first step is to sketch out the route described:

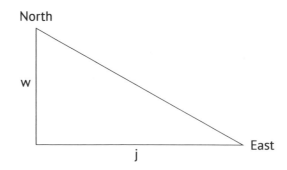

With this sketch it becomes clear that you are solving a right triangle. Finding the legs means finding the distance that both Wanda (w) and Jeff (j) traveled. You get:

$$w = 30mph \cdot 2hr = 60mi \qquad\qquad j = 36mph \cdot 4hr = 144mi$$

Next, use the Pythagorean Theorem to find the hypotenuse:

$a^2 + b^2 = c^2$	Pythagorean Theorem
$60^2 + 144^2 = c^2$	substitute
$3600 + 20736 = c^2$	calculate
$24336 = c^2$	calculate
$156 = c$	find the square root

NOTE: If you recognize that both legs are divisible by 12 [i.e., $\frac{60}{12}$ = 5 and $\frac{144}{12}$ = 12], you will recognize the Pythagorean proportion of 5:12:13. Alternatively, you could calculate the hypotenuse as 13 × 12 = 156.

Now, according to your finding, Wanda and Jeff are 156 miles apart after 4 hours. To find the amount of time it takes for them to cover the remaining distance we set up the classic converging travel equation, using *t* for total travel time:

t(speed of Wanda + speed of Jeff) = distance traveled	starting equation
t(30mph + 36mph) = 156mi	substitute
$t = \frac{156}{66}$ = 2.36hr	divide both sides by 66 and calculate

The total **distance** for the trip is the perimeter of the triangle: $60mi + 144mi + 156mi = 360mi$. The amount of **time** for the total trip is $4hr + 2.36hr = 6.36hr$. NOTE: Remember that Jeff and Wanda started at the same time. Plugging these figures into your formula for average speed:

$$average\ speed = \frac{distance}{time} = \frac{360mi}{6.36hr} = 56.6mph$$

Enter **56.6** as your answer. NOTE: The average speed is higher than either Jeff or Wanda individually. This is because the problem asks for the average COMBINED speed of Jeff and Wanda. Remember to read the question carefully.

13. B.

This problem tests your understanding of the difference between median and average. First, find the number of Chocolate Candy Bars, given the question's average cost per item of $2.09. Because the number of Chocolate Candy Bars is unknown, assign the variable *x* and use the average formula:

$$\frac{sum\ of\ [each\ cost\ of\ item \cdot each\ item\ count] + cost\ of\ Chocolate\ Candy\ Bars \cdot x}{sum\ of\ item\ counts + x} = avg\ cost$$

NOTE: In this case, you should make use of the on-screen calculator.

$\frac{1.76(4) + 3.99(2) + 4.52(2) + 3.27(3) + 2.00(5) + .67(6) + 1.15(x)}{4 + 2 + 2 + 3 + 5 + 6 + x} = 2.09$	
$\frac{47.93 + 1.15x}{22 + x} = 2.09$	simplify all constants
$47.93 + 1.15x = 2.09(22 + x)$	multiply by the denominator
$47.93 - 45.98 = 2.09x - 1.15x$	subtract $44.1 + 1.15x$ from both sides
$1.95 = .94x$	simplify
$2.07 = x$	divide both sides by .94

You are dealing with a **count** of items, so you must round to the nearest whole number. The correct answer choice is **B**. NOTE: You can verify your result by recalculating the average with 2 Chocolate Candy Bars.

14. B.

This problem asks you to add Chocolate Candy Bars to the table in order to achieve a **median** price of $1.88. The approach to this question is much simpler. Recall that the median value is dependent on the count of entries in a set: it will be the value of the middle item by count. If there is an even number of entries in the set, then the median value will be the average of the **two** middle values. Looking over the chart, you can see that there are no items in the data set with a value of $1.88. This tells you that the median must be an average of two values. You can see that $1.88 lies between $1.76 (Oatmeal Cookies) and $2.00 (CFL Light Bulbs). First, confirm that $1.88 is in fact the average of these two values (it is). Next, sort the set of values from lowest to highest, remembering to have an entry for each count of each value. Your data set will look like this:

{.67, .67, .67, .67, .67, .67, 1.76, 1.76, 1.76, 1.76, 2, 2, 2, 2, 2, 3.27, 3.27, 3.27, 3.99, 3.99, 4.54, 4.54}

Count the number of entries greater than $1.88 and the number of entries lower than $1.88. In this case, you find 12 entries above $1.88 and 10 entries below. So you will need to add **2** entries below $1.88. Chocolate Candy Bars are $1.15 so you will need to add 2 Chocolate Candy Bars in order to reach a median value of $1.88. The correct answer choice is **B**.

15. A, B, C, D.

This problem tests your knowledge of absolute value and exponents. You are given $y \neq 0$ and must determine which answer choices are positive. The only way to solve this is to review each answer against the given information.

A $(y^2)^3$: This is a nested exponent. There are two approaches to this problem. First, you may multiply the nested exponents together: $y^{2 \times 3} = y^6$. This results in an even exponent, which evaluates to a positive number. Second, you can evaluate the inner term of y^2, which results in a positive number. Applying the outer exponent of 3 to a positive number results in a positive number.

B y^{-2} : the exponent is −2 which is even, so this will be positive.

C $y^2 \cdot y^{-4}$: This expression has two exponents of the same base, so you add the exponents together to simplify the term to y^{-2}. Like **B**, this has an even exponent, which will always result in a positive value.

D y^0 : Any non-zero number raised to the 0 power evaluates to the number 1, which is positive.

E $\frac{1}{y^{-5}}$: −5 is an odd exponent, so this expression will evaluate to a negative number when y is negative. Do **NOT** select **E**.

16. C.

This problem tests your ability to solve a system of two equations. You are given one equation, so the first step is to find the equation for the second line. You are given that the line intersects the points (0,4) and (12,−2). First, find the slope of the line using the slope equation:

$$m = \frac{y^2 - y^1}{x^2 - x^2} = \frac{-2-4}{12-0} = -\frac{6}{12} = -\frac{1}{2}$$

Next, you use the slope-intercept $y - b = m(x - a)$ to create a formula. Substitute the value you just found for m. Try to choose the given point that will make your work easier, remembering the x coordinate is a and the y coordinate is b. In this case choose (0,4) to obtain:

$$y - 4 = -\frac{1}{2}(x - 0)$$

$$y = -\frac{1}{2}x + 4 \qquad \text{add 4 to both sides}$$

$$\frac{1}{2}x + y = 4 \qquad \text{move the } x \text{ term to the left}$$

Now that your line equation is in the same order as the given, it is easier to see how to proceed. You need to multiply the new line equation by 7 in order to eliminate the y term when adding the equations. After adding the given and your line equation together, solve for x. Below is the algebra:

$$\frac{7}{2}x + 7y = 28 \qquad \text{the new equation, multiplied by 7}$$

$$4x - 7y = 17 \qquad \text{the given from the question}$$

$$\frac{7+8}{2}x = 28 + 17 \qquad \text{add the two equations}$$

$$\frac{15}{2}x = 45 \qquad \text{simplify}$$

$$x = 6 \qquad \text{multiply both sides by the reciprocal of the } x \text{ coefficient}$$

Now, use the value of x to solve for y by substituting into either equation:

$$\frac{1}{2}(6) + y = 4 \qquad \text{substitute known value for } x$$

$$y = 4 - 3 = 1 \qquad \text{isolate the variable and calculate}$$

So the point of intersection is (6,1) or answer choice **C**. NOTE: You can test the other equation to verify your work.

17. D.

You are given that CB bisects the right-angle $\angle ACE$. So, $\angle ACB = \angle BCE = \frac{\angle ACE}{2} = \frac{90°}{2} = 45°$.

Since CD bisects $\angle ACB$, $\angle ACD = \angle DCB = \frac{\angle ACB}{2} = \frac{45°}{2} = 22.5°$.

So, $\angle DCE = \angle DCB + \angle BCE = 22.5° + 45° = 67.5°$.

18. D.

This problem tests your ability to set up a geometric word problem. The given data lays out the dimensions of a right triangle. The clue you are given is that the start of the glider is 40 feet above the ground (distance to the ground is **always** measured along a line perpendicular to the ground). The glider starts its journey 40 feet above the ground and ends 10 feet above ground. Therefore, the height of the triangle is 30 feet. You are given the distance between the two buildings as 40 feet. You thus have the two legs of the triangle at 30 and 40. You should recognize this as a multiple of the Pythagorean Theorem proportions of 3:4:5 and so arrive at 50 for the last side. The calculation is:

$$a^2 + b^2 = c^2 \qquad \text{Pythagorean Theorem}$$

$$30^2 + 40^2 = c^2 \qquad \text{substitution}$$

$$900 + 1600 = c^2 \qquad \text{calculate}$$

$$2500 = c^2 \qquad \text{simplify}$$

$$\sqrt{2500} = c = 50 \qquad \text{calculate}$$

QUANTITATIVE REASONING
ANSWER KEY: SECTION 4

The correct answer choice is **D**. REMEMBER: The negative result of the square root can be ignored in this instance because we are looking for a distance, which will always be a positive number.

19. B.

This problem tests your ability to combine percentages in order to achieve a desired result. The initial percentage of lemon juice is 15%. You are asked to add a solution with 47% lemon juice until you achieve a final juice percentage of 23%. First, start with the percentage formula $P = \frac{J}{L}$. P is the percentage, J is the amount of juice, and L is the amount of lemonade. There are 12 cups of lemonade, but remember that you are going to add an unknown amount of concentrate to the initial amount of lemonade, so set L = 12 + C, with C being concentrate. The amount of juice will have to be calculated from the given information. Your percentage formula can be rearranged to read J = PL, but remember that the final amount of juice (J) will be the initial amount plus 47% of the added concentrate (C). First calculate the initial amount of juice: J = PL = (.15)(12) = 1.8 cups. Now you can write the amount of juice (J): 1.8 + .47C. Finally, you are given that the final percentage of lemon juice is 23%, or P = .23. You are now ready to write out the equation:

$$.23 = \frac{1.8 + .47C}{12 + C} \qquad \text{given}$$

$$.23(12 + C) = 1.8 + .47C \qquad \text{multiply by the denominator}$$

$$12 + C = 7.826 + 2.043C \qquad \text{divide by .23}$$

$$4.174 = 1.043C \qquad \text{simplify}$$

$$4 = C \qquad \text{solve}$$

4 Cups must be added so the correct answer choice is **B**. REMEMBER: You have the online calculator to help you with the final calculations.

20. 3.3

This problem tests your ability to convert between time units and find a rate of travel. You are given the distance (2,802 miles), the rate of travel (65 MPH), and the number of hours traveled each day (24 – 8 – 3 = 13 hours). From this you are asked to determine the total number of days spent traveling. First, find the number of total hours traveled:

2802 *mi* ÷ 65 *MPH* = 43.1 *hours*

Next, divide by the hours spent traveling each day:

43.1 *hr* ÷ 13 *hrs per day* = 3.3 *days*

The correct answer is **3.3**.

1. **B.**

   The *quintessence* of something is its purest form, and here connects to the object's "sleek and ergonomic design." *Quietude* is tranquility, *decrepitude* refers to a state of collapse from age or illness, and *residue* is the balance or remainder of something—none of which fit the context. Watch out for *provenance*, which specifically refers to an object's point of origin or journey of ownership. Here, however, the term does not match the sentence's focus on design.

2. **B, D.**

   When one is *assayed*, one is evaluated. This matches the key word of "*measure*" in the sentence. In contrast, to *augment* is to add to, and to *expiate* is to make amends. For the second blank, *equivocated* is to have lied or misled. It has a negative tone, in line with the sentence's context of "*disrepute.*" To *muster* is to gather or assemble, and to *predetermine* is to settle beforehand. This last might describe executive action when faced with an evaluation, but there is not enough context to determine this from the sentence. The grammar of this choice also fits awkwardly with the wording of "*as to.*"

3. **B, E.**

   Since Toby's writing style was not a match, you have a clue that the passage is setting up opposites. Tabloids are known for their *sensationalism* and their *torridity*, or passion. Some tabloids certainly get into lots of legal battles, but their writing does not express *pugnacity* or the desire to fight. Toby, however, was not these things; you are looking for an opposite for blank (i). While his writing style might be *terse* or concise, the lack of sensationalism and torridity is better expressed by *academic* or formal fact-based writing.

4. **B, F, H.**

   For the first blank, the advisors' fears point you to *allay*, which is to calm or pacify. *Stint* is to set limits, which does not make sense in this context. *Incite* or motivate might fit, but there is nothing in the sentence that suggests the king wanted to feed his advisors' fears. *Vigilance* (wakefulness) and *retaliation* (repayment through action) might be warranted toward refugees in certain instances, but they are not actions prescribed by policy or law, the context given in the last part of the sentence. Only *sanctuary* (shelter) is a legal prescription, and stems from medieval times. Finally, *transmuted*, which means to change or transform into something different, fits the final blank. *Transfigured* is to only change outwardly, while to *defray* something is to provide money or payment. Neither fits the policy context of the last blank.

5. **B, E, I.**

   The practice of wearing crown jewels can be described as *ostentatious*, or showy and pretentious. *Panoramic* (an unobstructed and comprehensive view) does not work as a description of wearing jewels. *Palpable* (tangible) is not the best available descriptor for the context; this can be double-checked with the term for the second blank, where *opulence* (displaying wealth or affluence) describes such jewels themselves. In contrast, *rapacious* describes acts or persons of plunder, and *viable* means workable—both of which could apply in a certain context, but not in the context given here. Crown jewels are owned by monarchies, which are held by families—previous owners would be *progenitors*, or ancestors, suggested by the context clue of "*royal houses.*" A *hierarchy* (arrangement by rank) or *oligarchy* (government by a privileged few) mark other forms of organization.

6. **C, D, H.**

   This is a question that relies on relationships to deduce the correct answers. *While* is a context clue that tells you that the first half of the sentence will sit in relation and opposite to the second half. The will *enumerated*, or listed, the man's many wrongdoings. One may *extol* (praise) or *concoct* (make up) wrongdoings in certain situations, but a quick scan of the phrasing and answer choices for blank (iii) tells you that you want a word that might *counter* the children's grief (even if it fails). Praising or concocting one's wrongdoings usually causes distress to family members. For blank (ii) you want a term related to the will's enumeration, or *veracity* (truthfulness).

Turpitude (depravity) relates to the man's wrongdoings, but it is the will here that is the subject. *Ingenuity* means cleverness and does not fit the context. For the last blank, *mollify* is to soothe, something highly applicable to grief. *Mitigate* is close in meaning—to lessen in intensity—but it does not strongly follow the opposites drawn in the sentence or fit so closely with grief and is therefore a lesser choice. *Inure*, or to harden or habituate something, does not fit the context.

7. **B.**

   This set of answer choices is tricky. Answer choice A matches the first sentence and might seem to be a thesis statement. However, the rest of the paragraph does not discuss the link between psychotherapy and psychology but the vagueness and lack of clarity with regard to psychology. The correct answer choice is thus B. Answer choices C and D are both directly mentioned in the passage, but they are the author's premises in support of his main point.

8. **D.**

   This one is also a bit tricky. Here, keep in mind your answer to the previous question and your eyes on the author's main point. While answer choices A, B, and C all contradict various statements in the passage, it is answer choice D that directly contradicts his main point of the ill-defined nature of psychology.

9. *The minute you allow that, then you have acknowledged that you are no longer able to trust in your courts and in your law-enforcing machinery, and civil liberties are not very well off when anything like that happens.*

10. **A.**

    Here, the author specifically gives the "long line of courageous people" a singular value as an example for today (Lines 30–32), or answer choice A. Answer choices B, C, and D are all mentioned in connection to the "long line," but are not what the author values in her mentioned example.

11. **C.**

    The only clear inference here is C. Roosevelt's mention of continuing "the tradition in the future" (Line 32) indicates a belief that such a fight will be necessary. There is no guarantee that the youth will fight (A) or that democracy will be the result (B).

12. **C, D, E.**

    This is a straight reading comprehension passage, asking you to confirm the content that you just read. C, D, and E are all directly given by the author as causes for the disparity in treatments and survival among the AYA population (last sentence of the first paragraph). Answer choice B also appears in this sentence, but as a consideration for the age-specific guidelines, not a cause by itself. And while age defines the AYA group, age differentials (A) are never mentioned in the passage.

13. **D.**

    This question asks that you infer the answer from what is articulated in the passage. It can best be approached through elimination. The passage does not say that doctors lack training or that patients' media habits have a bearing on treatments, so A and C can be eliminated. And because hospital beds in pediatric units do not address the author's argument that specific treatment facilities for AYA patients are needed, you can eliminate B. This only leaves D. Films or comparative studies are not mentioned in the passage, but the described film would highlight the unique conditions of AYA patients—the author's main point.

14. **A, B, D, E.**

    This is a straight reading comprehension question. Only C is not mentioned in the passage. The author gives all of the rest as examples prior to her main point in the paragraph's last sentences.

15. B.

If you know what either *sycophantic* ("flattering") or *appellations* ("titles") means, you know the correct answer is B. If you do not know this information, however, you can look carefully at the context for some clues. The phrase equals "*patron*" and "*client*"—social roles for those who sponsor or commission work, and have the money to do so. They are generally well above the labourer class that Wollstonecraft discusses. Only answer choice B names something connected to class structures: "*titles.*"

16. C, D.

Here, A and E have no connections to the passage. From the previous question (and the last sentence), you know that the author believes that the roles of patron and client appear only when there are not fair labor practices; C is correct. The remaining two choices, B and D, say contradictory things; only one can be correct. In the next-to-last sentence, the author specifically states that salary should reward industry—but not be so great as to promote idleness. D is the correct choice.

17. A, D.

Indigent and *impecunious* both mean poor or without financial means. *Reticent* and *staid* are also synonyms, but mean reserved or sedate—hardly a descriptor for homeless residents who have lost everything.

18. A, C.

Your context clues tell you that the candidate lost supporters and voters due to his actions, giving you a negative tone. This takes out *acceded* (agreed) and *demurred* (hesitated), which have positive or neutral connotations. This still leaves you a number of answer choices with a negative tone. You can pull out the two best fits through context. While the candidate could *castigate* (severely criticize) or *malign* (bad-mouth) political issues, they do not work in this case with the directional term *on*. The candidate could, however, *pontificate* (speak in a dogmatic matter) or *inveigh* (speak with invective) *on* the issues.

19. B, E.

To *impair* and *aggrieve* both mean to injure. Another pair is *exsiccate* and *desiccate*, meaning to dry up, but they do not match the sentence context. *Delineate* is to depict or sketch, while *aggregate* is to gather—both too neutral for the described ruination of a career.

20. B, F.

Immutable means unchangeable, and *sacrosanct* means most sacred or inviolable. Both are characteristics often given to the divine or to deities. *Iconoclastic* attacks traditions, and is not specifically religious. *Obtuse* (blunt or stupid) and *monotonous* (sameness) do not form a pair, while *imperceptive*, or lacking perception, usually does not describe the divine, which is usually conceived as all-knowing.

QUANTITATIVE REASONING
ANSWER KEY: SECTION 6

1. **C.**

   This problem tests your understanding of probability. Drawing from a bag containing 3 orange, 6 red, and 5 blue marbles, you are asked to compare the probability of drawing marbles in a particular order. The probability of drawing a particular marble on a given draw will be:

   $$\frac{number\ of\ marbles\ of\ the\ desired\ color}{number\ of\ marbles\ in\ the\ bag}$$

   First, calculate the number of marbles in the bag: 3 + 6 + 5 = 14. The probability of a series of draws is equal to the product of the probabilities of each draw. In other words, find the probability for each draw, then multiply the series of probabilities together. To calculate for Quantity A, the series of draws is: blue, blue, red, orange. For the first draw there are 5 blue marbles out of 14; for the second, 4 blue marbles out of 13; for the third draw, 3 marbles out of 12; and for the final draw 6 marbles out of 11. Writing out the product you have:

   $\frac{5}{14} \cdot \frac{4}{13} \cdot \frac{3}{12} \cdot \frac{6}{11}$ expression for Quantity A

   Next, calculate for Quantity B. The series of draws is: red, orange, red, red. For the first draw, there are 6 red marbles out of 14; for the second, 3 marbles out of 13; for the third, 5 out of 12; and for the final draw, 4 marbles out of 11. Writing out the product you have:

   $\frac{6}{14} \cdot \frac{3}{13} \cdot \frac{5}{12} \cdot \frac{4}{11}$ expression for Quantity B

   From here you can see that the denominators are exactly alike. Also looking at the numerators, the products will be the same. Therefore the probabilities are equal. There is no need to calculate the exact probabilities. The correct answer choice is **C**.

2. **B.**

   This problem tests your knowledge of geometry and the ability to set up an algebra problem. First, you are given that the figure on the right is a trapezoid and the figure on the left is a rectangle. You are also given that the rectangle is half the area of the trapezoid. Begin by placing the figure's area formulas into an equation:

   $2x \cdot 3x \cdot 2 = \frac{2+6}{2} \cdot 3$ Area of Rectangle × 2 = Area of Trapezoid

   $12x^2 = 4 \cdot 3 = 12$ simplify

   $x^2 = 1$ divide both sides by the common factor of 12

   $x = 1$ calculate

   Because you are looking for area, discard the negative square root. The correct answer choice is therefore **B**. You can confirm this result by substituting x into the Area calculation for the rectangle: 2(1) · 3(1) = 6, which is half of 12, the area of the trapezoid that you found in line 2.

3. **B.**

   This problem is a test of your understanding of similar triangles. You are asked to compare the shadow length of two upright objects (a flagpole and a woman) in order to determine the height of the flagpole. The equation for the relationship of the two objects is:

   $$\frac{height\ of\ flagpole}{length\ of\ flagpole's\ shadow} = \frac{height\ of\ woman}{length\ of\ woman's\ shadow}$$

You can plug in the known values and solve for the height (*h*) of the flagpole:

$$\frac{h}{144 \text{ in}} = \frac{6 \text{ ft}}{1.5 \text{ yds}}$$ Given information

$$\frac{h}{144 \text{ in}} = \frac{6 \times 12 \text{ in}}{1.5 \times 36 \text{ in}}$$ Convert values to same unit of length (inches)

$$h = \frac{6 \times 12 \times 144}{1.5 \times 36} \text{ in}$$ Isolate the variable

$$h = 192 \text{ in}$$ Solution

Quantity B (192.5 inches) is greater than Quantity A (192 inches), so the correct answer is B.

4. C.

This problem tests your ability to use geometry to solve a problem and is best approached by sketching out the solution. You are asked to determine how many boxes and/or separators can be extracted from a 46" × 64" sheet of cardboard.

First, to find Quantity A, you need to determine the number of 16" × 30" pizza boxes that can be extracted from a single 46" × 64" sheet of cardboard. Comparing the box dimensions (16") and the cardboard dimensions, you may notice that 16" divides evenly into 64". Sketching a large rectangle of 64" × 46", place the smaller pizza box rectangles inside so that the 16" edges are on the long edge of the large rectangle. You will then notice that a strip of cardboard measuring 16" × 64" remains. You can cut two more boxes of 16" × 30" from this strip, leaving a 4" × 16" section of waste. Because this waste area is too small to make a box, you have to stop, having cut 6 boxes from a single sheet of cardboard.

Now, to find Quantity B, we can use the results from Quantity A to determine that it will take 4 sheets of cardboard to create the requested 24 boxes. The remaining question is, how many sheets of cardboard are required to cut out 24 of the 14"-round pizza separators? This can be found by dividing the diameter of the circle (*d* = 14) into the edge lengths of the rectangular piece of cardboard: $\frac{64}{14}$ = 4 with a remainder of 10". Moving in the other direction: $\frac{46}{14}$ = 3 with 4 inches remaining. You can thus fit 12 (4 × 3) separators onto a single sheet of cardboard. The number of sheets required to make the separators is $\frac{24}{12}$ = 2 sheets. Add these 2 to the 4 sheets required for the boxes and you get a value for Quantity B of 6.

Quantity A is equal to Quantity B, so the correct answer choice is C.

5. C.

This problem asks you to compare the value of 4 to the real solutions of the equation: $3x^3 + 5x^2 + 6x + 9 = 305$. The best strategy to accomplish this is factoring the polynomial. Because you are given a value to compare, you can try the given value in the polynomial to test if answer choice C is valid.

$3x^3 + 5x^2 + 6x + 9 \; ? \; 305$ The given equation

Here you replace the equals sign with a question mark to remind you that this is a test to find the relationship between the left and right sides.

$3(4)^3 + 5(4)^2 + 6(4) + 9 \; ? \; 305$ Substitute the test value

$305 = 305$ Solve

This demonstrates that at least one real solution for the polynomial is 4. Now factor out $(x - 4)$:

$3x^3 + 5x^2 + 6x + 9 = 305$ The given equation

$3x^3 + 5x^2 + 6x - 296 = 0$ Subtract 305 from both sides

Now divide $x - 4$ from the polynomial using polynomial division:

$$
\begin{array}{r}
3x^2 + 17x + 74 \qquad\qquad \text{Solution} \\[4pt]
(x - 4) \,\big)\, \overline{(3x^3 + 5x^2 + 6x - 296)} \\
\underline{3x^3 - 12x^2} \qquad\qquad\qquad \\
17x^2 + 6x - 296 \\
\underline{17x^2 - 68x} \qquad\quad \\
74x - 296 \\
\underline{74x - 296}
\end{array}
$$

The resulting polynomial of $3x^2 + 17x + 74$ does not have any real solutions. The quickest way to discover this is to use the quadratic formula:

$$x = \frac{-b \pm \sqrt{(b^2 - 4ac)}}{2a}$$

$$x = \frac{-17 \pm \sqrt{(17^2 - 4(3)(74)}}{2(3)}$$ Substitute coefficient values

$17^2 - 4(3)(74) = -599$ Calculate the radicand

Because the radicand is a **negative** value, there are no more real solutions. This means that 4 was the only real solution and therefore Quantity A is equal to Quantity B. The correct answer choice is C.

6. **C.**

This problem tests your understanding of the relationship between the hypotenuse and the legs of a right triangle. The sketch consists of a rectangle inscribed in a triangle, with two of the sides congruent with the legs of the triangle. You are also given that the leg of one side of the rectangle is half the length of the height of the triangle (h). Now for convenience you label the other leg b, and each of the shorter segments of the triangle per the diagram.

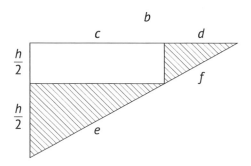

You now use the properties of similar triangles to find expressions for c and d. Start with the ratio:

$$\frac{(c + d)}{c} = \frac{h}{\frac{h}{2}}$$ Similar triangle theorem

$\dfrac{(c + d)}{c} = 2$	Simplify the right side
$c + d = 2c$	Multiply both sides by c
$d = c$	Subtract c from both sides

Now relate c and d to b:

$c + d = b$	Shown on the diagram
$c + c = b$	Substitute from above
$2c = b$	Simplify
$c = \dfrac{b}{2}$	Express c in terms of b

You have now demonstrated that the other side of the rectangle is equal to $\dfrac{b}{2}$. Next, put together the area formulas:

Area of the triangle = $\dfrac{1}{2}\,bh$

Area of the rectangle = $\dfrac{h}{2} \times \dfrac{b}{2} = \dfrac{1}{4}\,bh$

Shaded Area = Area of Triangle − Area of Rectangle	Formula
$= \dfrac{1}{2}\,bh - \dfrac{1}{4}\,bh$	Substitute values
$= \dfrac{1}{4}\,bh$	

Therefore the area of the rectangle equals the shaded area. Quantity A is equal to Quantity B, so the correct answer is **C.**

7. **C.**

This problem tests your ability to translate a probability question into a simple geometric exercise. To start, the probability of X being in any specific location can be expressed as:

$$\frac{\textit{number of locations for X in a region}}{\textit{number of all possible locations of X}}$$

Next, you can think of Line P as sitting on a number line. You can then relate the points on the line numerically, where lower values are to the left and greater values are to the right. You are given Line P containing Point A and Point B where A < B. Additionally, Point X is randomly placed on the Line such that $\overline{AX} = 2 \cdot \overline{BX}$.

Quantity A is the probability of X being in Region 2 between A and B (A < X < B). To solve this, set up the equation:

$\overline{AB} = (\overline{AX}) + (\overline{BX})$	Geometric relationship of the points
$\overline{AB} = 2 \cdot \overline{BX} + \overline{BX}$	Substitute the given
$\overline{AB} = 3 \cdot \overline{BX}$	Solve

This demonstrates there is only one solution in Region 2. Note that it is not important to know **what** the solution is; rather, you are looking for the **NUMBER** of **possible** solutions.

Quantity B is the probability of *X* being in Region 3 to the right of B (*X* > B). To solve, set up the equation:

$\overline{AX} = \overline{AB} + \overline{BX}$ Geometric relationship of the points

$2 \cdot \overline{BX} = \overline{AB} + \overline{BX}$ Substitute the given

$\overline{BX} = \overline{AB}$ Solve

This demonstrates there is also only one solution in Region 3. There are a total of two possible solutions. Using our starting ratio to find the probability of *X* being in Region 2:

$\dfrac{\textit{number of locations for X in Region 2}}{\textit{number of all possible locations of X}} = \dfrac{1}{2} = 50\%$ Solve for Quantity A

Since you know that there is also only one location in Region 3, Quantity B will also be 50%. Quantity A is therefore equal to Quantity B so the correct answer choice is **C.**

8. **D.**

   This problem tests your understanding of the relationship between a circle and an inscribed triangle. $\triangle ABC$ is a right triangle. You are also given the chord length $\overset{\frown}{BC}$ = 45°. From this you know that the inscribed angle $\angle BAC$ = 22.5°. The diagram shows $\angle ABC$ = 90° so you can find $\angle ACB$ with:

$$\angle ACB = 180° - \angle ABC - \angle BAC = 180° - 90° - 22.5° = 67.5°$$

   Next, the diagram shows chord $\overline{BD} \perp \overline{AC}$ so you can use the properties of similar right triangles to show that $\angle ABD = \angle ACB = 67.5°$.

   The correct answer is **D.**

9. **B.**

   This problem tests your ability to set up a geometric series. You are given that each employee hired costs $15/hr. The amount of revenue produced by each employee starts as $20/hr, but each additional employee produces only 90% of the previous hire. For the second hire on, then, produce an equation to reflect this percentage deduction:

   2nd: $20/hr × .9 = $18/hr
   3rd: $18/hr × .9 = $16.20/hr
   4th: $16.20/hr × .9 = $14.58/hr

   You are asked to determine how many employees the manager can hire who will each generate more revenue than they cost. Since the fourth employee costs $15/hr while only generating $14.58/hr, the manager cannot hire four employees. The correct answer choice is B.

10. C.

This problem tests your understanding of ratios. Given the relationship $5x = 4y = 2z$, you are to find the least possible value of the expression: $x^2 + 2y + z$. The first step is to solve the variables.

$5x = 4y = 2z$	Given relationship
$\dfrac{x}{4} = \dfrac{y}{5} = \dfrac{z}{10}$	Divide by least common multiple of the coefficients
$x = 4, y = 5, z = 10$	Solution

Now plug this solution into the expression:

$4^2 + 2(5) + 10 = 36$

The correct answer is C.

11. D.

This number theory problem tests your understanding of prime factors and number composition. The first step is to find the smallest **3-digit** number which has 3 prime factors. Choose the two smallest possible primes: 2 and 3. Find the smallest prime which, when multiplied with 2 and 3, is a 3-digit number. This happens to be 17: 2(3)(17) = 102. 101 is a prime number, so with 102 you have found the smallest 3-digit number with 3 prime factors. Call this a.

Now find the smallest **2-digit** number with 3 prime factors. The three smallest prime factors are 2, 3, and 5: 2(3)(5) = 30, which is a 2-digit number. Call this b.

This gives you: $ab = (2 \cdot 3 \cdot 17) \cdot (2 \cdot 3 \cdot 5) = 2^2 \cdot 3^2 \cdot 5 \cdot 17 = 3060$. As you can see, 3060 has exactly 4 prime factors: 2, 3, 5, 17.

The correct answer choice is **D.**

12. D.

This question tests your ability to read a graph and interpret a trend line. In order to fit the equation to the line, you first need to evaluate the slope of the line, then try the extreme values to see the variation. Note that you are **not** looking for an exact equation for the line; rather, you are looking for the **best** fit. The easiest way to calculate this is to find the variations from the trend line at the extremes and compare:

(A) has a positive slope and so can be eliminated.
(B) has a positive slope and so can be eliminated.
(C) has a negative slope. The equation varies from the trend line by 2 at the closest and by 9 at the extreme.
(D) has a negative slope. The equation varies from the trend line by 1.5 at the closest and by .5 at the extreme.
(E) has a positive slope and so can be eliminated.

Answer choice D has the least variation from the graph line and is the correct answer.

QUANTITATIVE REASONING
ANSWER KEY: SECTION 6

13. C.

This problem asks you to first sort the data on the chart in reference to variation from the trend line, and to then calculate the average variance of the middle quartiles.

To calculate the variation from the trend line, simply find the difference between each datum and the trend line along the vertical axis. Doing this will yield the set:

$$\{-1, -6, 2.5, 1.25, -5.25, 5.5, 2, -2.5, 2.25, 6.5, 1, -.5, 4.25, -5, 3.5, -5, -2.5, .5, -3, 2.5\}$$

Next, sort the set from least to greatest:

$$\{-6, -5.25, -5, -5, -3, -2.5, -2.5, -1, -.5, .5, 1, 1.25, 2, 2.25, 2.5, 2.5, 3.5, 4.25, 5.5, 6.5\}$$

A quartile is one-quarter of the data set by count. This data set has 20 elements and therefore the quartiles are calculated as follows:

Quartile 1 = elements 1 through 5 $\{-6, -5.25, -5, -5, -3\}$
Quartile 2 = elements 6 through 10 $\{-2.5, -2.5, -1, -.5, .5\}$
Quartile 3 = elements 11 through 15 $\{1, 1.25, 2, 2.25, 2.5\}$
Quartile 4 = elements 16 through 20 $\{2.5, 3.5, 4.25, 5.5, 6.5\}$

The middle two quartiles are Quartiles 2 and 3. To calculate their average variance, calculate the average of their elements:

$$\frac{-2.5 - 2.5 - 1 - .5 + .5 + 1 + 1.25 + 2 + 2.25 + 2.5}{10} = \frac{3.0}{10} = .3$$

Comparing this result to the answers you see that the closest answer is **C.** Note that because you are using a graph to visually **estimate** the variations, your answer will not always exactly match the choices.

14. A.

This problem tests your ability to generate a line equation and to solve a system of two equations. You are given a line equation for Line L: $3x - 4y = 10$. You are then asked to find the point of intersection with a perpendicular line that passes through $(3, 4)$. The first step is to convert the given equation to slope-intercept form:

$3x - 4y = 10$ Given equation for Line L
$y = \frac{3}{4}x - \frac{5}{2}$ Isolate variable y to get slope-intercept form

The slope for a line perpendicular to Line L is the inverse reciprocal of $\frac{3}{4}$. Use this value to generate a new line equation:

$(y - 4) = -\frac{4}{3}(x - 3)$ Point-slope form
$3y - 12 = -4x + 12$ Multiply both sides by 3
$4x + 3y = 24$ Equation (1) for the perpendicular line

At this point the fastest way to get your answer is to plug in the values from the answer choices and see if they work. Starting with answer choice A:

$3\left(5\frac{1}{25}\right) - 4\left(1\frac{7}{25}\right) ? 10$ Substitute values into Line L

$15\frac{3}{25} - 4\frac{28}{25} ? 10$ Multiply terms

$10 = 10$ Solve; solution is possible for Line L

Now try the perpendicular line:

$4\left(5\frac{1}{25}\right) + 3\left(1\frac{7}{25}\right) ? 24$ Substitute values for *x* and *y* into Equation (1) from above

$20\frac{4}{25} + 3\frac{21}{25} ? 24$ Multiply terms

$24 = 24$ Solve; solution is possible for perpendicular line

Answer choice A lies on both Line L and the perpendicular line and so **MUST** be the intersection of the two lines. The correct answer choice is **A.**

15. **3 hr 5min**
This problem tests your ability to translate a word problem into a series of percentage calculations. The time it will take Gretchen to transcribe the 6,000-word document can be expressed as follows:

intial time to type + time to fix typos + time to fix wrong words

First, calculate the time to type up the document:

$$\frac{6000 \text{ words}}{120 \text{ words/min}} = 50 \text{ min}$$

Next, calculate the number of typos committed by Gretchen (30%):

$$6,000 \text{ words} \cdot .3 = 1,800 \text{ words}$$

Calculate the number of typos missed (5%) and the time it takes to correct them:

$$1,800 \text{ words} \cdot .05 = 90 \text{ words} \cdot .5 \text{ min} = 45 \text{ min}$$

Then find the time it takes to fix the incorrect words substituted by the word processor (5%):

$$1,800 \text{ words} \cdot .05 \cdot 1 \text{ min} = 90 \text{ words} \cdot 1 \text{ min} = 90 \text{ min}$$

The total time to transcribe the document is:

$$50 \text{ min} + 45 \text{ min} + 90 \text{ min} = 185 \text{ min} = 3 \text{ hr } 5\text{min}$$

Enter your answer in the text box. Be sure to use the correct units.

QUANTITATIVE REASONING
ANSWER KEY: SECTION 6

16. B.

This problem tests your ability to calculate the standard deviation of a data set. The first step is to calculate the mean value of the data.

$$\frac{13 + 14(3) + 15(2) + 17(7) + 18 + 20(5) + 21 + 25}{1 + 3 + 2 + 7 + 1 + 5 + 1 + 1} = \frac{368}{21} = 17.52$$

Next, calculating the differences from the data points to the mean value, you get:

# Guessed	# Students	Difference
13 Blocks	1	4.5
14 Blocks	3	3.5
15 Blocks	2	2.5
17 Blocks	7	.5
18 Blocks	1	.5
20 Blocks	5	2.5
21 Blocks	1	3.5
25 Blocks	1	7.5

Now calculate the mean of the squares of the differences:

$$\frac{4.5^2 + 3(3.5^2) + 2(2.5^2) + 7(.5^2) + (.5^2) + 5(2.5^2) + 3.5^2 + 7.5^2}{21} = \frac{171.25}{21} = 8.154$$

Now take the square root of 8.154 and you have the standard deviation.

$$\sqrt{8.154} = 2.855$$

Rounding from 2.855 results in a value of 2.9. The correct answer choice is **B.**

17. B.

This problem tests your ability to interpret a word problem, apply percentages, and convert time units. You are given a weekly revenue of $1,000 / week per station less 70% in expenses, a monthly rental cost of $4,500, and an initial layout cost of $250,000. You are asked to calculate the minimum number of stations required to recoup the initial expense over a period of two years (or 104 weeks). Start with a basic formula:

income − rent > initial cost

For income, use x to represent the number of stations and set up the formula:

$1000 / week • (1 − .7) • x • 104 weeks$	Initial formula
$1000 • .3 • x • 104$	Simplify units
$31,200x$	Simplify to one term

Rent is simply the cost over two years (24 months): $4500 • 24 = $108,000.

Now plug everything into your basic formula:

$31,200x − $108,000 > $250,000	Starting formula
$31,200x > $358,000	Add $108,000 to both sides
x > $358,000/$31,200	Divide by $31,200
x > 11.47	Solve for x

You see there must be at least 11.47 stations. However, you cannot have part of a station so you need to round up to the nearest whole number, which is 12. The correct answer choice is B.

18. 41,040

This problem tests your understanding of factorials, prime factors and factors of numbers. Given the quantity 20! you are asked to find the number of distinct factors. Because 20! is an unusually large number you will have to find all the prime factors and use this information to calculate the number of distinct factors.

20! is the product of all integers from 1 to 20 and can be written:

$$1 \cdot 2 \cdot 3 \cdot 4 \cdot 5 \cdot 6 \cdot 7 \cdot 8 \cdot 9 \cdot 10 \cdot 11 \cdot 12 \cdot 13 \cdot 14 \cdot 15 \cdot 16 \cdot 17 \cdot 18 \cdot 19 \cdot 20$$

The prime factors of this product will consist of the prime factors of each integer from 1 to 20 and are, in order of its integers:

$$\{2, 3, 2, 2, 5, 2, 3, 7, 2, 2, 2, 3, 3, 2, 5, 11, 2, 2, 3, 13, 2, 7, 3, 5, 2, 2, 2, 2, 17, 2, 3, 3, 19, 2, 2, 5\}$$

Reordered by numeral:

$$\{2, 2, 2, 2, 2, 2, 2, 2, 2, 2, 2, 2, 2, 2, 2, 2, 2, 2, 3, 3, 3, 3, 3, 3, 3, 3, 5, 5, 5, 5, 7, 7, 11, 13, 17, 19\}$$

Thus 20! can be written: $2^{18} \cdot 3^8 \cdot 5^4 \cdot 7^2 \cdot 11^1 \cdot 13^1 \cdot 17^1 \cdot 19^1$

The number of factors can be found by calculating the number of distinct permutations of the prime factors. This is calculated by finding the product of 1 plus the exponent of each of the prime factors. We do this because the factor 1 is found when all exponents are set to 0. The resulting calculation is: $19 \cdot 9 \cdot 5 \cdot 3 \cdot 2 \cdot 2 \cdot 2 \cdot 2 = 41,040$.

Enter 41,040 in the text box.

QUANTITATIVE REASONING
ANSWER KEY: SECTION 6

19. A, B, C, D.

This problem tests your ability to relate geometry and algebra and use algebraic manipulation.

You are given the relationship $a + c = b$ where $b > a$. You are then asked to indicate which equations are true. You will have to test each answer choice to see if it is true.

$a^2 + 2ac + c^2 \,?\, b^2$	Answer choice A
$a^2 + 2ac + c^2 \,?\, (a + c)^2$	Substitute from the given relationship
$a^2 + 2ac + c^2 = a^2 + 2ac + c^2$	Expand the exponent

Answer choice A is true.

$bc - c^2 \,?\, ac$	Answer choice B
$b - c \,?\, a$	Divide by c
$b = a + c$	Isolate variable b

Answer choice B is true.

For answer choice C, you want to find a convenient substitution that will allow you to simplify the expression. In this instance you can replace the term bc by:

$a + c = b$	Given equation
$ac + c^2 = bc$	Multiply by c

Now you are ready to attack the problem:

$b^2 - bc = a^2 + ac$	Answer choice C
$b^2 - (c^2 + ac) = a^2 + ac$	Substitution
$b^2 = a^2 + ac + c^2 + ac$	Isolate the b term
$b^2 = a^2 + 2ac + c^2$	Simplify
$b = a + c$	Take the square root

Answer choice C is true. Note: We can do the last step because we are told a, b, c represent the sides of a rectangle and thus are guaranteed to be positive.

$2ac = ab + bc - c^2 - a^2$	Answer choice D
$a^2 + 2ac + c^2 = ab + bc$	Add $a^2 + c^2$ to both sides
$(a + c)^2 = ab + bc$	Factor the polynomial
$b^2 = ab + bc$	Substitution from the original given
$b = a + c$	Divide by b

Answer choice D is also true. Therefore, answer choices A, B, C and D are your true and correct answers.

20. B, C.

This problem tests your ability to translate a word problem into an inequality. You are told that Michael had an oil change performed on his vehicle and was charged a base price (*b*) plus 4.5% sales tax and a 3.5% convenience fee, each calculated on the base price. This can be written as:

$$b + b \cdot .045 + b \cdot .035 = b(1.0 + .045 + .035) = b \cdot 1.08 = 1.08b$$

Next, you are told that Michael gave the cashier $30 and received less than 6 dollars change. This can be written:

$$30 - 1.08b < 6$$

Now solve for the base price (*b*):

$30 - 1.08b < 6$	Given relationship
$24 < 1.08b$	Add 1.08b to both sides
$\dfrac{24}{1.08} < b$	Divide both sides by 1.08
$22.22 < b$	Calculate
$b > 22.22$	Move variable to the left for readability

The base price can be as little as $22.23, lower than $23.50—in which case, answer choice A will be false. Do not select.

Next, we need to find the greatest possible base price. Because Michael received change we start with:

$1.08b < 30$	Given
$b < \dfrac{30}{1.08}$	Divide both sides by 1.08
$b < 27.77$	Calculate

$27.77 is less than $28.20 so answer choice B must be true. Select answer choice B.

Finally, for the third statement we use the highest possible value for *b* to see the most Michael would pay in tax and convenience fees.

fees < 27.77 • .08

fees < 2.22

$2.22 is less than $2.46 so answer choice C must be true. Select answer choice C.

PRACTICE TEST 2
GRE ®
Graduate Record Examinations

This exam is 3 hours and 45 minutes long. Try to take this full exam in one sitting to simulate real test conditions.

While taking this exam, refrain from listening to music or watching TV.

When writing your responses for the Analyze an Issue and Analyze an Argument prompts, please use a computer, and turn off the spell-check feature to simulate real testing conditions.

If **circles** mark a question's answer choices, choose one answer. If **squares** mark a question's answer choices, choose more than one answer.

Use a basic calculator. Do not use a graphic or scientific calculator. On the real exam, you will have an on-screen calculator with only basic operation functions and a square root key.

Concentrate and GOOD LUCK!

ARGOPREP
ARGOPREP.COM/GRE

ANALYTICAL WRITING | ESSAY 1
ANALYZE AN ISSUE | 30 MINUTES

Teachers' salaries should be largely dependent on how well the teachers' students perform on standardized tests.

Discuss the extent to which you agree or disagree with the statement and explain your position. Citing specific examples, explain how the circumstances under which the recommendation could be adopted would or would not be advantageous in developing and supporting your view point.

GO TO THE NEXT PAGE

ANALYTICAL WRITING | ESSAY 2
ANALYZE AN ARGUMENT | 30 MINUTES

The following is from a memo released by a prominent pesticide company in Lincoln, Nebraska.

Wheat fields throughout the state are being ravaged by the wheat weevil, a crop pest that can eat through a pound of wheat in a day! The wheat weevil is highly mobile and has a short gestation period so an infestation can manifest in no time. To prevent your valuable crops from being destroyed, you must act now. Because the wheat weevil has already infected crops in Lincoln, you can be sure that they will inevitably make it to your land. Call us today so we can help you protect your livelihood. Just two easy treatments guarantee the safety and longevity of your crops.

Discuss the stated and unstated assumptions in the argument and discuss what the consequences might be if those assumptions are shown to be unwarranted.

GO TO THE NEXT PAGE

QUANTITATIVE REASONING
SECTION 3
20 QUESTIONS
35 MINUTES

1.

Quantity A	Quantity B

The Area of a regular Octagon with sides of length 4

The Area of a Square with sides of length 8

Ⓐ Quantity A is greater.
Ⓑ Quantity B is greater.
Ⓒ The quantities are equal.
Ⓓ The relationship cannot be determined from the information given.

2. A savings account offers 5% interest compounded daily.

Quantity A	Quantity B

The account balance after investing $1 per day for one year

The account balance after investing $65 at the end of every month

Ⓐ Quantity A is greater.
Ⓑ Quantity B is greater.
Ⓒ The quantities are equal.
Ⓓ The relationship cannot be determined from the information given.

3.

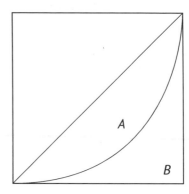

The Arc between region A and B is a quarter circle. The Triangle formed by region A and B is an isosceles right triangle.

Quantity A	Quantity B

Area of Region A

Area of Region B

Ⓐ Quantity A is greater.
Ⓑ Quantity B is greater.
Ⓒ The two quantities are equal.
Ⓓ The relationship cannot be determined from the information given.

4. The Earth rotates around its axis every 23 hours, 56 minutes, and 4 seconds.

Quantity A	Quantity B

The measure of the arc traversed by the hour hand on a clock from 10:15 to 1:07

The rotation of the Earth measured in degrees during the same time

Ⓐ Quantity A is greater.
Ⓑ Quantity B is greater.
Ⓒ The quantities are equal.
Ⓓ The relationship cannot be determined from the information given.

GO TO THE NEXT PAGE

5. The algae on the surface of a pond increases in size by 10% each day. At night the algae on the surface of the same pond is reduced by 5%.

Quantity A	Quantity B
The number of days it takes for the algae to go from 15% of the pond's surface to 50%	The number of days it takes for the algae to go from 50% of the pond's surface to 100%

Ⓐ Quantity A is greater.
Ⓑ Quantity B is greater.
Ⓒ The two quantities are equal.
Ⓓ The relationship cannot be determined from the information given.

6.

$$y = 2x^2 + x - 5$$

Quantity A	Quantity B
The distance between the y intercept and the value of x at the line of symmetry	The distance between the x intercepts

Ⓐ Quantity A is greater.
Ⓑ Quantity B is greater.
Ⓒ The two quantities are equal.
Ⓓ The relationship cannot be determined from the information given.

7.

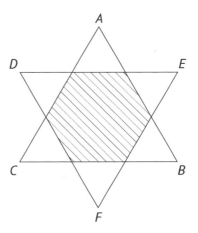

ABC is an equilateral triangle.
DEF is an equilateral triangle.

Quantity A	Quantity B
The shaded area is a regular hexagon	The sum of the unshaded areas

Ⓐ Quantity A is greater.
Ⓑ Quantity B is greater.
Ⓒ The two quantities are equal.
Ⓓ The relationship cannot be determined from the information given.

GO TO THE NEXT PAGE

QUANTITATIVE REASONING
SECTION 3

8. Find the length of $\overline{AB}$.

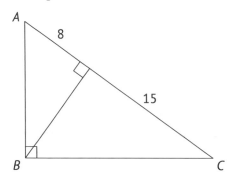

Ⓐ 11.3

Ⓑ $2\sqrt{30}$

Ⓒ $\sqrt{23}$

Ⓓ $2\sqrt{46}$

Ⓔ $2\sqrt{26}$

---

9. Find the distance between the point $(-4,5)$ and the intersection of the lines $2y - x = 0$ and $3x + 5y = 44$.

Ⓐ $3\sqrt{10}$

Ⓑ $\sqrt{145}$

Ⓒ $\sqrt{13}$

Ⓓ $2\sqrt{10}$

Ⓔ $\sqrt{10}$

10. Given right triangle *ABC*, find the slope of segments $\overline{AB}$ and $\overline{BC}$.

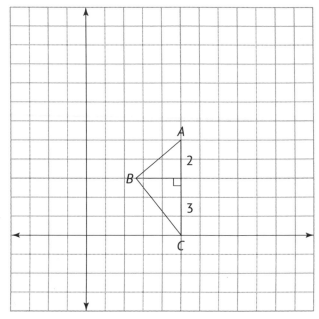

Ⓐ $\frac{2}{3}$ and $\frac{-3}{2}$

Ⓑ $\frac{2}{\sqrt{6}}$ and $\frac{-3}{\sqrt{6}}$

Ⓒ $\frac{2}{\sqrt{5}}$ and $\frac{-\sqrt{5}}{2}$

Ⓓ $\frac{-3}{\sqrt{7}}$ and $\frac{\sqrt{7}}{3}$

Ⓔ The slopes cannot be determined from the information given.

---

11. Given a cube with sides of length *x*, what is the increase in volume if the length of each side is increased by 2 units?

Ⓐ 8

Ⓑ $x^3 - 8$

Ⓒ $6x^2 - 6x + 8$

Ⓓ $3x^2 + 12x$

Ⓔ $6x^2 + 12x + 8$

GO TO THE NEXT PAGE

12. Given points $A(1, 3)$, $B(-3, 15)$, and $C(-6, 21)$, what is the distance from the midpoint of $\overline{AB}$ to Point C?

- (A) 31
- (B) 14
- (C) $\sqrt{5}$
- (D) 13
- (E) $\sqrt{13}$

13. The square of the sum of two numbers is 289. The product of the two numbers is 66. What is the sum of the squares of the two numbers? Enter your answer in the text box below.

14. A boat sails at 15 MPH for two hours on a course of 30°. It then swings to port (left) 30° and sails at 4 MPH for two more hours. It now swings 120° to port and sails two more hours at 15 MPH. How far is the boat from the starting point? Enter your answer in decimal form to the nearest hundredth in the box provided.

15.

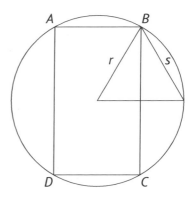

In the figure above the chord s is length 6 and the circle has a radius of 7. The radius intersecting $\overline{BC}$ does so at a right angle. Find the area of the rectangle $ABCD$. Enter your answer in the text box below rounded to the nearest whole number.

Use the graph below to answers questions 16 and 17. Select one answer unless otherwise indicated.

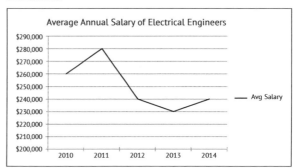

16. What was the approximate percentage decrease in average annual salary from 2011 to 2012?

- (A) 14.3%
- (B) 15.2%
- (C) 50%
- (D) 25%
- (E) 18.5%

GO TO THE NEXT PAGE

17. What was the average salary in 2015 if it was 10% greater than the median salary for the previous five years?

(A) $253,000
(B) $264,000
(C) $275,000
(D) $286,000
(E) $308,000

18. Three circles of the radius 1 are positioned so that any two circles contact each other at exactly one point. What is the area enclosed by the three circles?

(A) $\pi - \sqrt{3}$

(B) $2 - \dfrac{\pi}{6}$

(C) $\dfrac{\pi}{2}$

(D) $\sqrt{3} - \dfrac{\pi}{2}$

(E) $\dfrac{\pi^2}{\sqrt{3}}$

19. What is the greatest possible area for a right triangle with a hypotenuse of 5?

(A) 3.536
(B) 6.000
(C) 6.125
(D) 6.250
(E) There is not enough information to determine the answer.

20. The equation for a circle can be written $(x - a)^2 + (y - b)^2 = r^2$ where (a, b) is the center of the circle and r is the radius.

What is the center point of the circle

$$\frac{y + 4}{x - 4} = \frac{15}{(x - 4)(y - 2)} - \frac{x - 2}{y - 2} ?$$

(A) (4, 4)
(B) (2, 2)
(C) (2, 4)
(D) (3, 1)
(E) (1, 3)

STOP

VERBAL REASONING
SECTION 4

20 QUESTIONS
30 MINUTES

For questions 1 to 6, you are to choose <u>one</u> answer for each blank from the corresponding column of choices.

1. Myron could not shake his intense _____ over the situation, issuing apology after apology in the days that followed.

   Ⓐ disquietude
   Ⓑ wanderlust
   Ⓒ compunction
   Ⓓ prelude
   Ⓔ filibuster

2. The young socialite had spoken in a(n) (i)_____ tone when discussing fashion trends over dinner, yet he (ii)_____ himself before a visiting designer the next day.

Blank i	Blank ii
Ⓐ frenzied	Ⓓ prostrated
Ⓑ imperious	Ⓔ absconded
Ⓒ impervious	Ⓕ complemented

3. Climate change often evokes heated debates. Few can deny, however, that areas once lush and (i)_____ are now becoming (ii)_____, uninhabitable and fallow.

Blank i	Blank ii
Ⓐ fecund	Ⓓ diaphanous
Ⓑ puerile	Ⓔ barren
Ⓒ besmirched	Ⓕ bombastic

4. The long-tail boat cruised down the Mekong River as the passengers aboard enjoyed the (i)_____ scenery. The boat ride was the first (ii)_____ they had had since participating in the (iii)_____ week's flood clean-up activities.

Blank i	Blank ii
Ⓐ picturesque	Ⓓ preclusion
Ⓑ tumultuous	Ⓔ respite
Ⓒ ornate	Ⓕ cacophony

Blank iii
Ⓖ baleful
Ⓗ melancholy
Ⓘ reprieved

5. While active euthanasia (i)_____ much media attention, other issues in nursing homes (ii)_____ themselves on the public only when an ethically charged case (iii)_____ state or national law.

Blank i	Blank ii
Ⓐ deflects	Ⓓ ingratiate
Ⓑ garners	Ⓔ interpolate
Ⓒ impinges	Ⓕ pique

Blank iii
Ⓖ improvises
Ⓗ deposes
Ⓘ impugns

GO TO THE NEXT PAGE

VERBAL REASONING
SECTION 4

6. The notion that all religions of the world can unite under one force is far-fetched. Yet the widespread adoption of certain religious (i)_____ could change the world for the better. For example, Buddhist ideas of non-violence could not only be (ii)_____ to all religions but could also serve as a means of (iii)_____ military tensions.

Blank i
Ⓐ ideologies
Ⓑ exegesis
Ⓒ platitudes

Blank ii
Ⓓ inane
Ⓔ germane
Ⓕ irrelevant

Blank iii
Ⓖ assuaging
Ⓗ oscillating
Ⓘ osculating

Questions 7 and 8 are based on the following passage. Select one answer unless otherwise indicated.

The Yogi practices exercises by which he attains control of his body, and is enabled to send to any organ or part an increased flow of vital force or "prana," thereby strengthening and invigorating the part, or organ. He
5 knows all that his western scientific brother knows 5
about the physiological effect of correct breathing, but he also knows that the air contains more than oxygen and hydrogen and nitrogen, and that something more is accomplished than the mere oxygenating of the
10 blood. He knows something about "prana," of which 10
his western brother is ignorant, and he is fully aware of the nature and manner of handling that great principle of energy, and is fully informed as to its effect upon the human body and mind. He knows that by rhythmical
15 breathing one may bring himself into harmonious 15
vibration with nature, and aid in the unfoldment of his latent powers. He knows that by controlled breathing he may not only cure disease in himself and others, but also practically do away with fear and worry and
20 the baser emotions. 20

7. Choose the sentence that best expresses the main point of the passage.

8. According to the passage, the author introduces "prana" in order to accomplish what? Choose <u>all</u> that apply.

Ⓐ introduce the foundation of the yogi's expertise
Ⓑ demonstrate the yogi's superiority to western science
Ⓒ encourage practitioners' happiness
Ⓓ define the term
Ⓔ explain how yogic practices cure disease

GO TO THE NEXT PAGE

Questions 9 to 12 refers to the following passage on comparative human-animal psychology. Select one answer unless otherwise indicated.

That the mind of each human being forms a region inaccessible to all save its possessor, is one of the commonplaces of reflection. His neighbor's knowledge of each person's mind must always be indirect, a matter
5 of inference. How wide of the truth this inference may 5 be, even under the most favorable circumstances, is also an affair of everyday experience: each of us can judge his fellow-men only on the basis of his own thoughts and feelings in similar circumstances, and
10 the individual peculiarities of different members of 10 the human species are of necessity very imperfectly comprehended by others.

The science of human psychology has to reckon with this unbridgeable gap between minds as its chief
15 difficulty. The psychologist may look into his own 15 mind and study its workings with impartial insight, yet he can never be sure that the laws which he derives from such a study are not distorted by some personal twist or bias. For example, it has been suggested that
20 the philosopher Hume was influenced by his tendency 20 toward a visual type of imagination in his discussion of the nature of ideas, which to him were evidently visual images. As is well known, the experimental method in psychology has aimed to minimize the danger of
25 confusing individual peculiarities with general mental 25 laws. In a psychological experiment, an unbiased observer is asked to study his own experience under certain definite conditions, and to put it into words so that the experimenter may know what the contents of
30 another mind are like in the circumstances. 30

Thus language is the essential apparatus in experimental psychology; language with all its defects, its ambiguity, its substitution of crystallized concepts for the protean flux of actually lived experience, its lack
35 of terms to express those parts of experience which are 35 of small practical importance in everyday life, but which may be of the highest importance to mental science. Outside of the psychological laboratory language is not always the best guide to the contents of other
40 minds, because it is not always the expression of a 40 genuine wish to communicate thought. "Actions speak louder than words," the proverb says; but when words are backed by good faith they furnish by far the safest

indication of the thought of others. Whether, however,
45 our inferences are made on the basis of words or of 45 actions, they are all necessarily made on the hypothesis that human minds are built on the same pattern, that what a given word or action would mean for my mind, this it means also for my neighbor's mind.

50 If this hypothesis be uncertain when applied to our 50 fellow human beings, it fails us utterly when we turn to the lower animals. If my neighbor's mind is a mystery to me, how great is the mystery which looks out of the eyes of a dog, and how insoluble the problem presented by
55 the mind of an invertebrate animal, an ant or a spider! 55 We know that such minds must differ from ours not only in certain individual peculiarities, but in ways at whose nature we can only guess.

9. In the second paragraph, the author introduces the example of Hume in order to:

Ⓐ support her point that psychology and philosophy have a great deal in common
Ⓑ discuss one of the forefathers of psychological thought
Ⓒ illustrate the bias inherent in relying on one's own mind as the standard by which to derive mental laws
Ⓓ provide an example of the experimental method in psychology

_____

10. Choose the sentence that best illustrates the author's presented basis for the study of human psychology.

_____

11. Based on the passage, we can infer that:

Ⓐ animals' lack of language prevents us from understanding their minds
Ⓑ experimental psychology cannot be used in animal psychology
Ⓒ the mental laws of human psychology do not hold true in animal psychology
Ⓓ Hume's work on the nature of ideas was flawed

_____

GO TO THE NEXT PAGE

VERBAL REASONING
SECTION 4

12. Which of the following best surmises the author's drawn relationship between human and animal psychologies?

Ⓐ If we cannot understand our neighbor's mind, we cannot understand an animal's

Ⓑ The mental laws of human psychology are knowable and certain, while those of animal psychology are unknown and variable

Ⓒ The shared assumed patterns across human minds cannot be extended to animal minds

Ⓓ Philosophers have been working on the links between human and animal psychologies since Hume

Ⓔ Language in the laboratory will eventually form the bridge between human and animal psychologies

Question 13 is based on the following passage excerpted from a nursing manual of the 1920s.

A full history of the advances in medicine and surgery that have been made during the last half century is not only most interesting, but is as thrilling as a tale of adventure. Many of those who have investigated the
5 origin and transmission of disease have worked without 5 financial reward, and some have even risked their lives deliberately that others might be saved from illness and death. Among these may be mentioned Dr. James Carroll, who exposed himself to the bite of the yellow-
10 fever mosquito and thus contracted the disease; Dr. 10 Jesse Lazear, who died from the same disease; and Dr. Walter Reed, who risked his life to prove the mosquito the carrier of the yellow-fever germ. By the researches and heroic work of these men and their co-workers,
15 Havana was made healthful, the Panama Canal became 15 possible, and the world was given a shining example of the value of preventive measures when applied to problems of health.

13. The primary purpose of the passage is to:

Ⓐ discuss the poverty of medical researchers

Ⓑ provide a full history of advances in medicine and surgery

Ⓒ narrate the adventures of medical researchers

Ⓓ argue for the value of preventive medical measures

Ⓔ sing the praises of medical pioneers

Questions 14 to 16 are based on the following excerpt from a 1902 lecture on zoogeography. Select one answer unless otherwise indicated.

During the last decennium Zoogeography has developed in a very peculiar direction, which, in a large part, is directly opposite to the methods introduced by Wallace. The professed aim of the latter was the
5 creation of a zoogeographical division of the earth's surface into regions, realms and the like, the purpose of which was the subordination of the facts of animal distribution under a fixed scheme; and since it was self-evident from the beginning that the distribution
10 of animals ought to express the physical conditions of the earth's surface, it was assumed that the proposed zoogeographical divisions correspond to the chief features of the distribution of the conditions of life.

Soon, however, it was discovered that it is impossible
15 to give a division of the earth's surface that could claim general recognition. It is true that each of the proposed schemes was actually supported by more or less numerous instances of distribution, and that in many cases the physical factors influencing and
20 explaining these divisions were easily understood; but there was always alongside of the supposed normal conditions a number of exceptional cases, where the actual distribution of certain animals or animal groups was directly the opposite.

14. According to the author, what was the PRIMARY purpose of Wallace's work?

- (A) To divide the earth's surface into various units
- (B) To determine the major features of various animal groups
- (C) To create a classification system for the geographic distribution of animals
- (D) To find and explain all exceptions to the rules of distribution

15. According to the passage, what is the basic assumption that underlies early approaches to the study of zoogeography?

- (A) All animals can be classified and categorized
- (B) Any proposed zoogeographical divisions based on animal distribution correspond to geographical features that affect life conditions
- (C) Animals dwell where they can survive
- (D) Wallace's methods were correct
- (E) We can always find and define where animals live

16. Which of the following is MOST like zoogeography, as described in the passage?

- (A) The categorization of plant species via their genes
- (B) The study of cultures of the subarctic over time
- (C) A listing of housing types via geographic region
- (D) Jacques Cousteau's many underwater studies around the world
- (E) A detailed examination of the plants and trees in New England

For questions 17 to 20, select two answers that best complete the blank and produce two sentences that are alike in meaning.

17. Several _____ police incidents at the hotel kicked off the convention's weekend, sending waves of concern among participants.

- [A] coeval
- [B] reprobate
- [C] convivial
- [D] coincident
- [E] concomitant
- [F] dissident

18. While the benefactor's reasons for his large donation appeared _____, many on the board suspected that he had ulterior motives for his generosity.

- [A] sanctimonious
- [B] altruistic
- [C] magnanimous
- [D] reprehensible
- [E] raucous
- [F] refractory

---

19. Alison's carefree and _____ nature was at odds with the serious, silent nature of her work environment.

- [A] decorous
- [B] quiescent
- [C] prolix
- [D] voluble
- [E] munificent
- [F] malevolent

---

20. Foreign revolutions often _____ a coeval economic collapse that can linger for decades after violence has ceased.

- [A] eviscerate
- [B] adumbrate
- [C] prognosticate
- [D] enervate
- [E] propagate
- [F] engender

STOP

QUANTITATIVE REASONING
SECTION 5

20 QUESTIONS
35 MINUTES

1.

Quantity A	Quantity B
Sum of integers from 0 to 50 which are evenly divisible by 5.	Sum of all integers from 0 to 40 which are evenly divisible by 3.

Ⓐ Quantity A is greater.
Ⓑ Quantity B is greater.
Ⓒ The two quantities are equal.
Ⓓ The relationship cannot be determined from the information given.

2. A circle is divided into 5 arcs where the longest division is exactly twice the length of the shortest division.

Quantity A	Quantity B
The measure of the longest arc	One-third of the circumference of the circle

Ⓐ Quantity A is greater.
Ⓑ Quantity B is greater.
Ⓒ The two quantities are equal.
Ⓓ The relationship cannot be determined from the information given.

3.

$$ab < 1$$
$$ac < 1$$
$$cb < 1$$
$$abc = 1$$
$$b > 1$$

Quantity A	Quantity B
$\dfrac{1}{a + c}$	b

Ⓐ Quantity A is greater.
Ⓑ Quantity B is greater.
Ⓒ The two quantities are equal.
Ⓓ The relationship cannot be determined from the information given.

4.

The average of a, b, and c is 32.
The average of b, c, and d is 23.

Quantity A	Quantity B
The average of a and d	The average of a, b, c, and d

Ⓐ Quantity A is greater.
Ⓑ Quantity B is greater.
Ⓒ The two quantities are equal.
Ⓓ The relationship cannot be determined from the information given.

GO TO THE NEXT PAGE

5. All of the arcs inscribed on the square have equal radii. Each of the arcs touches its neighbor at exactly one point.

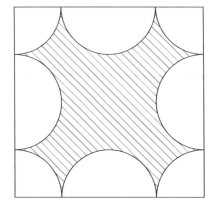

Quantity A	Quantity B
The area of the shaded region	The area of the unshaded region

Ⓐ Quantity A is greater.
Ⓑ Quantity B is greater.
Ⓒ The two quantities are equal.
Ⓓ The relationship cannot be determined from the information given.

6.

$$f(x) = Ax^2 + Bx + 7$$
$$f(3) = 34$$
$$f(4) = 51$$

Quantity A	Quantity B
A	B

Ⓐ Quantity A is greater.
Ⓑ Quantity B is greater.
Ⓒ The two quantities are equal.
Ⓓ The relationship cannot be determined from the information given.

7.

$$\frac{4x^3 - 12x^2 - 36x + 27}{(2x - 3)} = 0$$

Quantity A	Quantity B
solutions for x	0

Ⓐ Quantity A is greater.
Ⓑ Quantity B is greater.
Ⓒ The two quantities are equal.
Ⓓ The relationship cannot be determined from the information given.

GO TO THE NEXT PAGE

8.

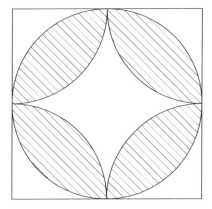

The figure above is a circle inscribed in a square. Each of the 4 arcs interior to the circle have a radius equal to half the length of the sides of the square.

Quantity A	Quantity B
The area of the shaded portion of the figure	The area of the un-shaded portion of the figure

Ⓐ Quantity A is greater.
Ⓑ Quantity B is greater.
Ⓒ The two quantities are equal.
Ⓓ The relationship cannot be determined from the information given.

9. A single sheet of paper which is .2 mm thick is tightly rolled into a cylinder with a radius of .5 meters and 1 meter tall. Approximately how long is the sheet of paper when it is un-rolled?

Ⓐ 3,927 mm
Ⓑ 0.25 mm
Ⓒ 1,250 m
Ⓓ 3,927 m
Ⓔ 3,927 Km

10. 6 triangles, each with an area of $\sqrt{3}$, are placed side by side so that they form a regular hexagon. What is the perimeter of the hexagon?

Ⓐ $6\sqrt{3}$
Ⓑ 6
Ⓒ 12
Ⓓ $12\sqrt{3}$
Ⓔ 18

Use the graph below to answer questions 11 to 13. Select one answer choice unless otherwise indicated.

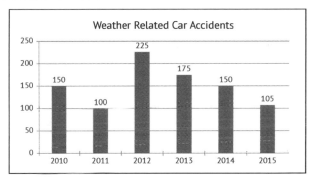

11. In 2013, 57.4% of car accidents were not weather related. How many car accidents occurred that year?

Ⓐ 375
Ⓑ 320
Ⓒ 355
Ⓓ 305
Ⓔ 410

GO TO THE NEXT PAGE

QUANTITATIVE REASONING
SECTION 5

12. For one of the years from 2010 to 2015, the number of total car accidents was 500 and 45% were weather-related. What year was that?

  Ⓐ 2010
  Ⓑ 2012
  Ⓒ 2013
  Ⓓ 2014
  Ⓔ 2015

13. A report stated that police responded to 800 car accidents from 2010 to 2012. What percentage were weather-related?

  Ⓐ 12.5%
  Ⓑ 20%
  Ⓒ 41%
  Ⓓ 59%
  Ⓔ 62%

14. What is the length of an edge of a regular pyramid with the base of an equilateral triangle and a surface area of 96?

  Ⓐ 11.31
  Ⓑ 7.44
  Ⓒ 5.66
  Ⓓ 10.29
  Ⓔ The answer cannot be determined from the information given.

15. Given the two circles $x^2 + y^2 = 2x + 14y + 1$ and $\frac{8y - 6x}{x^2 + y^2} = 1$, find the distance between the respective centers.

  Ⓐ $\sqrt{74}$
  Ⓑ 5
  Ⓒ 10
  Ⓓ $5\sqrt{10}$
  Ⓔ The answer cannot be determined from the information given.

16.

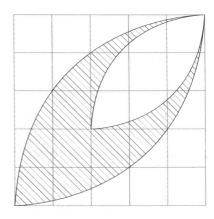

Each of the arcs are quarter circles. Find the area of the shaded region.

  Ⓐ $4\pi - 8$
  Ⓑ $\frac{25\pi}{4} - \frac{25}{2}$
  Ⓒ $8\pi - 16$
  Ⓓ $25 - \frac{25\pi}{4}$
  Ⓔ 13

17. A rail car with 18,000 pounds of corn grain with 2% inert dust delivers its load to a drying facility. First the dust is filtered out. Next, the grain has a starting moisture content of 28% (by weight) and so is dried to 15% moisture content (by weight). After drying, the inert dust is mixed back into the corn to a maximum constituent of 2% (by weight). How much does the load of corn now weigh? Enter your answer to the nearest tenth in the text box.

GO TO THE NEXT PAGE

18. A passenger jet burns 1500 pounds of fuel at each take-off and landing. Additionally it burns 100 pounds of fuel per person per 500 miles traveled. A flight leaves Los Angeles with 183 persons aboard and lands in Hawaii and then Tokyo for a distance of 6501 miles. If jet fuel costs \$0.2511/pound, how much did the fuel cost per person for this flight? Enter your answer in the text box provided.

20. Find all the possible solutions for x in following system of equations:

$$3x - 4y = 8$$
$$2y + x^2 = 3$$

Ⓐ $-\frac{1}{2}$

Ⓑ $-\frac{7}{2}$

Ⓒ $-\frac{37}{8}$

Ⓓ 2

Ⓔ 0

19.

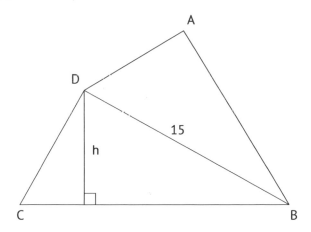

$\triangle ABD$ is similar to $\triangle BCD$.

$$h = 7\frac{1}{17}$$

What is the perimeter of quadrilateral ABCD? Enter your answer in the text boxes.

Note: Answer is in mixed fraction form.

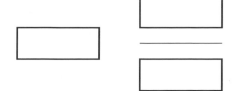

VERBAL REASONING
SECTION 6

20 QUESTIONS
30 MINUTES

For questions 1 to 6, you are to choose one answer for each blank from the corresponding column of choices.

1. Historically held to be _____ of virtue, many of America's early presidents had in fact owned slaves and participated in vast real estate deals concerning lands formerly held by Native peoples.

Ⓐ paragons
Ⓑ ciphers
Ⓒ founders
Ⓓ prophets
Ⓔ felons

2. Neighbors whispered that (i)_____ from bullies in her youth had turned the (ii)_____ widow into a recluse, but her family knew the real reason for her seclusion.

Blank i	Blank ii
Ⓐ quips	Ⓓ devout
Ⓑ ordeals	Ⓔ retiring
Ⓒ escapades	Ⓕ taut

3. (i)_____ beliefs have animated various communities around the world to (ii) _____ various practices that they consider (iii)_____ to their values.

Blank i	Blank ii
Ⓐ Orthodox	Ⓓ belie
Ⓑ Occult	Ⓔ expurgate
Ⓒ Putative	Ⓕ beleaguer

Blank iii
Ⓖ antagonistic
Ⓗ contentious
Ⓘ endemic

4. (i)_____ diction creates the clearest, most (ii)_____ circumstances for a successful career that requires public speaking. This (iii)_____ the notion that reading aloud at a young age is important for future success.

Blank i	Blank ii
Ⓐ Lucid	Ⓓ propitious
Ⓑ Loquacious	Ⓔ reparable
Ⓒ Lucrative	Ⓕ strident

Blank iii
Ⓖ corroborates
Ⓗ abolishes
Ⓘ satiates

5. The (i)_____ organization (ii) _____ its fundraising goals for the third year in a row, despite its (iii)_____ expression of its own mission.

Blank i	Blank ii
Ⓐ despotic	Ⓓ rallied
Ⓑ inarticulate	Ⓔ traversed
Ⓒ sedulous	Ⓕ transcended

Blank iii
Ⓖ munificent
Ⓗ middling
Ⓘ adroit

GO TO THE NEXT PAGE

6. The (i)_____ policy only incensed communities, who (ii)_____ over limited resources and (iii)_____ any further ameliorative political action.

Blank i	Blank ii
Ⓐ prodigal	Ⓓ equivocated
Ⓑ stolid	Ⓔ squabbled
Ⓒ deprecatory	Ⓕ malingered

Blank iii

Ⓖ dilated
Ⓗ scotched
Ⓘ remonstrated

GO TO THE NEXT PAGE

Questions 7 to 9 are based on the following 17th-century passage written by a working astronomer. Select one answer unless otherwise indicated.

In the present small treatise I set forth some matters of great interest for all observers of natural phenomena to look at and consider. They are of great interest, I think, first, from their intrinsic excellence; secondly,
5 from their absolute novelty; and lastly, also on account of the instrument by the aid of which they have been presented to my apprehension.

The number of the Fixed Stars which observers have been able to see without artificial powers of sight up
10 to this day can be counted. It is therefore decidedly a great feat to add to their number, and to set distinctly before the eyes other stars in myriads, which have never been seen before, and which surpass the old, previously known, stars in number more than ten times.

15 Again, it is a most beautiful and delightful sight to behold the body of the Moon, which is distant from us nearly sixty *semi*-diameters of the Earth, as near as if it was at a distance of only two of the same measures; so that the diameter of this same Moon appears about
20 thirty times larger, its surface about nine hundred times, and its solid mass nearly 27,000 times larger than when it is viewed only with the naked eye; and consequently any one may know with the certainty that is due to the use of our senses, that the Moon certainly does not
25 possess a smooth and polished surface, but one rough and uneven, and, just like the face of the Earth itself, is everywhere full of vast protuberances, deep chasms, and sinuosities.

Then to have got rid of disputes about the Galaxy or
30 Milky Way, and to have made its nature clear to the very senses, not to say to the understanding, seems by no means a matter which ought to be considered of slight importance. In addition to this, to point out, as with one's finger, the nature of those stars which every one of
35 the astronomers up to this time has called *nebulous*, and to demonstrate that it is very different from what has hitherto been believed, will be pleasant, and very fine. But that which will excite the greatest astonishment by far, and which indeed especially moved me to call the
40 attention of all astronomers and philosophers, is this, namely, that I have discovered four planets, neither known nor observed by any one of the astronomers before my time, which have their orbits round a certain bright star, one of those previously known, like Venus
45 and Mercury round the Sun, and are sometimes in front of it, sometimes behind it, though they never depart from it beyond certain limits. All of which facts were discovered and observed a few days ago by the help of a telescope devised by me, through God's grace first
50 enlightening my mind.

7. The author uses "nebulous" (Line 35) in order to:

    (A) show how all astronomers think alike
    (B) refer to the stars' locations in a nebula
    (C) give the technical term for stars
    (D) describe astronomers' hazy, incomplete knowledge of the nature of stars
    (E) both B and D

8. The primary purpose of the passage is to:

    (A) wax poetic on all things astronomy
    (B) persuade philosophers and astronomers to pursue new discoveries
    (C) present new knowledge on the moon
    (D) prove which planets revolve around the sun
    (E) describe the author's discoveries using a telescope

9. The passage mentions all of the following EXCEPT:

    (A) the discovery of four planets
    (B) the viewing of a comet
    (C) current disputes regarding the Milky Way
    (D) the distance to the moon
    (E) the stars identifiable to the naked eye

GO TO THE NEXT PAGE

Questions 10 to 12 are based on the following discussion of anxiety disorders. Select one answer unless otherwise indicated.

All individuals experience some sort of anxiety or fear in their lifetimes. Likewise, most are able to effectively manage such feelings from significantly affecting their lives. However, in some cases, individuals are
5 unable to regulate and categorize fear and anxiety, and consequentially develop disordered patterns of response leading to anxiety disorders and phobias. These individuals can develop avoidant coping strategies to deal with the fear and often experience
10 functional disability as a result. Understanding such deviations from the population norm and how natural inclinations and emotions become disordered requires a comprehensive understanding of what anxiety and fear are, and how they emerge early in life. How exactly
15 do phobias and disordered anxieties arise? Where do infants derive their senses of fear and anxiety? The study of the possible etiology of fear and anxiety serves to provide critical research on phobias and anxiety disorders and provide a more complete understanding
20 of their pathology, potentially leading to possible treatment and prevention methods.

Past research has suggested that phobias and anxiety disorders are mainly acquired through conditioned responses, such as classical and operate conditioning
25 beginning in infancy and progressing throughout life. However, recent research has suggested that phobias and anxiety disorders may be acquired through observational learning and social referencing. A study by de Rosnay, Cooper, Tsigaras and Murray showed
30 that infants modify their affective behavior towards a stranger following observations of mothers modeling anxious behaviors during interactions with a stranger. While other elements such as genetics, temperament, and parenting style have undergone a great deal of
35 research, areas such as social referencing as a means of anxiety acquisition and development have yet to receive adequate attention.

10. At the end of the first paragraph, the author poses the question, "Where do infants derive their senses of fear and anxiety?" Select the sentence in the passage that best answers the question.

_____

11. The author mentions "genetics, temperament, and parenting style" in Line 33 in order to:

Ⓐ highlight areas of research that have historically received attention
Ⓑ discuss in detail the key factors that lead to the development of fear in adolescents
Ⓒ advocate for more research in these areas
Ⓓ pinpoint the root causes of anxiety
Ⓔ provide alternative explanations for reasons phobias develop

_____

12. The author mentions which of the following with regard to people who are unable to regulate their fear? Select <u>all</u> that apply.

Ａ They develop avoidant coping strategies
Ｂ Their overall functioning can be impaired
Ｃ They are less prone to social referencing
Ｄ They are prone to anxiety disorders and phobias

_____

GO TO THE NEXT PAGE

Questions 13 to 16 refer to the following excerpt from a speech delivered by U.S. Vice President Spiro Agnew in November of 1969. Select one answer unless otherwise indicated.

As with other American institutions, perhaps it is time that the networks were made more responsive to the views of the nation and more responsible to the people they serve. I am not asking for government
5 censorship or any other kind of censorship. I am asking whether a form of censorship already exists when the news that forty-million Americans receive each night is determined by a handful of men responsible to their corporate employers, and filtered through a handful of
10 commentators who admit to their own set of biases.

The questions I am raising tonight should have been raised by others long ago. They should have been raised by those Americans who have traditionally considered the preservation of freedom of speech and freedom
15 of the press their special provinces of responsibility and concern. They should have been raised by those Americans who share the view of the late Justice Learned Hand, that "right conclusions are more likely to be gathered out of a multitude of tongues than through
20 any kind of authoritative selection."

Advocates for the networks have claimed a first-amendment right to the same unlimited freedoms held by the great newspapers of America. The situations are not identical. Where *The New York Times* reaches
25 800,000 people, NBC reaches twenty times that number with its evening news. Nor can the tremendous impact of seeing television film and hearing commentary be compared with reading the printed page.

A decade ago, before the network news acquired such
30 dominance over public opinion, Walter Lippmann spoke to the issue: "There is an essential and radical difference," he stated, "between television and printing.... The three or four competing television stations control virtually all that can be received over
35 the air by ordinary television sets. But, besides the mass-circulation dailies, there are the weeklies, the monthlies, the out-of-town newspapers, and books. If a man does not like his newspaper, he can read another from out of town, or wait for a weekly news
40 magazine. It is not ideal. But it is infinitely better than the situation in television. There, if a man does not like what the networks offer him, all he can do is turn them off, and listen to a phonograph."

"Networks," he stated, "which are few in number,
45 have a virtual monopoly of a whole medium of communication." The newspapers of mass circulation have no monopoly of the medium of print. A "virtual monopoly of a whole medium of communication" is not something a democratic people should blithely
50 ignore. And we are not going to cut off our television sets and listen to the phonograph because the air waves do not belong to the networks; they belong to the people. As Justice Byron White wrote in his landmark opinion six months ago, "It is the right
55 of the viewers and listeners, not the right of the broadcasters, which is paramount."

13. The passage gives all of the following EXCEPT which to differentiate between network news and newspapers? Select **all** that apply.

A The number of viewers
B The cost difference between a television and a newspaper
C People enjoy television more than phonographs
D The experience of seeing and hearing is not like that of reading
E The number of television stations versus the number of available printed news publications

14. Which of the following, if true, would have most weakened Agnew's argument?

Ⓐ Most television reporters had also worked in print journalism
Ⓑ Newspaper editors had biases
Ⓒ Television networks bitterly competed against one another
Ⓓ In 1969, most Americans did not own or watch television
Ⓔ Hundreds of Americans had already filed monopoly complaints with the Federal Communications Commission (FCC)

GO TO THE NEXT PAGE

15. Agnew uses the words of Justice Byron White (Line 53) to do what?

Ⓐ argue that media ownership equals media censorship
Ⓑ back the first-amendment rights of newspapers
Ⓒ prove the existence of a "virtual monopoly of a whole medium of communication"
Ⓓ support his claim that broadcast airwaves belong to the American people
Ⓔ name viewers and listeners as the appropriate content programmers for media

16. Which of the following would most resemble Agnew's described media monopoly?

Ⓐ A sole U.S. energy company, owned by its employees
Ⓑ The top three U.S. agribusiness corporations owning all food inputs and outputs
Ⓒ U.S. gas companies operating 80 percent of the oil wells in Nigeria
Ⓓ Four U.S. companies producing 80 percent of all U.S. cellphones
Ⓔ All computer manufacturers copyrighting the experience of using their products

For questions 17 to 20, select two answers that best complete the blank and produce two sentences that are alike in meaning.

17. Amy epitomized the _____ student who continually sought the favor of her instructors through flattery.

Ⓐ collegial
Ⓑ sycophantic
Ⓒ obsequious
Ⓓ obdurate
Ⓔ esurient
Ⓕ parsimonious

18. Bill was quite the _____ ; he threw lavish fetes for all his friends.

Ⓐ epicurean
Ⓑ stoic
Ⓒ philanthropist
Ⓓ gourmandizer
Ⓔ pragmatist
Ⓕ opportunist

19. Though the small surrounding villages worked arduously to maintain their independence, they were eventually _____ by the larger province.

Ⓐ amalgamated
Ⓑ usurped
Ⓒ emancipated
Ⓓ exculpated
Ⓔ absolved
Ⓕ annexed

20. Cecilia's _____ behavior often shocked her parents, who were themselves polite and soft-spoken.

Ⓐ passé
Ⓑ torpid
Ⓒ impertinent
Ⓓ hermetic
Ⓔ impudent
Ⓕ incorporeal

289

1. A.

This problem asks you to compare the area of an octagon to the area of a square. First, the simpler Quantity B is calculated using the formula for the area of a square:

$$Area = side^2 = 8^2 = 64$$

Next, calculate Quantity A.

The easiest way to calculate the area of a regular octagon only knowing the length of a side is to sketch out the octagon and divide into regions whose areas are easy to calculate.

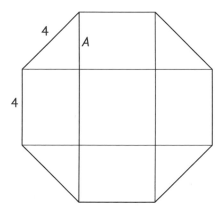

With this sketch the octagon is divided into (1) a square with area 4 × 4, (2) 4 rectangles each with an area of 4 × A, and (3) 4 triangles each with an area $\frac{1}{2} A^2$. From these pieces we can derive an area formula as follows:

$$Area\ of\ Octagon = 4^2 + 4 \cdot \frac{1}{2} A^2 + 4 \cdot 4 \cdot A$$

A can be calculated using the Pythagorean Theorem:

$4^2 = A^2 + A^2$	Pythagorean Theorem
$16 = 2A^2$	Simplify
$4 = A\sqrt{2}$	Calculate
$A = \frac{4}{\sqrt{2}} = 2\sqrt{2}$	Isolate variable and simplify

Now substitute value for A into the original Area Formula:

$Area\ of\ Octagon = 4^2 + 2 \cdot (2\sqrt{2})^2 + 4 \cdot 4 \cdot 2\sqrt{2}$	Substitute for A
$16 + 16 + 32\sqrt{2} = 77.25$	Calculate

77.25 is greater than 64, therefore Quantity A is greater than Quantity B. The correct answer choice is A.

QUANTITATIVE REASONING
ANSWER KEY: SECTION 3

2. A.

This problem tests your skill with a geometric series. You are asked to compare two different schemes of investment which earns daily interest of 5%. In Quantity A you invest $1 per day, while in Quantity B you invest $65 at the end of each month. Logically, whichever Quantity is larger at the end of the first month will be larger at the end of the year. You are given that Quantity B at the end of the month is $65, so all you have to do is find Quantity A.

You may recall the formula for calculating the future value of an investment with compound interest and payments:

$$\text{future value} = \text{payment} \cdot (1 + \text{interest}) \, \frac{(1 + \text{interest})^{\text{term}} - 1}{\text{interest}}$$

in which case, the problem is trivial. However, it may be easier to remember the much simpler compound interest formula and use an estimation technique:

$$FV = \text{present value} \cdot (1 + \text{interest})^{\text{term}}$$

The first step is to calculate the value of the dollar invested on the first day. This first dollar will have compounded interest for days numbered 2 through 30, so the term is 29 days:

$$FV \text{ dollar on day } 1 = \$1 \cdot (1 + .05)^{29} = \$4.12$$

It is quite a bit of work to calculate how much each day's investment will be at the end of the month, so to save time you can calculate a few values and use their average in order to get an estimate for Quantity A:

FV dollar on day 6 $= \$1 \cdot (1 + .05)^{24} = \$3.23$
FV dollar on day 12 $= \$1 \cdot (1 + .05)^{18} = \$2.41$
FV dollar on day 18 $= \$1 \cdot (1 + .05)^{12} = \$1.80$
FV dollar on day 24 $= \$1 \cdot (1 + .05)^{6} \ = \$1.34$

This gives you 6 values to generate your estimate:

$$\text{Estimate} = 30 \text{ days} \, \frac{(\$4.12 + \$3.23 + \$2.41 + \$1.80 + \$1.34 + \$1.00)}{6} = \$69.55$$

At $69.55, Quantity A outpaces Quantity B. The correct answer choice is A.

Note: compare this value with the one you get using the compound interest with payments formula:

$$\text{future value} = 1 \cdot (1 + .05) \, \frac{(1 + .05)^{30} - 1}{.05} = \$69.76$$

3. A.

This problem asks you to interpret a geometric drawing in order to determine the relationship between the labeled regions. From the given information you can deduce that the diagram is a square with a diagonal and quarter circle arc overlaid. From this information you can calculate the relative size of the regions.

Region A consists of the quarter circle minus the unlabeled triangle. And since we know that the quarter circle is inscribed in a square this makes the formula for region A:

Area A = Area of Quarter Circle   Area of Triangle

Region B consists of the area of the square minus the quarter circle:

Area B = Area of Square – Area of Quarter Circle

You now set up the inequality:

Area of Quarter Circle – Area of Triangle ? Area of Square – Area of Quarter Circle

If we label each side of the square *r* we can now insert the formulas for the respective areas:

$\frac{1}{4}\pi r^2 - \frac{1}{2}r^2 \; ? \; r^2 - \frac{1}{4}\pi r^2$	Area formulas
$\frac{1}{4}\pi - \frac{1}{2} \; ? \; 1 - \frac{1}{4}\pi$	Divide by r^2
$\pi - 2 \; ? \; 4 - \pi$	Multiply by 4
$2\pi \; ? \; 6$	Add $2 + \pi$ to both sides
$6.28... > 6$	Evaluate *pi*

The left side of the inequality is greater than the right so Quantity A is greater than Quantity B. The correct answer choice is A.

4. **A.**

    This problem asks you to compare the measure of two arcs. In order to find Quantity A first remember that the hour hand on a clock travels two circumferences every day while the earth only rotates once per day. Therefore the hour hand on a clock moves at twice the rate at which the earth rotates. This means that for any fixed length of time the hour hand will traverse a greater arc than the earth will rotate. Quantity A is greater than Quantity B. The correct answer choice is A.

5. **A.**

    This problem tests your skill with geometric series. You are given that each day the algae on the surface of a pond grows by 10% but then retracts 5% each night. You are asked to compare the number of days it takes the algae to grow from 15% to 50% to the time it takes to grow from 50% to 100% of the pond surface. Begin by calculating the growth for each day:

    $$(1 + .10)(1 - .05) = (1.10)(.95) = 1.045$$

    Now set up the formula for geometric growth:

    $$start\ amount \cdot growth\ rate^{time} = end\ amount$$

    $$growth\ rate^{time} = \frac{end\ amount}{start\ amount}$$

    At this point you can see that you don't actually need to calculate the number of days. Because the growth rate is the same for both Quantities you can see that whichever quantity is greater will result in a greater value for $\frac{end\ amount}{start\ amount}$. Therefore you only need to compare the ratios of the starting and ending amounts.

$\dfrac{50\%}{15\%} ? \dfrac{100\%}{50\%}$ Starting and Ending values for Quantity A and B

$3.\overline{33} > 2$ Calculate

This shows that Quantity A is greater than Quantity B. The correct answer choice is A.

6. **B.**

This problem tests your understanding of a parabola. You are given the parabolic equation $y = 2x^2 + x - 5$ and asked to compare the location of the line of symmetry with the distance between the x intercepts. You can get to both quantities by using the quadratic formula. Starting with Quantity A:

$x = \dfrac{-b \pm \sqrt{b^2 - 4ac}}{2a}$ Quadratic formula

$x = \dfrac{-1 \pm \sqrt{1^2 - 4(2)(-5)}}{2(2)}$ Substitute coefficients

$x = \dfrac{-1 \pm \sqrt{41}}{4}$ Substitute coefficients

$x = -\dfrac{1}{4} \pm \dfrac{\sqrt{41}}{4}$ Simplify

Stopping here you get the line of symmetry in the first expression, namely $= -\dfrac{1}{4}$. The y-intercept has a value of 0 for x by definition so Quantity A is $-\dfrac{1}{4}$.

To work on Quantity B, find the intercepts:

$x_1 = -\dfrac{1}{4} + \dfrac{\sqrt{41}}{4}$ Intercept 1

$x_2 = -\dfrac{1}{4} - \dfrac{\sqrt{41}}{4}$ Intercept 2

Because you know that intercepts are on a line the distance is simply the absolute value of the difference between the points:

$distance = |x_1 - x_2|$ Distance formula for points on a line

$distance = \left(-\dfrac{1}{4} + \dfrac{\sqrt{41}}{4}\right) - \left(-\dfrac{1}{4} - \dfrac{\sqrt{41}}{4}\right)$ Substitute values

$distance = \dfrac{\sqrt{41}}{4} + \dfrac{\sqrt{41}}{4} = \dfrac{\sqrt{41}}{2} = \dfrac{6.4}{2} = 3.2$ Substitute values

Quantity B is greater than Quantity A so the correct answer choice is B.

7. **C.**

This problem tests your knowledge of regular polygons. The diagram is a regular hexagon as formed by overlaying two triangles to form a 6-pointed star. You are asked to compare the area of the hexagon with the area of the small triangles projecting from each side. You are given no dimensions or values to use.

293

QUANTITATIVE REASONING
ANSWER KEY: SECTION 3

The first step is to determine what sort of triangles are formed. Since the shaded area is a *regular* hexagon you can calculate the exterior angles at each corner:

exterior angle = 180 – interior angle

$$interior\ angle = \frac{180(number\ of\ sides - 2)}{number\ of\ sides}$$

Now plug in the values:

$$interior\ angle = \frac{180(6 - 2)}{6} = 120 \qquad \text{Substitute}$$

$$exterior\ angle = 180 - 120 = 60 \qquad \text{Substitute}$$

From this you see that the exterior angles are 60° which means they are all equilateral triangles. Next draw a line to bisect each interior angle to the opposite corner. Because the interior angles are 120° the bisecting line creates triangles with interior angles of 60° which are also six equilateral triangles.

Both the un-shaded and shaded triangles are equilateral triangles with sides of the same length and are therefore congruent. There are six shaded triangles and six un-shaded triangles, therefore Quantity A is equal to Quantity B. The correct answer choice is C.

8. **D.**

    This problem tests your knowledge of the proportionality of a right triangle. In order to find $\overline{AB}$, you need to use the proportion

    $$\frac{\overline{AC}}{\overline{AB}} = \frac{\overline{AB}}{\overline{AD}}$$

    In order to make the math more readable, let $c = \overline{AB}$. Now you are ready to solve:

$\frac{23}{c} = \frac{c}{8}$	proportion of similar triangles
$23(8) = c^2$	cross multiply
$184 = c^2$	calculate
$\sqrt{184} = c$	take the square root of both sides
$2\sqrt{46} = c$	simplify the radical

    The correct answer choice is **D**.

9. **B.**

    This problem tests your use of the distance formula and the ability to solve a system of equations. You are asked to find the distance between the point (–4, 5) and the intersection of two lines. The first step is to solve the system of equations for the point of intersection:

1) $2y - x = 0$	given equation #1
2) $3x + 5y = 44$	given equation #2
1) $-3x + 6y = 0$	multiply equation #1 by 3
$11y = 44$	add equation #2 and the modified #1
$y = 4$	solve for y

1) $2(4) - x = 0$ substitute value of y into equation #1

        $8 = x$ solve for x

You now have the intersection point $(8, 4)$. Applying the Distance Formula, you get:

$$\sqrt{(x_1 - x_2)^2 + (y_1 - y_2)^2} = Distance$$ Distance Formula

$$\sqrt{(8 - -4)^2 + (4 - 5)^2} =$$ substitute values for x and y

$$\sqrt{144 + 1} = \sqrt{145}$$ calculate and simplify

The distance is $\sqrt{145}$. The correct answer choice is **B**.

10. B.

This problem tests your understanding of the proportions on a right triangle. Because of the orientation of the triangle, you can determine the rise for each segment. The missing part of the slope is the run, which corresponds to the height of the triangle (the unlabeled segment that intersects the hypotenuse at a right angle). Fortunately, this value can be found using the ratios of the proportions of a right triangle. Let the height of the triangle be h. Use the ratios of the hypotenuses to find h:

$$\frac{short\ leg\ of\ the\ small\ triangle}{hypotenuse\ of\ the\ small\ triangle} = \frac{short\ leg\ of\ the\ large\ triangle}{hypotenuse\ of\ the\ large\ triangle}$$

$$\frac{2}{\overline{AB}} = \frac{\overline{AB}}{5}$$ substitute values from the given figure

$$10 = \overline{AB}^2$$ multiply both sides by $5\overline{AB}$

You stop here because you will use the Pythagorean Theorem to solve for h:

$$2^2 + h^2 = \overline{AB}^2$$ Pythagorean Theorem with substitutions from given figure

$$h^2 = \overline{AB}^2 - 2^2$$ isolate the h term

$$h^2 = 10 - 4$$ substitute from previous calculation; calculate the exponent

$$h = \sqrt{6}$$ find the root

Now you have all the information you need to write the slopes. Remember: It is customary to convert a fraction containing a radical so that the radical appears in the numerator.

$$slope\ \overline{AB} = \frac{2}{\sqrt{6}} = \frac{\sqrt{6}}{3}$$

$$slope\ \overline{BC} = \frac{-3}{\sqrt{6}} = \frac{-\sqrt{6}}{2}$$

11. E.

This is a problem testing your ability to multiply a cube polynomial. You are told that the initial figure is a cube. A cube's calculation for volume is $V = S^3$ where S is the length of a side. Secondly, you are given the length of the sides of the cubes. $S_1 = x$ is the original cube's side length, and $S_2 = x + 2$ is that of the second cube. The final solution you are looking for is the difference in the volumes of the cubes, or $V_2 - V_1$. First, write out the initial expression. Then use substitution to put everything in terms of x.

$$V_2 - V_1 = S_2^3 - S_1^3$$ substitute your expressions into the volume formula

$$= (x + 2)^3 - x^3$$ substitute in the two cubes' side lengths

$$= x^3 + 6x^2 + 12x + 8 - x^3 \qquad \text{expand the exponent}$$
$$= 6x^2 + 12x + 8 \qquad \text{simplify}$$

At this point you do not have enough information to solve for x. This is confirmed by the selection of answer choices: answer choice A is 8, which is clearly less than your answer. The remaining choices are expressions. The correct answer choice is **E**.

12. D.

This problem asks you to find a midpoint and a distance in a Cartesian coordinate system. First, find the midpoint between A(1, 3) and B(−3, 15) using the midpoint formula:

$$Midpoint\,(A, B) = \frac{x_a + x_b}{2}, \frac{y_a + y_b}{2} \qquad \text{Formula for Midpoint}$$

$$\left(\frac{1 + 3}{2}, \frac{3 + 15}{2}\right) = (-1, 9) \qquad \text{calculate}$$

Next, find the distance from the midpoint (−1, 9) to point C (−6, 21) using the distance formula:

$$\sqrt{(x_c - x_{mid})^2 + (y_c - y_{mid})^2} \qquad \text{Distance Formula}$$

$$\sqrt{(-6 - -1)^2 + (21 - 9)^2} \qquad \text{substitute}$$

$$\sqrt{(-5)^2 + (12)^2} \qquad \text{calculate}$$

From here, recognize the 5 and 12 from the 5:12:13 Pythagorean triple.

$$\sqrt{25 + 144} = \sqrt{169} = 13 \qquad \text{solve the root}$$

The distance is 13. The correct answer choice is *D*.

13. 157.

This problem tests your ability with algebra and polynomials. You are asked to find the sum of the squares of two numbers. You are given the square of the sum of the two numbers, which is 289. You are also given the product of these same numbers, which is 66. You will employ a strategy to look for a useful substitution in order to solve this problem. To begin, let the two numbers be represented by x and y. This means that the sum of the squares you are looking for can be represented by the expression $x^2 + y^2$. This is important to remember so you do not waste time solving for x and y individually. Now write the first given:

$$(x + y)^2 = 289 \qquad \text{given}$$
$$(x + y)(x + y) = 289 \qquad \text{expand the square}$$
$$x^2 + 2xy + y^2 = 289 \qquad \text{calculate the polynomial by multiplying the expressions}$$

At this point you can see that you have the target expression, but first you need to deal with the extra term $2xy$. To do so, write the product of the two numbers as $xy = 66$. From this, you can see the substitution:

$$x^2 + 2(66) + y^2 = 289 \qquad \text{substitute for } xy$$
$$x^2 + 132 + y^2 = 289 \qquad \text{calculate}$$
$$x^2 + y^2 = 289 - 132 = 157 \qquad \text{subtract 132 from both sides and solve}$$

The sum of the two squares is **157**. Enter your answer in the box.

14. 21.93 Miles.

This problem tests your ability to calculate the sides of a triangle. The easiest way to answer this problem is to sketch out the course of the boat.

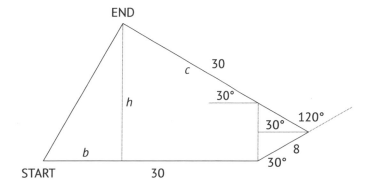

Now use your knowledge of a 30-60-90 triangle to work out the measurements for h and b. First write down the relationships:

$$short\ leg = \frac{1}{2}\ hypotenuse$$

$$long\ leg = \frac{\sqrt{3}}{2}\ hypotenuse$$

Starting with the small 30-60-90 triangle formed after the first turn you see the hypotenuse is 8. The next turn happens to form another 30-60-90 triangle in the opposite direction with a hypotenuse of 30. To find h you then get:

$$h = \frac{8}{2} + \frac{30}{2} = 19$$

To find b you use:

$$b = 30 + \frac{\sqrt{3}}{2}\ 8 - \frac{\sqrt{3}}{2}\ 30 = 30 - 11\sqrt{3}$$

Now use the Pythagorean Theorem, plugging in the values for h and b:

$$distance = \sqrt{(19^2 + (30 - 11\sqrt{3})^2)} = 21.93$$

Enter 21.93 miles in the text box.

15. 91.

This problem tests your ability to use the Pythagorean Theorem. You are given: $s = 6$ and $r = 7$. From this you need to find the area of rectangle *ABCD*. To start, you will find it helpful to add a couple of labels to the diagram:

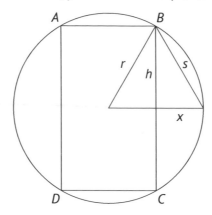

You start by calculating h and x using the Pythagorean theorem:

$h^2 = r^2 - (r - x)^2$	Pythagorean Theorem for base of triangle opposite x
$h^2 = s^2 - x^2$	Pythagorean Theorem for x
$s^2 - x^2 = r^2 - (r - x)^2$	Substitute
$s^2 - x^2 = r^2 - r^2 + 2rx - x^2$	Expand the exponent
$6^2 - x^2 = 7^2 - 7^2 + 2(7)x - x^2$	Substitute values
$36 = 14x$	Simplify
$x = \dfrac{36}{14}$	Solve for x

Next, find h using the simplest equation:

$$h^2 = 6^2 - \frac{36}{14}$$

$$h = \sqrt{36 - \frac{36}{14}} = 6\sqrt{\left(1 - \frac{1}{14}\right)} = 6\sqrt{\frac{13}{14}}$$

Now relate the area of the triangle to the dimension that you know:

Area of the rectangle $= \overline{BC} \cdot \overline{CD}$

First find a calculable expression for $\overline{CD}$:

$\overline{CD}^2 = 4r^2 - \overline{BC}^2$	Pythagorean Theorem
$\overline{CD} = \sqrt{4r^2 - \overline{BC}^2}$	Take the square root
$\overline{CD} = \sqrt{4r^2 - (2h)^2}$	Substitute

Now substitute the known values into the area formula:

Area of the rectangle = $2h \cdot \sqrt{4r^2 - 4h^2}$ Substitution

Area of the rectangle = $2\left(6\sqrt{\dfrac{13}{14}}\right) \cdot \sqrt{4(7^2) - 4 \cdot \left(6\sqrt{\dfrac{13}{14}}\right)^2} = 91$ Substitute and calculate

Be sure to follow instructions and round to the nearest whole number. Enter **91** in the text box.

16. A.

This problem tests your skill with calculating percentages. To find the percentage decrease, use the formula:

$$percent\ decrease = \frac{starting\ value - end\ value}{starting\ value}$$

Substituting the values from the chart you get:

$$\frac{280,000 - 240,000}{280,000} = \frac{40,000}{280,000} = 14.3\%$$

The correct answer choice is **A**.

17. B.

This problem tests your understanding of median, and how to calculate an increase by percentage. First, create a set of the data points on the chart using the salary value for each year:

{260,000, 280,000, 240,000, 230,000, 240,000}

Now sort the set by value:

{280,000, 260,000, 240,000, 240,000, 230,000}

The median is the center element: 240,000. Now calculate the 10% increase:

salary 2015 = $240,000 • 1.10 = $264,000

The correct answer choice is **B**.

18. D.

This problem tests your ability to translate a word problem into a geometry problem and calculate a complex area. You are looking for the area enclosed by three adjacent circles, each with a radius of 1. The first thing to do is sketch out a diagram of the figure description:

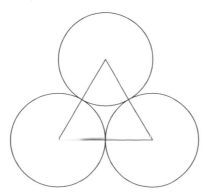

From this you see the lines connecting the centers of the circles form an equilateral triangle with side lengths of 2. Additionally each point of the triangle cuts a sector from its associated circle. From this you can create the formula:

Enclosed Area = Area of Triangle – Area of the Sectors

Since you know the triangle is equilateral, you also know that each sector has an angle measuring 60°. The area of these sectors is:

$3 \cdot \dfrac{60}{360} \pi r^2$ Formula for Area of the Sectors

$\dfrac{1}{2} \pi (1)^2 = \dfrac{1}{2} \pi$ Substitute and simplify

The area of the triangle is next:

$height = \dfrac{\sqrt{3}}{2} \cdot hypotenuse$ Height of a 30-60-90 triangle

$height = \dfrac{\sqrt{3}}{2} \cdot 2 = \sqrt{3}$ Substitute 2 for the hypotenuse

The base of the triangle is 2. Therefore the Area of the Triangle is:

$\dfrac{1}{2} base \cdot height = \dfrac{1}{2} (2) \cdot \sqrt{3} = \sqrt{3}$

Plugging these two Area values into your starting formula, you now calculate the enclosed area: $\sqrt{3} - \dfrac{\pi}{2}$, which cannot be simplified. The correct answer choice is **D**.

19. **D.**

This problem tests your ability to work with polynomials and use reasoning to understand an inequality. You are asked to find the greatest area of a right triangle given a hypotenuse of 5. Start by creating variables for the legs of the triangle. You can say that the length of the first leg of the triangle is x, while the second can be stated as x plus some value a. The resulting formula for the area of the triangle looks like this:

$Area = \dfrac{1}{2} x(x + a)$

Because you know this is a right triangle, you can plug the expressions for the triangle's legs and the hypotenuse's value of 5 into the Pythagorean Theorem:

$x^2 + (x + a)^2 = 5^2$ Pythagorean Theorem

$x^2 + x^2 + 2ax + a^2 = 25$ Expand the exponent

$2x^2 + 2ax = 25 - a^2$ Simplify and subtract a^2 from both sides

$4 \cdot \dfrac{1}{2} x(x + a) = 25 - a^2$ Factor the left side

$4 \cdot Area = 25 - a^2$ Substitute

$Area = \dfrac{1}{4} (25 - a^2)$ Divide both sides by 4

At this point you see that because a has a coefficient of -1, the Area will be smaller as a becomes larger. Thus you achieve the greatest Area when a is 0. Use this value to calculate the greatest possible Area:

$$Area = \frac{1}{4}(25 - 0^2) = \frac{25}{4} = 6.25$$

You have shown the greatest possible area of a triangle with the hypotenuse of 5 is 6.25. The correct answer choice is **D**.

20. D.

This problem tests your ability to use algebraic manipulation to transform an equation into a common form and then extract the required data. First you will need to cross multiply:

$\dfrac{y+4}{x-4} = \dfrac{15}{(x-4)(y-2)} - \dfrac{x-2}{y-2}$	The given equation
$(x-4)(y-2)\dfrac{y+4}{x-4} = 15\dfrac{(x-4)(y-2)}{(x-4)(y-2)} - (x-4)(y-2)\dfrac{x-2}{y-2}$	Multiply by the lowest common denominator
$(y-2)(y+4) = 15 - (x-4)(x-2)$	Simplify
$y^2 + 2y - 8 = 15 - (x^2 - 6x + 8)$	Expand the factors
$x^2 - 6x + y^2 + 2y = 15$	Move the variables to the left side and simplify all constants
$x^2 - 6x + 9 - 9 + y^2 + 2y + 1 - 1 = 15$	Add and subtract constant values to complete the squares
$(x-3)^2 - 9 + (y+1)^2 - 1 = 15$	Factor the polynomials
$(x-3)^2 + (y+1)^2 = 25$	Add 10 to both sides

You now have an equation in the form shown in the problem: $(x-a)^2 + (y-b)^2 = r^2$. In this instance $a = 3$, $b = -1$, and $r = 5$. The center lies at $(3, -1)$. The correct answer choice is **D**.

VERBAL REASONING
ANSWER KEY: SECTION 4

1. **C.**

   Myron might have felt both *disquietude* (unease) and *compunction* (remorse) over the situation, but the apologies mentioned in the second half of the sentence are only directly linked to remorse, or answer choice C. The remaining nouns—*wanderlust* (strong desire to travel), *prelude* (action or event that precedes something else), and *filibuster* (long speech used to impede legislative action)—do not fit the context.

2. **C, D.**

   Here, the word "yet" moves you in a direction opposite that of the first half of the sentence. Since you do not have enough context to choose the first blank—*frenzied* (madly excited), *imperious* (haughty), and *impervious* (incapable of being affected) could all describe the socialite's tone—complete the second blank first. Here, only *prostrated*, or to cast oneself on the ground in humility or adoration, fits the sentence, as the socialite cannot *abscond* (depart and hide) or *complement* (make perfect) himself in this context. The opposite of *prostrated* and its demonstrated adoration is then *impervious*, the correct answer for the first blank.

3. **A, E.**

   Phonetically, *puerile* might remind you of *pure* or *putrid*, but it actually means infantile or immature. *Fecund* is a synonym for your context clue of *lush*. *Besmirched* is soiled, usually in relation to a reputation—it has nothing to do with the soil that is indirectly referenced here. *Now* moves the sentence in the opposite direction for Blank ii, with *barren* the opposite of lush and matching the context clues of *inhospitable* and *fallow* (uncultivated).

4. **A, E, H.**

   The *picturesque* or striking scenery provided a source of enjoyment. *Tumultuous* might also describe a landscape for some, but rarely one that provides *enjoyment*. A *respite* is both a delay in punishment and an interval of rest or relief; the second meaning fits the context here. For the last blank, *baleful* tends to indicate a state of threat or menace and is too strong for the given context. *Reprieved* plays on the previously given terms, and is a synonym for *respite*. The best fit for this blank, however, is *melancholic* or gloomy.

5. **B, D, I.**

   For the first blank, euthanasia *garners* (gathers or stores up) a lot of media attention; it does not *deflect* (turn aside) media attention or *impinge* (make an impression or have an effect) upon the media. For the second blank, only *ingratiate* and *interpolate* require an object (here, "themselves") so you can eliminate *pique* (to wound or excite). To *interpolate* or interject oneself on the public does not make sense, so the correct answer for blank ii is *ingratiate*, or become popular with. You can also match this term's sensibility with the first blank to double check your answer. For the final blank, an ethically charged case *impugns* (challenges) the law. *Improvise* (to perform on the spur of the moment) and *depose* (to dethrone) do not fit the context.

6. **A, E, G.**

   Ideologies are deeply held ideas or notions. *Platitudes* are trite remarks, which can also be made in religious contexts. However, something trite will likely not *change the world*, the context clue of the second sentence. From the contextual set-up of *not only...but could also*, you know that the last two blanks support each other. *Germane* means appropriate or suitable, while to *assuage* is to relieve or ease. *Osculating* (to come into close contact) and *oscillating* (to vibrate or swing back and forth, like a pendulum) do not fit the context, but can be confusing in their similar spellings if you do not recognize the terms.

7. *He knows something about "prana", of which his western brother is ignorant, and he is fully aware of the nature and manner of handling that great principle of energy, and is fully informed as to its effect upon the human body and mind.* Here, you are looking for the sentence that comes closest to capturing the multiple ideas of the passage. This sentence asserts that the yogi knows of *prana* and is intimately familiar with its effects, essentially giving him greater knowledge than his western peers. Do not be thrown off by the order of the sentence, which splits *prana* at the beginning from its effects at the end.

8. **A, B.**

   This question is a straight reading comprehension question. The passage does not directly mention happiness, so answer choice C can be eliminated. And when the last sentence mentions the curing of disease, it is in relation to controlled breathing rather than *prana*, so answer choice E can be eliminated. Answer choice D is a bit tricky. At one point the author calls *prana* a "vital force," at another "that great principle of energy." In this case, both act as descriptors rather than explicit definitions, as you are still left wondering, *what* great principle of energy? So D can be eliminated. This leaves A and B, each of which summarizes a sentence in which the term can be found. A and B are thus correct.

9. **C.**

   In the second paragraph, the sentence that mentions Hume specifically starts with the phrase, "For example." This tells you that this sentence is directly connected to the preceding statement. Here, the previous sentence states that a psychologist can never be sure that the laws derived from his own thought process are not biased by the individualized way in which his or her own mind works. This is paraphrased by answer choice C.

10. *Whether, however, our inferences are made on the basis of words or of actions, they are all necessarily made on the hypothesis that human minds are built on the same pattern, that what a given word or action would mean for my mind, this it means also for my neighbor's mind.* Pay special attention to the wording here: this question is not asking you for a main idea or premise, but for the author's strongest statement regarding the presumed basis for human psychology. The last sentence of the third paragraph lays outs the basic hypothesis that underlies all human psychology: that all human minds rely on a similar pattern. The positioning of this sentence just before the author turns to animal psychology, where it acts as a "period" or "end-stop" on the author's previous points, also serves to highlight its importance in the author's argument.

11. **B.**

   This question asks you to *infer* based on the passage. The easiest one to eliminate here is D, since the passage makes no judgment on Hume's work. Both A and C cannot be inferred from the passage: while animal minds are clearly mysterious, the passage does not locate that mystery in any one thing, like the lack of language or different mental laws. In contrast, the experimental psychology mentioned in answer choice B relies on language (see the first sentence of the third paragraph). Since animals do not share language with us, we can infer that they cannot be subjected to experimental psychology. Answer choice B is correct.

12. **C.**

   This question specifically asks you to choose the BEST summary of the author's drawn relationship between human and animal psychologies. Be prepared in these cases to have several answer choices that might be close to each other, or might both be supported by the passage – you will then have to make a value judgment as to which is the best or closest to the question's request. Begin by eliminating any choices not supported by the passage at all. Here, D and E do not appear in the passage. Answer choice A puts two elements of the passage together: our indirect knowledge of our neighbor's mind (first paragraph), and the mystery of animal minds (last paragraph). However, the passage does not draw links between these two things so you can eliminate A. B is too specific: it addresses mental laws, which are never mentioned in relation to animals in the last paragraph. This only leaves answer choice C, which in fact summarizes the last sentence of the third paragraph and the first sentence of the fourth. This is your correct answer.

13. **E.**

   This question is perhaps a bit unfairly hard. While answer choices A, C, and D use terms or phrases from the passage, none of these topics are treated to much degree in the passage. No full history (choice B) is provided, although several historical specifics are mentioned. You are thus left with answer choice E. To double-check this answer, you can see if everything else—adventures, names and accomplishments, research results—serve as premises to support your chosen main point (they do).

VERBAL REASONING
ANSWER KEY: SECTION 4

14. C.

Wallace's work is specifically discussed in the first paragraph. For this question, B and D can be eliminated as they are not mentioned in the passage in connection with Wallace's work. A and C *both* describe aspects of his work; however, dividing the earth's surface into units is part of the *aim* of Wallace's work, while the creation of a fixed scheme (classification system) was its *purpose*. C is the correct answer.

15. B.

Here, you want to be careful to stay within the confines of the passage. Answer choices A, C, and E might all be assumptions involved in the study of zoogeography, but the passage mentions none of them. The second paragraph specifically tells you that Wallace's early scheme was soon found to be inadequate; thus, you can eliminate D. This leaves you with B, which summarizes the early assumption described in the last sentence of the first paragraph.

16. C.

For this question, you need to understand the subject of zoogeography as described by the passage: the mapping of animal life in relation to geography. Only C mentions the study of a subject in relation to geography, and this is the correct answer. D and E propose studies in particular environments, but do not study geography; B proposes a study in relation to time, which is not a major consideration in zoogeography. The mapping of plant life in relation to genes, proposed in answer choice A, runs parallel to the subject of zoogeography, but remains an inferior choice in relation to C.

17. A, D.

Both *coeval* and *coincident* refer to events happening at the same time, and can describe the mentioned police incidents. *Convivial* describes something festive, a tone that does not match the concern and seriousness expressed in the sentence. *Concomitant* describes something that accompanies a sentence's subject, and does not have a paired term. *Reprobate* (hardened in sin) and *dissident* (rebellious) might describe police incidents, but the terms are not similar in meaning.

18. B, C.

Altruistic (unselfish) and *magnanimous* (coming from a nobility of character) are both positive moral descriptions for an action. Their positive connotations fit the context of the sentence, which requires a positive first half to counter the negative second half, as indicated by the keyword "while." The remaining answer choices all carry negative connotations: *sanctimonious* refers to a hypocritical devoutness to something; *reprehensible* actions demand or deserve reproof; *raucous* is boisterous; and *refractory* actions are unmanageable ones.

19. C, D.

The structure of the sentence lets you know that you are looking for words opposite "serious" and "silent". *Prolix* (overly verbose; long and wordy) and *voluble* (glib or talkative) both describe someone who is a great talker. None of the remaining words form a pair: *decorous* describes someone who is proper; to be *quiescent* is to be at rest; *munificent* is to be generous; and *malevolent* is someone who is harmful or wishing ill on others.

20. E, F.

These answer choices represent three pairs of words. To *eviscerate* is to deprive of meaning or significance, similar to *enervate*, which is to deprive of force or strength. To *adumbrate* is to foreshadow something, while *prognosticate* is to forecast or predict. And *propagate* is to spread or disseminate, while *engender* is to produce or give rise to. In the context of the sentence, only the last pair works: a collapse that lingers for decades is not weakened by revolution, and one that is "coeval" (at the same time; see question #17) cannot be foreshadowed.

1. A.

This problem tests your ability to use number theory in order to calculate the sum of an arithmetic series. Recall the formula for the sum of a series:

$$sum = number\ of\ terms \cdot \frac{first + last}{2}$$

To find the number of terms use the formula:

$$number\ of\ terms = \left(\frac{last - first}{difference\ between\ consecutive\ terms}\right) + 1$$

For Quantity A you are to find the sum of the numbers from 0 to 50 evenly divisible by 5:

$$sum = \left(\frac{50 - 0}{5} + 1\right) \cdot \frac{0 + 50}{2} = 11 \cdot 25 = 275$$

For Quantity B you are to find the sum of the numbers from 0 to 40 evenly divisible by 3. Because 40 is not divisible evenly by 3 you need to find the greatest term less than 40 that is evenly divisible by 3. To do this simply round off: $40 \div 3 = 13.3\overline{3}$ to get 13, which multiplied by 3 is 39. Now plug the numbers into the formula:

$$sum = \left(\frac{39 - 0}{3} + 1\right) \cdot \frac{0 + 39}{2} = 14 \cdot \frac{39}{2} = \frac{1521}{6} = 273$$

Quantity A is greater than Quantity B. The correct answer choice is **A.**

2. D.

This problem asks you to set up an inequality by translating a geometric relationship. You are given that a circle is divided into 5 arcs with the longest arc being exactly twice the length of the shortest arc. You can solve this problem using either the arc lengths or the measure of the angles. Using the measure of the arcs is a bit simpler.

Quantity A is the measure of the longest arc. You can find the longest possible arc with the following:

a is the shortest arc measure
L is the amount of arc added to a

$a + 2a + (a + L_1) + (a + L_2) + (a + L_3) = 360°$	Sum of the arcs equals the circle
$5a + (L_1) + (L_2) + (L_3) = 360°$	Simplify by gathering terms
$5a = 360° - (L_1) + (L_2) + (L_3)$	Isolate the variable
$a = \dfrac{360° - (L_1) + (L_2) + (L_3)}{5} = \dfrac{360°}{5} - \dfrac{(L_1) + (L_2) + (L_3)}{5}$	Solve for a
$a = 72° - \dfrac{(L_1) + (L_2) + (L_3)}{5}$	Simplify the solution

From here you can see that the greatest a can be is 72°. This greatest value will occur when all the L terms are equal to 0. This means that the greatest arc (2a) can only be 144°, which is *greater* than one-third of the circumference of the circle. To find the smallest measure for a, you can reason that since the largest possible angle is 2a, then any L term can be no larger than a. Substitute a for the L terms into the equation for the sum of the arcs:

$$a + 2a + (a + a) + (a + a) + (a + a) = 360°$$ The sum of the arcs is the circle

$$9a = 360$$ Simplify

$$a = 40$$

This shows that the smallest measurement for arc *a* is 40°. This makes the greatest arc (*2a*) in this instance only 80° which is *smaller* than one-third the circumference of the circle. Because you cannot determine whether the largest arc is smaller or greater than one-third the circumference, the correct answer choice is **D**.

3. **B.**

This problem tests your ability to use number theory and the property of reciprocals in order to solve an inequality. You are given several pieces of information, all relating the variables *a*, *b*, and *c* to the number 1. To solve this problem start with the last two given statements:

$$abc = 1$$ Given

$$ac = \frac{1}{b}$$ Divide by *b*

Next, relate *a* and *c* to *b*:

$$ab < 1$$ Given

$$a < \frac{1}{b}$$ Divide by *b*

Note: because we are given that *b* is positive we know the inequality will not change direction.

Now let *x* be a positive number such that: $\frac{1}{x} = a$. Return to the inequality:

$$\frac{1}{x} < \frac{1}{b}$$ Substitution

$$x > b$$ Reciprocal inequality

Using the same chain of reasoning for *c*:

$$cb < 1$$ Given

$$c < \frac{1}{b}$$ Divide by b

Let *y* be a positive number such that: $\frac{1}{y} = c$.

$$\frac{1}{y} < \frac{1}{b}$$ Substitution

$$y > b$$ Reciprocal inequality

If *y* > *b* and *x* > *b* then *xy* > *b*.

Now return to the given equation:

$$abc = 1$$ Given

$$\frac{1}{x} \cdot b \cdot \frac{1}{y} = 1$$ Substitution

$$b = xy$$ Multiply by *xy*

Because you have already demonstrated that $xy > b$ then $b = xy$ cannot be true. Therefore a and c cannot be *positive* numbers. This only leaves negative numbers:

$ab < 1$ — Given

$a < \dfrac{1}{b}$ — Divide by b

Now let x be a *negative* number such that: $\dfrac{1}{x} = a$.

$\dfrac{1}{x} < \dfrac{1}{b}$ — Substitution

$x < b$ — Reciprocal inequality of a negative number

Using the same chain of reasoning for c:

$cb < 1$ — Given

$c < \dfrac{1}{b}$ — Divide by b

Let y be a *negative* number such that: $\dfrac{1}{y} = c$.

$\dfrac{1}{y} < \dfrac{1}{b}$ — Substitution

$y < b$ — Reciprocal inequality of a negative number

You now have a situation where it is possible that $xy = b$. So looking at Quantity A: $\dfrac{1}{a+c}$ you can easily see that Quantity A will be a negative value while Quantity B will be positive. The correct answer choice is **B**.

4. **D.**

This problem tests your ability to simplify a system of equations in order to find the range of answers. You are given two averages:

$$\frac{a+b+c}{3} = 32 \text{ and } \frac{b+c+d}{3} = 23$$

You are asked to compare Quantity A which is the average of a and d. Start by simplifying the averages:

$\dfrac{a+b+c}{3} = 32$ — Average 1 given

$a + b + c = 96$ — Multiply by 3; call this equation (1)

$\dfrac{b+c+d}{3} = 23$ — Average 2 given

$b + c + d = 69$ — Multiply by 3; call this equation (2)

$a - d = 27$ — (1) − (2)

$a + d = 2d + 27$ — Add $2d$ to both sides

$\dfrac{a+d}{2} = 2d + \dfrac{27}{2}$ — Divide by 2

QUANTITATIVE REASONING
ANSWER KEY: SECTION 5

You now have an expression for the average of a and d. From here you see it is not possible to reduce the number of variables further, so you will have to compare this expression against Quantity B to see if you can resolve the problem.

For Quantity B start with:

$a + b + c = 96$	Equation (1)
$a = 96 - b - c$	Isolate the a variable
$\dfrac{a + b + c + d}{4} = \dfrac{96 - b - c + b + c + d}{4}$	Substitute for a on the right hand side
$= \dfrac{96 + d}{4}$	Simplify

You now have an expression for Quantity B. Compare:

Quantity A ? Quantity B

$2d + \dfrac{27}{2}$? $\dfrac{96 + d}{4}$	Substitution
$8d + 54$? $96 + d$	Multiply by 4
$7d$? 42	Subtract $54 + d$ from both sides

At this point you can see that the relationship cannot be resolved because you cannot determine the value of d. You cannot determine the relationship from the information given. The correct answer choice is **D**.

5. **B.**

This problem tests your ability to generate an algebraic equation from a geometric diagram. The arcs in the diagram have equal radii and touch at exactly one point. Quantity A is the shaded region and can be written:

Shaded Area = Area of the square – unshaded area

First calculate the area of the square using r as the radius:

Area of the square = $4r \cdot 4r = 16r^2$

Now calculate the area enclosed by the arcs:

unshaded area = $4 \cdot \dfrac{1}{2}\pi r^2 + 4 \cdot \dfrac{1}{4}\pi r^2 = 3\pi r^2$

Now compare the two quantities:

Quantity A ? Quantity B

$16r^2 - 3\pi r^2$? $3\pi r^2$	Comparison of the Quantities
$16r^2$? $6\pi r^2$	Add $3\pi r^2$ to both sides
$8 < 3\pi$	Divide by $2r^2$
$8 < 3(3.14)$	Substitute approximation for π

Quantity B is greater than Quantity A. The correct answer choice is **B**.

6. **B.**

    This problem tests your ability to solve a system of equations. Start by substituting the given values into the given functions. For $f(3)$:

$f(x) = Ax^2 + Bx + 7$	Given
$f(3) = A(3)^2 + B(3) + 7$	Substitution
$34 = 9A + 3B + 7$	Substitute and simplify
$27 = 9A + 3B$	Subtract 7 from both sides
$9 = 3A + B$	Divide by 3
$36 = 12A + 4B$	Multiply by 4

    Now do the same for $f(4)$:

$f(4) = A(4)^2 + B(4) + 7$	Substitution
$34 = 16A + 4B + 7$	Substitute and simplify
$27 = 16A + 4B$	Substitute and simplify

    Now solve the system of equations:

$36 = 12A + 4B$	From $f(3)$
$27 = 16A + 4B$	From $f(4)$
$9 = -4A$	$f(3) - f(4)$
$A = -\dfrac{9}{4}$	Solve for A

    Now use $f(4)$ to find B:

    $$34 = 16A + 4B + 7$$

$27 = 16\left(-\dfrac{9}{4}\right) + 4B$	Substitute
$65 = 4B$	Simplify
$\dfrac{65}{4} = B$	Solve for B

    B is greater than A, therefore Quantity B is greater than Quantity A. The correct answer choice is **B**.

7. **D.**

    This problem tests your ability to determine the range of a function. You are given the following equation and asked to compare x and 0:

    $$\frac{4x^3 - 12x^2 - 36x + 27}{2x - 3} = 0$$

    For this type of problem it is easiest to use a process of elimination. The first thing to note is that, because the expression is equal to zero the only valid solutions of x will occur when:

    $$4x^3 - 12x^2 - 36x + 27 = 0$$

QUANTITATIVE REASONING
ANSWER KEY: SECTION 5

The best approach to solve this problem is the process of elimination. Because you are comparing solutions for x to the value zero you can start by checking if 0 is a valid solution:

$4(0)^3 - 12(0)^2 - 36(0) + 27 > 0$ Substitute

Answer choice C can be eliminated.

Next, look to see if there is a solution for x that is *greater* than 0. For this you only have to prove that there is a positive solution for x. There is no need to find the actual solution. Start by choosing a couple of convenient values for x. Start with $\frac{1}{2}$:

$4\left(\frac{1}{2}\right)^3 - 12\left(\frac{1}{2}\right)^2 - 36\left(\frac{1}{2}\right) + 27\ ?\ 0$ Substitute

$\quad\quad \frac{1}{2} - 3 - 18 + 27 > 0$ Simplify the exponents

From this conclusion you can reason that if there is some number x *greater* than $\frac{1}{2}$ which results in the expression being *less* than zero, there must be some value between $\frac{1}{2}$ and that number for which the expression *will be* zero (i.e. a solution for x).

Now try the value 2 for x:

$4(2)^3 - 12(2)^2 - 36(2) + 27\ ?\ 0$ Substitute
$\quad\quad 32 - 48 - 72 + 27 < 0$ Simplify the exponents

You have shown there is a solution for x which is *greater* than 0.

Now, see if there is a solution which is *less* than 0. Remember you have already established that for $x = 0$ the polynomial is 27 (and greater than 0), so you are looking to see if there is a negative number which will result in the polynomial having a value less than zero. For convenience choose the value -10:

$4(-10)^3 - 12(-10)^2 - 36(-10) + 27\ ?\ 0$ Substitute
$\quad\quad -4000 + 1200 + 360 + 27 < 0$ Simplify the exponents

From this you have shown there is at least one value for x which is *less* than 0 that will be a solution for the polynomial.

Because there is both a positive and a negative solution the answer cannot be determined. The correct answer choice is **D**.

8. **A.**
    This problem tests your ability to calculate an area from a geometric diagram. For this problem it will help to add two lines bisecting the diagram. Then label the un-shaded area of one square A and the radius of the arcs as r:

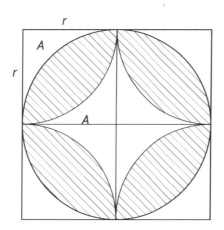

This divides the diagram into 4 equal squares where the shaded region in each of these smaller squares is: $r^2 - 2A$.

The area of region A can then be found with the equation: region $A = r^2 - \dfrac{1}{4}\pi r^2$.

Substitute the expression for the area of region A back into the shaded region formula:

$r^2 - 2A$ Shaded region formula

$r^2 - 2\left(r^2 - \dfrac{1}{4}\pi r^2\right)$ Substitute

$r^2 - 2r^2\left(1 - \dfrac{1}{4}\pi\right)$ Factor

$r^2\left(1 - 2\left(1 - \dfrac{1}{4}\pi\right)\right)$ Factor

$r^2\left(1 - 2 + \dfrac{1}{2}\pi\right)$ Simplify

$r^2\left(-1 + \dfrac{1}{2}\pi\right)$ Simplify

The area of the un-shaded region is then expressed:

un-shaded area = square − shaded area

$un\text{-}shaded\ area = r^2 - \left(r^2\left(-1 + \dfrac{1}{2}\pi\right)\right)$ Substitution

$= r^2\left(1 - 1\left(-1 + \dfrac{1}{2}\pi\right)\right)$ Distributive

$= r^2\left(1 + 1 - \dfrac{1}{2}\pi\right)$ Simplify the signs

$= r^2\left(2 - \dfrac{1}{2}\pi\right)$ Simplify

Now compare the two areas:

shaded region ? unshaded region

QUANTITATIVE REASONING
ANSWER KEY: SECTION 5

$r^2\left(-1+\frac{1}{2}\pi\right)\ ?\ r^2\left(2-\frac{1}{2}\pi\right)$ Substitution

$\left(-1+\frac{1}{2}\pi\right)\ ?\ \left(2-\frac{1}{2}\pi\right)$ Divide by r^2

$\pi > 3$ Add $\frac{\pi}{2}$ to both sides and simplify

From this you see that the shaded area of each small square is greater than the un-shaded area, so it follows that the shaded area of the entire diagram is greater than the un-shaded area. The correct answer choice is **A**.

9. **D.**

This problem asks you to use your knowledge of cylinders to calculate the length of a roll of paper. In order to solve this problem use the fact that the volume of the paper will be the same in both the cylinder and as a flat sheet.

$$volume\ of\ cylinder = volume\ of\ sheet$$

$$height \cdot \pi r^2 = height \cdot length \cdot thickness$$

Now plug in the values given in the problem:

$1m \cdot \pi(.5m)^2 = 1m \cdot length \cdot .2mm$ Substitution

$1m \cdot \pi(.5m)^2 = 1m \cdot length \cdot .0002m$ Convert to common units

$\frac{1m \cdot \pi(.5m)^2}{1m \cdot .0002m} = length$ Isolate the variable

$3926.99m = length$ Calculate

The answer rounds to $3,927m$. The correct answer choice is **D**.

10. **C**

This problem asks you to calculate the side of a hexagon only knowing the area of a triangle. You are also told that the hexagon formed is regular, which tells you that the triangles forming the hexagon must be equilateral. From this use your knowledge of a 30-60-90 triangle to calculate the length of the sides of each triangle.

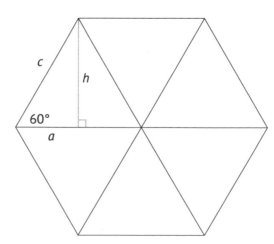

Use the relationship of the 30-60-90 triangle: $h = \frac{\sqrt{3}}{2}c$, $a = \frac{1}{2}c$. Start with the area of the equilateral triangle:

$$A = \frac{1}{2} \cdot 2a \cdot h \qquad \text{Formula for the Area of a Triangle}$$

$$\sqrt{3} = \frac{1}{2} \cdot 2 \cdot \frac{1}{2}c \cdot \frac{\sqrt{3}}{2}c \qquad \text{Substitution}$$

$$\sqrt{3} = \frac{\sqrt{3}}{4}c^2 \qquad \text{Simplify}$$

$$4 = c^2 \qquad \text{Isolate the variable}$$

$$2 = c \qquad \text{Solve}$$

Remember you only need the positive square root here because you have been given a triangle with a positive area. This shows that each side of the hexagon are 2 units, therefore the *perimeter* = 6 • 2 = 12. The correct answer choice is **C**.

11. D.

This problem asks you to convert a percentage to a number. Given that 57.4% of accidents were non-related to weather, this tells you that 42.6% of accidents *were* weather related. First calculate the total number of accidents from the data on the chart:

$.426 \cdot total = 175\ accidents$

$total = \dfrac{175\ accidents}{.426} = 410.8\ accidents$

The closest answer shown is 410, so the correct answer choice is **D**. You can double-check your answer: 410 • .426 = 174.66 which rounds to 175.

12. B.

This problem asks you to use a known percentage to determine which datum fits the given. Calculate the number of weather related accidents using the given information: 500 · .45 = 225. Scanning the chart you see that only 2012 had this number of weather related accidents, so the correct answer choice is **B**.

13. D.

This problem asks you to calculate a percentage from the data collected from 2010 to 2012. Using the total of 800 accidents, calculate the percentage:

$$percent = \frac{150 + 100 + 225}{800} = \frac{475}{800} = 59\%$$

The correct answer choice is **D**.

14. B.

This problem asks you to calculate the length of an edge of an equilateral triangle (*c*). You are given a regular pyramid which has an equilateral triangle as a base. Since a regular triangle will have three sides of equal length, it follows that all sides of the pyramid will have an equal area. Additionally, because you are given that the base is a triangle it follows that the pyramid has 4 sides. This information tells you that each face has an area of:

QUANTITATIVE REASONING
ANSWER KEY: SECTION 5

$96 \div 4 = 24$. Now use this to calculate the length of the sides for each triangle.

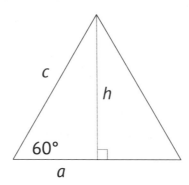

First, use the relationship of the 30-60-90 triangle in order to find a and h:

$$h = \frac{\sqrt{3}}{2}\, c, a = \frac{1}{2}\, c$$

Next, plug the appropriate substitutions into the formula for the area of a triangle:

$area = \frac{1}{2} \cdot base \cdot height$	Formula for the Area of a Triangle
$24 = \frac{1}{2} \cdot c \cdot \frac{\sqrt{3}}{2}\, c$	Substitution
$24 \cdot \frac{4}{\sqrt{3}} = c^2$	Isolate the variable by cross-multiplying
$7.44 = c$	Calculate

Only the positive square root is used because length is always a positive value. The correct answer choice is **B**.

15. B.

This problem asks you to find the distance between the center of two circles given their respective equations. The first task is to transform the equations into the general formula for a circle:

$$(x - a)^2 + (y - b)^2 = r^2$$

Starting with the first equation:

$x^2 + y^2 = 2x + 14y + 1$	Given
$x^2 - 2x + y^2 - 14y = 1$	Move the variables to the left
$x^2 - 2x + 1 - 1 + y^2 - 14y + 49 - 49 = 1$	Add constant terms in order to complete the square
$(x - 1)^2 - 1 + (y - 7)^2 - 49 = 1$	Complete the squares
$(x - 1)^2 + (y - 7)^2 = 51$	Add 50 to both sides

You have your first center point: $(1, 7)$. Now for the second equation:

$$\frac{8y - 6x}{x^2 + y^2} = 1 \qquad \text{Given}$$

$$8y - 6x = x^2 + y^2 \qquad \text{Multiply by denominator}$$

$$x^2 + 6x + y^2 - 8y = 0 \qquad \text{Move the variables to the left}$$

$$x^2 + 6x + 9 - 9 + y^2 - 8y + 16 - 16 = 0 \qquad \text{Add constant terms in order to complete the square}$$

$$(x + 3)^2 - 9 + (y - 4)^2 - 16 = 0 \qquad \text{Complete the squares}$$

$$(x + 3)^2 + (y - 4)^2 = 25 \qquad \text{Add 25 to both sides}$$

You have your second center point: $(-3, 4)$. Now apply the Distance between Points formula:

$$distance = \sqrt{(1-(-3))^2 + (7 - 4)^2} = \sqrt{(16 + 9)} = \sqrt{25} = 5$$

You can discard the negative square root because distance is always positive. The correct answer choice is **B**.

16. C.

This problem asks you to use a graph diagram to calculate the area of a non-standard region bounded by 4 quarter circle arcs. If you divide the graph diagonally from top right to bottom left you can label your diagram as below.

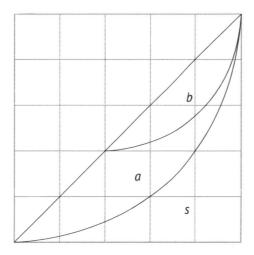

Using the graph, you see that each side of the square is 5 units. Additionally, notice that the large arc has a radius of 5 while the smaller arc has a radius of 3. Set up the equation to find region *a*:

$$a = area\ of\ triangle - region\ s - region\ b$$

You can see there is an isosceles right triangle inscribed within the quarter circle described by arc *b* which has legs of length 3. You can now find the area of region *b* by subtracting the area of the triangle from the area of the quarter circle:

$$b - quarter\ circle - area\ of\ small\ triangle$$

ARGOPREP
ARGOPREP.COM/GRE

$b = \frac{1}{4}\pi(3)^2 - \frac{1}{2}(3)^2$ Substitution

$b = \frac{9}{4}\pi - \frac{9}{2}$ Simplify

Now find s:

s = *area of the square – quarter circle under arc a*

$s = 5^2 - \frac{1}{4}\pi(5)^2$ Substitution

$s = 25 - \frac{25}{4}\pi$ Simplify

Returning to the equation for a:

$a = \frac{1}{2} \cdot 5^2 - \left(25 - \frac{25}{4}\pi\right) - \left(\frac{9}{4}\pi - \frac{9}{2}\right)$ Substitution

$a = \frac{25}{2} - 25 + \frac{25}{4}\pi - \frac{9}{4}\pi + \frac{9}{2}$ Simplify the signs

$a = \frac{16}{4}\pi - \frac{16}{2} = 4\pi - 8$ Simplify the fractions

Referring back to the diagram, remember that region a represents *half* the shaded area so the final answer is: $8\pi - 16$. The correct answer choice is **C**.

17. **15,247.1 lbs.**

This problem tests your ability to calculate percentages and mixing. You start with 18,000 pounds of grain which contains 2% inert dust. First calculate the amount of grain (98%) left after filtering the dust:

18,000 *lbs* • .98 = 17,640 *lbs*

Next you are told that the grain has a moisture content of 28%. This means the grain has 72% solids at start:

17,640 *lbs* • .72 = 12,700.8 *lbs*

After drying the moisture content is only 15%, with the 12,700.8 *lbs* of solids now 85% of the weight:

grain weight • .85 = 12,700.8 *lbs*

$$grain\ weight = \frac{12,700.8\ lbs}{.85} = 14,942.1\ lbs$$

Finally, you are told that dust is re-introduced to make up 2% of the total weight. This means that 14,942.1 *lbs* of grain is only 98% of the total weight:

final weight • .98 = 14,942.1 *lbs*

$$final\ weight = \frac{14,942.1\ lbs}{.98} = 15,247.1\ lbs$$

Enter **15,247.1 *lbs*** in the text box.

18. **$334.71.**

In this problem you are asked to calculate the fuel cost per person for a passenger traveling from Los Angeles to Hawaii to Tokyo.

First calculate how much fuel is used in the trip described. For each take-off and landing the plane uses 1,500 *lbs* of fuel. You have a take-off from Los Angeles, a landing and a take-off from Hawaii, and finally the landing in Tokyo.

fuel for landing and take-offs = 1,500 *lbs* • 4 = 6,000 *lbs*

Now calculate the amount of fuel burned in the air using the information given in the problem:

$$183 \text{ } persons \bullet \frac{100 \text{ } lbs}{500 \text{ } miles \cdot person} \bullet 6{,}501 \text{ } mile = 237{,}936.6 \text{ } lbs$$

Now divide the total amount of fuel used by the number of passengers and multiply by the price:

$$\frac{237{,}936.6 \text{ } lbs + 6{,}000 \text{ } lbs}{183 \text{ } persons} \bullet \frac{\$.2511}{lb} = \$334.71$$

You have calculated the price of fuel per passenger as **$334.71.** Enter your result in the text box.

19. **$45\dfrac{5}{17}$ or $\dfrac{770}{17}$**

This problem asks you to use your knowledge of the ratios of similar triangles to find the perimeter of a quadrilateral.

You are given that $\triangle ABD$ is similar to $\triangle BCD$, $h = 7\dfrac{1}{17}$, and $\overline{BD} = 15$. First apply the Ratio of Similar Triangles:

$\dfrac{h}{\overline{BD}} = \dfrac{\overline{AD}}{\overline{BD}}$ Ratio of Similar Triangles

$h = AD$ Multiply both sides by $\overline{BD}$

Now use the Pythagorean Theorem to find $\overline{AB}$:

$\overline{AB}^2 = \overline{BD}^2 - \overline{AD}^2$ Pythagorean Theorem

$\overline{AB}^2 = 15^2 - \left(7\dfrac{1}{17}\right)^2$ Substitution

$\overline{AB}^2 = 225 - \dfrac{14400}{289}$ Expand the exponent

$\overline{AB}^2 = \dfrac{65025}{289} - \dfrac{14400}{289} = \dfrac{50625}{289}$ Subtract using a common denominator

$\overline{AB} = \dfrac{225}{17}$ Take the square root; discard the negative result

Now you can return to using the ratio of similar triangles to find the remaining sides:

$\dfrac{\overline{BC}}{\overline{BD}} = \dfrac{\overline{BD}}{\overline{AB}}$ Ratio of Similar Triangles

$\dfrac{\overline{BC}}{15} = \dfrac{15}{\dfrac{225}{17}}$ Substitute values

QUANTITATIVE REASONING
ANSWER KEY: SECTION 5

$\overline{BC} = \dfrac{225}{\frac{225}{17}} = 17$	Solve for $\overline{BC}$
$\dfrac{\overline{DC}}{h} = \dfrac{\overline{BC}}{\overline{BD}}$	Ratio of Similar Triangles
$\dfrac{\overline{DC}}{7\frac{1}{17}} = \dfrac{17}{15}$	Substitution
$\overline{DC} = \dfrac{17\left(7\frac{1}{17}\right)}{15} = \dfrac{17\left(\frac{120}{17}\right)}{15} = 8$	Solve for $\overline{DC}$

The perimeter is then:

$\overline{AB} + \overline{BC} + \overline{CD} + \overline{AD}$	Perimeter Formula
$\dfrac{225}{17} + 17 + 8 + 7\frac{1}{17} = 45\frac{5}{17}$	Calculate

The correct answer is **$45\frac{5}{17}$ or $\dfrac{770}{17}$**. Enter your answer in the boxes provided. Remember that the numerator goes in the top box and the denominator goes in the bottom.

20. **B, D.**

This problem asks you to solve a system of equations, one of which is a polynomial.

$2y + x^2 = 3$	Given equation (1)
$2x^2 + 4y = 6$	Multiply through by 2
$3x - 4y = 8$	Given equation (2)
$2x^2 + 3x = 14$	Add equations (1) and (2)
$2x^2 + 3x - 14 = 0$	Move all terms to one side of the equation
$(2x + 7)(x - 2) = 0$	Factor the polynomial

From this you see there are 2 solutions for $x : \{-\frac{7}{2}, 2\}$. Select answer choices **B** and **D**.

VERBAL REASONING
ANSWER KEY: SECTION 6

1. A.
The phrase "in fact" lets you know that this sentence will convey opposites in its two halves. A *paragon* is a perfect model, which when tied to virtue stands as the opposite of the moral corruption represented by slavery and land grabs. *Founders* is a trick option, as America's early presidents are often referred to as the country's founding fathers; the term means one who begins or establishes something. A *cipher* is a person of no value, a *prophet* is one who predicts the future, and a *felon* is a criminal. None fit the context.

2. A, E.
Here, you need to know that *quips* can be sharp and cutting, and not just the smart or saucy remarks they often describe. The word choice of "from" also suggests A, since one usually describes *ordeals* (severely trying tests or experiences) or *escapades* (reckless adventures) as "with" someone or something. For the second blank, *retiring* describes someone who is withdrawn or secluded, matching the context of the sentence. There is nothing in the sentence to suggest that the widow is *devout* (pious) or *taut* (emotionally or mentally tense).

3. A, E, G.
Orthodox (traditional) beliefs have caused various communities to *expurgate* or remove various practices from their midst. For the first blank, *putative* (supposed or reputed) does not fit the context. Some of these beliefs may have been *occult* ones, tied to the supernatural, but there is nothing in this sentence to support this choice. For the second blank, *belie* (show to be false) does not properly fit the sentence's grammar, while *beleaguer* (attack, usually in a military context) better fits people or places than practices. For the third blank, a community would remove practices that were *antagonistic* or hostile to their values. *Endemic* is the opposite and means belonging to a specific group of people, while something that is *contentious* causes arguments but is not necessarily damaging.

4. A, D, G.
Lucid means clear. Do not be led astray by *loquacious* (talkative), which refers to speaking but does not describe one's diction. *Lucrative* is profitable and does not fit the context. For the second blank, *propitious* (favorable) suggests a positive outcome, in line with the context clue of "successful." *Reparable* describes something capable of being repaired, while *strident* labels something that has a harsh or grating sound or character. Neither fit the context. Lucid diction then *corroborates* or confirms the importance of reading aloud in children. It does not *abolish* (cancel) or *satiate* (satisfy) this importance.

5. B, F, H.
Since you have no context for the first blank of the sentence, you need to tackle the other two before you can fill in the first. The context clue of *despite* lets you know that the last two blanks move in opposite directions. If they *transcend* (surpass) their fundraising goals, they *middle through* their mission statement. *Adroit* is skillful, and would not explain the context of *despite*. Since you now know they have a *middling* mission statement, you can label them as *inarticulate* in the first blank.

6. A, E, H.
The policy was *prodigal*, or wasteful. This answer choice also ties to the context clue of the community's "limited resources." *Stolid* means dull or impassive, and has a very neutral tone in contrast to how "incensed" the community feels. *Deprecatory* expresses disapproval or protest, which in this context more accurately describes the community than the policy itself. For the second blank, the community *squabbled* (engaged in petty quarrels) over resources. To *equivocate* is to hedge or use ambiguous expressions, while one feigns illness to escape duty when one *malingers*. Neither fits the context. Finally, the community's response *scotched* or hindered any further political action. It did not *dilate* or expand such action, while *remonstrating* or protesting is not strong enough to counter the "ameliorative" (making better) efforts.

7. E.

This author is tricky, using both meanings of *nebulous* at once: (1) having the nature of or location within the astronomical phenomena of a nebula, and (2) hazy, vague, or confused. Throughout the passage the author criticizes the state of astronomical knowledge even as he reveals his discoveries, so this dual meaning keeps with his dual lines of argument.

8. E.

While answer choices B, C, and D partially draw on the language of the passage, they all infer information beyond what is presented. The passage is highly structured in its argument, so it is not the poetic diatribe suggested by answer choice A. The correct answer choice is E, reinforced by the fact that the last sentence of both the first and last paragraphs state as much.

9. B.

This is a straight content question. Only the viewing of a comet is not mentioned in the passage.

10. *A study by de Rosnay, Cooper, Tsigaras and Murray showed that infants modify their affective behavior towards a stranger following observations of mothers modeling anxious behaviors during interactions with a stranger.* Here, the order of the paragraphs, along with the subject of infants, are key. The question to be answered lies toward the end of paragraph 1. Carefully reading the next sentence, you see that it does not answer the posed question but sends you toward the content of the next paragraph: research that provides a more complete picture as to how phobias arise. In this second paragraph, only one mentioned set of research—the study by the four social scientists—directly mentions infants, providing your answer.

11. A.

This is a straight context question. The author specifically says that these three areas have had a great deal of research, or answer choice A. For this reason, the author specifically advocates for other areas to be researched, so you can eliminate C. The author does not name the three as key factors in the development of fear, as root causes of anxiety, or as alternative explanations for phobias. Answers B, D and E can thus also be eliminated.

12. A, B, D.

The 3rd sentence specifically mentions individuals who "are unable to regulate and categorize fear and anxiety," which can lead to anxiety disorders and phobias, or answer choice D. The next sentence describes such individuals with both A (avoidant coping strategies) and B (impaired functioning). Social referencing, as mentioned in answer choice C, does not appear until the 2nd paragraph. In that context it is clear that the role of social referencing is not yet clear, so C is *not* a correct choice.

13. B, C.

This is a straight reading comprehension question. In the third paragraph, Agnew mentions the number of readers versus viewers and, in the last sentence, asserts that reading is not like seeing and hearing. You can eliminate A and D. In the fourth paragraph, he relies on the words of Lippmann to give a number of print publications in relation to television stations, eliminating answer choice E. B and C, in contrast, are not mentioned anywhere in the passage.

14. D.

For questions like this, you first must identify and summarize the author's argument. Agnew is arguing that broadcast journalism is radically different from print journalism, and is both biased and has a greater sway over the American populace due to this difference. However, if most Americans in 1969 did not access broadcast journalism, Agnew's claims of bias and its ability to influence American politics are mute. Thus, D is the correct answer choice. All of the other answer choices mention things that might have also been true, but they do not have direct bearing on Agnew's claims.

15. D.

White's words end the last paragraph of the passage, and state that the needs of viewers and listeners have priority over those of the networks' broadcasters. This supports Agnew's claims that broadcasting belongs to the American people, and thus D is the correct answer choice. Do not be confused by E, which directly names the "viewers and listeners" of White's quotation but as media programmers, which is not mentioned in the passage. Likewise, do not be confused by A, B, and C, all of which reflect elements of the passage. White's words are specifically used to speak to the ownership of the broadcasting airwaves, so these answer choices are incorrect.

16. B.

Here, you must summarize the shape of Agnew's media monopoly, and then infer which of the answer choices is the most similar. Agnew's monopoly is not a sole company, does not operate overseas, does not produce a product, and does not copyright experiences, so you can infer that A, C, D, and E are not correct answers. B, on the other hand, depicts a handful of companies and is in control of what goes into and out of its production lines—very similar to the handful of networks discussed by Agnew, whose bias controls what stories go into their content and what is then aired and produced. B is the correct answer.

17. B, C.

Here, the context of seeking *favor* leads to the synonyms *sycophantic* and *obsequious*, both of which describe someone seeking attention through flattery. *Esurient* and *parsimonious* form another pair, but their connotation of greed or stinginess do not match the context.

18. A, D.

The only pair here is *epicurean* and *gourmandizer*, both being labels for someone who enjoys luxury, especially regarding food and drink. Bill may also be all of the other answer choices, but they do not fit the context of his *lavish fetes*.

19. B, F.

Usurped and *annexed* both describe the act of taking over or seizing land and/or power that belongs to another. *Emancipated* or set free also fits the context of the sentence but does not have a paired word.

20. C, E.

The terms *impertinent* (uncivil or insolent) and *impudent* (impertinent or shameless) are nearly synonyms and both describe behavior, the subject of this sentence. *Passé* means outmoded, *torpid* refers to something inactive or sluggish, and *hermetic* is isolated and not affected by outside behavior. These three could all refer to behavior, but have no similar paired words and can be eliminated. The last, *incorporeal*, describes something that is immaterial or insubstantial.

GRE® PREP

VOCABULARY

aberration: noun – deviating from the right path or usual course of action; a mental disorder, especially of a minor or temporary nature. *Everyone was sure that Yoo's poor race performance was an aberration, and that he would run faster at the championship meet.*

abstinence: noun – the giving up of certain pleasures such as food or drink. *During Lent, many people believe that abstinence from indulgences helps them be more reflective and open to spiritual guidance.*

abstract: adjective – theoretical, not applied or practical; not concrete; hard to understand. *The artwork was a bit too abstract for Janna to understand; all she saw was dots and lines, not the masterpiece everyone else claimed to see.*

acclaim: noun – loud applause; approval. *Gina's discovery of the gene mutation earned her great acclaim in the science community.*

acquiesce: verb – to accept the conclusions or arrangements of others; to accede; to give consent by keeping silent. *The teacher refused to acquiesce to the student's request for an extension on the assignment since ample time had already been allotted.*

admonish: verb – to advise against something; to warn; to scold gently; to urge strongly. *Andrew admonished Doug for failing to turn on the alarm after he left.*

advocate: verb – to support; to be in favor of. *David failed to advocate for his employees' needs; as a result, they all left and found better positions in another department.*

aesthetic; adjective – showing an appreciation of beauty in nature or art; artistic. *The designer's fresh aesthetic won over the judges at the fashion show.*

affinity: noun – natural attraction to a person or liking for a thing; relation; connection. *Emily has an affinity for unique craft beers and single-malt whiskey.*

aggrandizement: noun – to increase in rank or wealth; growth in power. *I attributed the lieutenant's aggressiveness towards his subordinates to his need for aggrandizement and validation.*

alienate: verb – to turn away the normal feelings of fondness toward anyone; to estrange. *Jess felt alienated by her peers after they discovered she she had inadvertently gotten them in trouble for skipping school.*

alleviate: verb – to make easier to endure; to relieve; to diminish. *Serena asked for an ice pack in hopes that it would alleviate her pain.*

altruistic: adjective – thoughtful of the welfare of others. *Father Merchant was known for his altruistic deeds; he gave freely to those in need and encouraged others to do the same.*

ambiguous: adjective – permitting more than one interpretation; not clearly defined. *Based on the union rep's ambiguous remarks, the workers were not sure whose side he was actually on.*

ambivalence: noun – condition of having conflicting attitudes. *The director's ambivalence toward his cast made way for lots of confusion and uncomfortable interactions.*

ameliorate: verb – to make better or more tolerable; to improve. *Seeing that tensions were flying, Berry stepped in and tried to ameliorate the situation by asking everyone to take a break and reconvene later.*

analogous: adjective – similar in certain qualities; comparable. *The engineer said that the new machine was analogous to the human heart.*

anonymity: noun - condition of being nameless or unknown. *The witness agreed to speak only under the condition of anonymity because he feared for his life.*

antithesis: noun – direct opposite. *While most people believe twins are exactly alike, Laura is the antithesis of her twin Kate in every way.*

apocryphal: adjective – of doubtful authenticity; counterfeit. *The Easter Bunny is one of the most recognizable apocryphal symbols in the world.*

arduous: adjective – hard to do; strenuous. *The marathon was more arduous than Victor anticipated, especially since it started to rain as soon as he started the hilly part of the course.*

articulate: adjective – able to put one's thoughts into words easily and clearly. *The attorney was able to clearly articulate the facts of his client's self-defense case and convince the jury of his client's innocence.*

augment: verb – to increase or enlarge; to become greater in size. *Ryan suggested to his manager that they augment the amount budgeted for the main event in order to make sure enough funds were available for adequate security.*

belittle: verb – to make something seem less important. *The candidate tried to belittle her competitor by repeatedly mentioning that she only had a community college degree.*

bequeath: verb – to leave money or property by a will; to pass along. *Dawn bequeathed her estate to her daughters to split evenly.*

bizarre: adjective – strikingly odd in appearance or style; grotesque. *The zombie movie had too many bizarre and gory scenes for Taylor; he turned it off before it was finished.*

blithe: adjective – happy and cheerful; gay. *Despite the unfortunate circumstances, Linda remained blithe and positive and tried to encourage those around her to see the silver lining.*

bombastic: adjective – high-sounding; marked by use of language without much real meaning. *The review board was not impressed with the doctor's bombastic plea and proceeded with the hearing to review whether or not he should keep his medical license.*

buffoon: noun – a clown; someone who amuses with tricks and jokes. *Sila often acted like a buffoon to make her friends and family laugh.*

cache: noun – a hiding place; something hidden in a hiding place. *The battle took a turn for the worse when the enemy bombers destroyed the cache of weapons the squadron had stored away for later use.*

cacophony: noun- discord; harsh sound. *Her thoughts were interrupted by a cacophony of construction noises from the nearby building site.*

cajole: verb – to persuade by pleasant words or false promises. *The private investigator tried to cajole the neighbor into lying for his client by offering him part of the insurance settlement his client stood to receive.*

callous: adjective – unfeeling; insensitive. *Cynthia was not expecting her husband's callous response to her suggestion that they see a therapist.*

capitulate: verb – to surrender; to cease resisting. *The rebels finally decide to capitulate when they realized they were surrounded and had no where to run or hide.*

capricious: adjective – changeable, fickle. *The weather in Chiang Mai has been so capricious lately that it has been nearly impossible to make outdoor plans based on the weather reports.*

carping: adjective – complaining. *Carl spent most of the trip carping about how uncomfortable his train seat was and how awful the food tasted.*

catalyst: noun – someone or something that brings about a change. *The conference was just the catalyst Evita needed to kick-start her new business venture.*

catharsis: noun – an emotional purification or relief. *The movie provoked more of a catharsis than even the directors imagined.*

caustic: adjective – stinging, biting. *The caustic environment caused Pamela to seek another place of employment.*

celestial: adjective – having to do with the heavens; divine. *The clouds and setting sun treated onlookers to a celestial display of colors and natural beauty.*

chimerical: adjective – absurd; wildly fanciful. *The chimerical effigies in the haunted house were hardly scary; more people laughed at them than were afraid of them.*

clairvoyant: adjective –having exceptional insight. *The fortune-teller claimed to be clairvoyant and insisted that the police take her vision of the impending threat seriously.*

clandestine: adjective – secret or hidden. *The clandestine passageway led to a secret garden full of poppies and intricate topiaries.*

colloquial: adjective – conversational; used in an informal speech or writing. *Wanting to better relate to his constituents, Robert abandoned his formal tone and spoke in a more colloquial manner during the town hall.*

commiserate: verb – to sympathize with; to feel sorrow for another's suffering. *Jack and his co-worker met up after work to eat ice cream and commiserate about their demanding boss.*

composure: noun – calmness. *Everyone was surprised by how well the bank teller was able to maintain her composure during the bank robbery.*

copious: adjective – abundant. *Reese drank copious amounts of coffee while trying to finish writing her book.*

dearth: noun – shortage. *The dearth of resources led to the quick demise of the colony.*

debilitate: verb – to weaken. *The spike strips debilitated the vehicle by deflating its tires.*

deference: noun – great respect. *The squadron always showed deference towards older, more decorated officers.*

deprecate: verb – to express strong disapproval of. *Mark grew tired of his mother-in-law constantly deprecating him and his profession.*

derogatory: adjective- tending to lower in estimation; degrading. *Bill neglected to pay his outstanding bill, so a derogatory mark was placed on his credit report.*

desecrate: verb – to treat with disrespect. *The tourists were arrested for desecrating the ancient temples of Angkor Wat.*

deter: verb – to discourage; to keep someone from doing something. *Laura did not let the slim possibility of success deter her from entering the competition.*

devoid: adjective – entirely without; lacking. *The campsite was devoid of any possible water source, and the rangers were forced to relocate.*

diatribe: noun – a denunciation; bitter verbal attack. *The politician's insult-laden diatribe angered many of the citizens and caused them to seriously reconsider whether or not to re-elect him.*

didactic: adjective – intended to instruct. *Once Sarah finished the didactic portion of the course, she enrolled in the practicum to gain hands-on experience treating patients.*

diffuse: adjective – spread out; wordy. *The hall monitor tried to diffuse the situation before it escalated and required the involvement of formal sanctions.*

disdain: noun – a feeling of contempt for anything that is regarded as unworthy; scorn. *The Queen looked on in disdain as the prisoner was escorted into the court to face charges of treason.*

dismantle: verb – to pull down; to take apart. *The sharp student used well-known facts to quickly dismantle the teacher's circumstantial argument.*

disparage: verb – to discredit; to belittle. *Sue grew tired of the disparaging remarks from her coach and decided to quit the team.*

ebb: verb – to decline. *The lottery winnings continued to ebb and Gretchen carelessly purchased big-ticket items and fancy trips.*

eclectic: adjective – consisting of selections from various sources. *Bryce was known for his eclectic sense of style and his quirky personality.*

efface: verb – to wipe out; to erase. *The thief attempted to efface the evidence of his crime to no avail; the police quickly captured him.*

effervescent: adjective – lively; giving off bubbles. *Corey's effervescent personality rubbed off on all those around him; it's no wonder he was always invited to parties.*

egregious: adjective – extraordinarily bad. *Sam's egregious error was hard to overlook no matter how unintentional it was.*

elucidate: verb – to make clear. *The event this weekend elucidated the need for better crowd management policies.*

embellish: verb – to decorate; to elaborate upon. *Katniss loved sparkly things and would often use glitter and crystals to embellish her shoes and accessories.*

emulate: verb – to try to equal or surpass. *Tina was committed to becoming the best ballerina around and often emulated Misty Copland's style and choreography to try to push herself to the next level.*

enigma: noun – a puzzle; a baffling situation. *The stone was a real enigma to the archeologists since they had never seen anything like it and nothing similar had been found on the entire continent.*

ephemeral: adjective – lasting for only a short time. *Rick had an ephemeral feeling of nostalgia every time he drove past his old house.*

equivocate: verb – to use ambiguous or unclear expressions in order to mislead; to be shifty; to hedge. *Unlike his competitor who was very clear about his stance on the matter, Harold preferred instead to equivocate on the issue.*

esoteric: adjective – understood by only a few; little known; obscure. *The once esoteric band became a national sensation after being featured on a popular online music blog.*

exacerbate: verb – to make a situation worse; to irritate. *William tried to help, but his involvement only exacerbated the situation.*

exemplary: adjective – serving as a model. *Justin was an exemplary mentor for the internal medicine residents.*

expedite: verb – to make easy and quick; to speed up. *The mail-forwarding service had several options available for those who wanted to expedite the delivery of their orders.*

expunge: verb – to erase; to remove completely. *The law student asked for his record to be expunged since his arrest was found to be unjustified.*

extol: verb – to praise highly. *The convent was extolled for having the best egg tarts in all of Portugal.*

fastidious: adjective – hard to please; dainty in taste. *Jasmine was so fastidious that no one knew what to get her for her birthday.*

fervor: noun – intense emotion; great warmth of feeling. *His fervor when discussing current events was a shock to the generally calm group.*

flagrant: adjective – outrageous; glaringly offensive. *The coach argued that the foul was flagrant and deserved a stiffer penalty.*

fledgling: adjective – newly developed; little known. *The fledgling start-up secured a large grant from an angle investor.*

forlorn: adjective – deserted; left alone and neglected; unhappy. *The forlorn gazelle grazed aimlessly hoping to stumble upon his herd.*

formidable: adjective – hard to overcome; to be dreaded. *The warped wall proved to be a formidable challenge for the competitive skate boarder.*

galvanize: verb – to arouse suddenly; to startle. *The massive oil spill quickly galvanized efforts to prevent the transport of crude via boats and barges.*

garbled: adjective – confused; mixed up. *The formatting was garbled making the document hard to read.*

garner: verb – to gather and store away; to collect. *Fanny was able to garner the support of her family to help her train for the obstacle course race.*

garrulous: adjective – talkative. *Wendy's garrulous nature was annoying to her roommate who preferred to be left alone in silence.*

gratuitous: adjective – freely given; unnecessary; uncalled-for. *The gratuitous violence in the movie was a distraction from the main storyline.*

gullible: adjective – easily deceived. *The con man took advantage of Austin's gullible nature and swindled him out of thousands of dollars.*

hackneyed: adjective – used too often; trite; commonplace. *The hackneyed décor made the café seem more like a chain restaurant rather than the trendy hotspot it purported to be.*

hedonist: noun – one who lives solely for pleasure. *Pai is a haven for hedonists given its remote location and rampant availability of drugs and alcohol.*

heretic: noun – a person who upholds religious doctrines contrary to the established beliefs of his church. *Joan of Arc was considered a heretic because she supposedly saw visions that contradicted the monarchy.*

homogeneous: adjective – similar; uniform in nature. *The rabbits had been carefully breed to ensure they all had homogenous phenotypes.*

hyperbole: noun – an exaggerated statement used as a figure of speech for rhetorical effect. *Although they were well aware that the motivational speaker's speech was full of hyperbole, they were motivated by the deeper implications of the speaker's rhetoric.*

iconoclast: noun – a person who attacks cherished beliefs or established institutions. *Gerald was proud of being labeled an iconoclast and stood by his decision to promulgate the hypocrisy of the well-respected university.*

imminent: adjective – about to occur. *Everyone knew the storm was imminent and prepared their houses by boarding up windows and placing sandbags around the perimeter.*

impassive: adjective – without feelings or emotion; insensible. *Greg sat looking impassively out the window, unable to feel anything after losing his beloved dog, Jake.*

incongruous: adjective – inappropriate; out of place. *The sale of alcohol was incongruous with the family-oriented nature of the event.*

incorrigible: adjective – too firmly fixed to be reformed or changed. *Helsa's behavior was incorrigible; after several intervention programs and various therapeutic approaches, it was clear nothing could assuage her aggression or limit her violent outbursts.*

indefatigable: adjective – tireless. *Pim's indefatigable efforts as a medical volunteer with the Peace Corps earned her national recognition and a scholarship from a local university.*

indigent: adjective – poverty stricken. *The government made a special effort to ensure the indigent population in the city had adequate housing and clothing during the brutally cold winter.*

ingratiate: verb – to make oneself acceptable. *Amy was constantly trying to ingratiate herself in hopes that her boss would notice and give her the promotion she desperately wanted.*

innocuous: adjective – harmless. *The bug looked big and scary, but in reality, it was rather innocuous.*

insurgent: noun – one who rises in revolt. *The insurgents launched a debilitating assault on the capital.*

intemperate: adjective – lacking in self-control. *John was intemperate when it came to chocolate; he just could not seem to stop eating it.*

jargon: noun – the specialized vocabulary of members of a group. *Most of the document was in the local jargon and was not easily understood by outsiders.*

judicious: adjective – wise; careful; showing sound judgment; prudent. *The principal handled the complaint judiciously, ensuring all parties had a chance to share their version of the story and that all facts were considered carefully.*

kindle: verb – to ignite; to arouse or inspire; to catch fire; to become aroused. *With the wind blowing furiously, Answar found it difficult to kindle the fire.*

lackluster: adjective – lacking brightness; dull; lacking liveliness, vitality, or enthusiasm. *Clint's lackluster response signaled that he might no longer be interested in serving as chair of the commission.*

laconic: adjective – brief or terse in speech; using few words. *Aldridge delivered a laconic but impactful speech after securing a win in the primary.*

lassitude: noun – state or feeling of being tired and listless; weariness. *The lassitude of the team was understandable given the arduous conditions they were forced to work under for several months.*

laudable: adjective – worthy of praise. *The board rewarded Ellen's laudable achievements by promoting her to project lead.*

lethargic: adjective – drowsy; dull; sluggish; indifferent. *The medication caused Dillon to be lethargic and foggy; he stayed home on the couch until he made a full recovery.*

levity: noun – lightness; lack of seriousness; fickleness. *Graham's sense of humor injected some much needed levity into the once tense atmosphere.*

listless: adjective – indifferent; marked by a lack of energy or enthusiasm. *The dog sat listlessly in the corner, not wanting to even go for a walk.*

lucid: adjective – easily understood; rational; clear; clear-minded. *It takes Tina about four cups of coffee to become lucid in the mornings.*

malicious: adjective- spiteful; intentionally mischievous or harmful. *Though he had no malicious intent, his negligence still caused a great deal of harm to those involved.*

marred: verb – injured; spoiled; damaged; disfigured. *The graffiti artist marred the newly erected statute in the square, covering it with spray paint and decals.*

meager: adjective – thin; lean; of poor quality or small amount. *Though he came from a meager background, Fred managed to make the most of what he had.*

meandering: verb – winding back and forth; rambling. *Meandering the streets and alley ways of a new city is one of the best ways to tap into the local culture.*

mitigate: verb – to make or to become milder or less severe; to moderate. *John hoped that drinking coffee would help mitigate the drowsiness caused by the medicine.*

nomenclature: noun – a systematic naming in an art or science. *The nomenclature of the chemical compound was more complicated than scientists originally suspected.*

nonchalance: noun – carelessness; lack of interest or concern. *Bert's nonchalance did little to help him convince his manager that he was ready for a promotion.*

obliterate: verb – to blot out leaving no traces; to destroy. *The nuclear bomb obliterated the old camp site, leaving nothing but charred and barren land behind.*

obscure: adjective – not clear or distinct; hidden; remote; not well known. *The obscure metal was once used by the ancient Romans to make swords and drinking vats.*

officious: adjective – meddling; giving unnecessary or unwanted advice or services. *Baxter's officious manner helped her gain friends, but once they discovered her true nature, they strayed away from her.*

opulent: adjective – wealthy; abundant. *The opulent stateroom was full of unique treasures and artifacts.*

overt: adjective – not hidden; open. *The overt sexism of the sportscaster did not go unnoticed; several people filed complaints with the network and the sportscaster was relieved of his duties.*

pariah: noun – an outcast. *Because of his shady past, the old man was treated like a pariah by a majority of the townspeople.*

parsimonious: adjective – too thrifty; stingy. *The parsimonious businessman amassed a small fortune as as a result of his frugality but rarely enjoyed the fruits of his labor because he was so focused on saving.*

paucity: noun – scarcity; smallness in number or amount. *The city was deeply impacted by the paucity of teacher's; they had to bring in teachers from a neighboring city to ensure they were able to staff all their classrooms at the start of the school year.*

peerless: adjective – having no equal; better than the rest. *Jasper's peerless athleticism made him the envy of football players throughout the state.*

perfidy: noun- treachery; betrayal of trust. *Pierce found it hard to grapple with the perfidy of his long-time training partner and friend.*

peruse: verb – to study; to read. *The director asked the panel to peruse the material before the interview started so that they could formulate specific questions about the candidate's credentials.*

philistine: adjective – narrow-minded; smugly conventional. *Heidi's philistine views were not warmly received by the stanchly liberal crowd.*

piety: noun – devotion and reverence, especially to god and family. *In addition to the pastor's piety, the congregation appreciated his sense of duty to the youth of the church and to the community.*

pique: verb – to hurt the feelings of or make resentful; to arouse; to excite. *The commercial piqued Jenna's curiosity about the new video game and prompted her to do some more research on its features.*

placate: verb – to soothe; to pacify. *Jade tried to placate the upset child with ice cream and candy to no avail.*

plagiarize: verb – to take ideas or writings from someone else and present them as one's own; to use without giving credit. *The thesis committee failed to approve the dissertation once they realized that a significant portion of it was plagiarized.*

ponderous: adjective – very heavy; bulky; labored and dull or tiresome. *Matt spent months in a ponderous state after his company failed; he hashed over every single business decision and transaction that could have made a difference in the outcome.*

pragmatic: adjective – practical; opinionated; concerned with actual practice rather than with theory or speculation. *The city council appointed Gerard to chair the budget committee because of his pragmatic approach to financial management.*

quandary: noun – condition of being doubtful or confused. *Weighing the benefits and potential drawbacks of the underwater pump left the environmentalists in a quandary.*

querulous: adjective – peevish; faultfinding; expressing or suggestive of complaint. *The camp staff became adept at ignoring the camper's querulous demands for attention.*

quixotic: adjective – idealistic and utterly impractical. *It is quixotic to think that we can ignore the inevitable consequences of climate change.*

rancor: noun – deep spite or malice; strong hate or bitter feeling. *His rancor towards his in-laws did little to ease the tensions between the families.*

rebuff: verb – to refuse in a sharp or due way; to snub; to drive or beat back. *The actress felt like she was rebuffed by the Academy for the third consecutive year.*

recalcitrant: adjective – refusing to obey or follow orders; unmanageably resistant. *Colin was expelled from the military academy for his recalcitrant attitude and his unwillingness to follow the rules.*

recluse: noun- a person who lives alone, away from others. *The kid in the neighborhood considered the old woman a recluse since she never came outside.*

redundant: adjective – wordy; exceeding what is necessary or normal; lavish; overflowing. *The newsletter was redundant; each article shared the same facts using different words and phrasing.*

refurbish: verb – to freshen or polish again; to make like new. *Although the laptop was refurbished, it looked and worked like new.*

rejuvenate: verb – to make young or fresh again. *Angela felt rejuvenated after spending the day at the spa.*

relic: noun – a thing or part that remains from the past; something kept as sacred because it belonged to a saint. *The pilgrims made the journey to Vezelay where the relics of Mary Magdalene were supposedly buried.*

repugnant: adjective – disgusting; loathsome; objectionable; incompatible. *The Ambassador held nothing back in his speech that condemned the repugnant actions of the opposition party.*

rescind: verb – to cancel; to repeal; to set aside. *The committee discovered that Stephen lied about his credentials and decided to rescind his offer of admission.*

residual: adjective – left over, remaining. *The residual crumbs on his mouth gave Oscar away when he tried to deny that he was the one who took the cookies from the jar.*

resilient: adjective – getting back strength or spirits quickly; springing back into shape or position. *The garden was resilient and bounced back quickly after being nearly destroyed by the storm.*

respite: noun – a temporary cessation or postponement, usually of something disagreeable; interval of rest. *After a long day wrangling unruly children at the slumber party, Kate treated herself to wine and a bubble bath, a much needed respite before the children woke up again.*

sagacious: adjective – very wise or shrewd. *The Dali Lama is a sagacious and unbiased leader revered for his wisdom and his commitment to fairness and equality.*

salutary: adjective – healthful; useful or helpful; remedial. *Esther acknowledged that although her father's lecture was hard to swallow, it was salutary and helped her refocus her behavior.*

sanction: noun – authorized approval or permission; support or encouragement; something that gives binding force to a law. *The Olympic Committee sanctioned the cyclers, stripping those who tested positive for doping of their medals.*

saturate: verb – to soak through and through; to fill completely. *The cloth was saturated with the dye in order to create a vibrant print.*

scapegoat: noun – one taking the blame for the mistake and crimes of others. *Dean Smith, wanting to avoid being held responsible for the email scandal, made Dean Hammonds the scapegoat and she took the fall instead.*

scoff: verb – to mock or jeer at; to make fun of. *The fans scoffed at the other team and mocked their odd looking mascot.*

scrupulous: adjective – very honest and conscientious; careful about claimed expense. *To avoid an unfavorable audit, the businessman kept scrupulous records of all his expenses.*

scrutinize: verb – to look at very carefully; to inspect minutely. *Every move the account administrator made was scrutinized since he was good friends with the bank manager who was recently indicted on fraud charges.*

sectarian: adjective – pertaining to a group within a larger group that is limited by common beliefs or interests; narrow-minded. *The small group of priests drew ire from religious leaders for perpetuating sectarian ideas that were not aligned with the larger mission of the faith.*

sequester: verb – to hide or keep away from others; to withdraw into seclusion; to confiscate; to segregate. *The judges were sequestered in a room so that they could deliberate without influence from outside sources.*

serene: adjective – unruffled; tranquil; unclouded. *The house was perched on the side of the hill and offered unobstructed views of the blue serene sea.*

skeptical: adjective – not easily persuaded or convinced. *Kim was skeptical of the sudden increase in test scores and asked the school board to launch an investigation.*

sobriety: noun – seriousness, gravity, or solemnity; absence of alcoholic intoxication. *Calvin celebrated 20 years of sobriety with cake and alcohol-free sparkling cider.*

taciturn: adjective –laconic; uncommunicative. *Discontent with her job, Sophia became withdrawn and taciturn; she spent most of her time in her office and barely returned calls or emails.*

tangential: adjective – diverging or digressing. *The conversation was tangential at best, barely focusing on the main point for more than a few seconds.*

tawdry: adjective – gaudy and cheap; vulgarly ornamental. *The display was tawdry and salacious and solicited much admonishment from offended customers.*

tedious: adjective – long or verbose and wearisome; tiresome; boring. *The problem sets were tedious and time-consuming; everyone complained that they were just busy work with no real value.*

temerity: noun – rashness; foolish or reckless boldness. *AJ's temerity in constantly challenging his manager cost him his promotion and landed him on probation.*

tenet: noun – a principle, doctrine, or belief held as a truth by a group. *The disciples worked hard to practice the tenets of their faith in all their endeavors.*

terse: adjective – using only a few words but clear to the point; polished. *Theresa was often terse when delivering her opening statement, believing that the jury only needed to hear a clear presentation of the facts.*

threadbare: adjective – frayed or shabby; used so often that it is stale. *The children played so much in their playroom that patches of the carpet had become threadbare.*

thwart: verb – to oppose directly; to baffle; to block; to frustrate. *The construction project was thwarted by activists who contented building the new bridge would destroy protected greenspace.*

tirade: noun – a long, angry, or scolding speech; a harangue. *The public was disappointed in the candidate's insult-laden tirade about the judge assigned to his case.*

trepidation: noun – a trembling; apprehension; a state of alarm and dread. *The team moved forward with trepidation, not sure what was ahead in the dense forest.*

unassailable: adjective – undeniable; unquestionable; not able to attack. *Erica's version of the story was unassailable; video evidence confirmed all the details she shared.*

undermine: verb – to dig or to make a tunnel under; to wear away and weaken the support of; to injure or to weaken in a slow or sneaky way. *Shannon hoped that her injuries were not going to undermine her ability to perform in the track meet.*

unequivocal: adjective – plain; very clear in meaning. *The professor was impressed by the student's unequivocal explanation of the complex theorem.*

ungainly: adjective – clumsy; awkward; hard to handle. *Tim had trouble maneuvering his way down the steps with the ungainly air cast on his ankle.*

unimpeachable: adjective – beyond doubt or reproach; unquestionable. *The prosecution believed their witness was unimpeachable; they were sure the jury would have no issues believing everything in his statement.*

unobtrusive: adjective – not readily noticeable; inconspicuous. *Given his height and large stature, it was nearly impossible for Tony to make an unobtrusive entrance into a room.*

unscathed: adjective – undamaged; unharmed. *The car was completely totaled in the accident leaving many shocked that the race car driver escaped the accident unscathed.*

untenable: adjective – that which cannot be maintained or occupied; incapable of being defended or held. *The social worker determined that the home was untenable for the children; there was no running water, no electricity, and only one bedroom.*

urbane: adjective – courteous suave; polished. *Jimmy was the epitome of urbane with his tailored suits, debonair personality, and fine taste in wine.*

utopian: adjective – excellent, but existing only in fancy or theory; given to dreams or schemes of perfection. *For Fran, the island was her own utopian escape from the stress of her job and her family.*

vacillate: verb – to say unsteadily; to totter; to waver; to fluctuate. *The vacillating fan provided intermittent relief to the hot and exhausted campers.*

validate: verb- to declare or make legally sound; to substantiate; to verify. *The results of the contest were unofficial until they were validated.*

venerate: verb – to regard with respect and reverence; to honor. *Pope John Paul II is venerated as one of the most influential Pope's in modern history.*

verbose: adjective – wordy; tedious. *The reporter was overly verbose and took an inordinate amount of time to get past the unnecessary details and to the point.*

viable: adjective – able to live or exist; practicable. *Many couples opt not to share news that they are expecting until after 12 weeks when they are certain that the fetus is viable.*

vicarious: adjective – taking the place of another; experienced through sympathetic participation in the experience of another. *Many people are afraid to travel or feel like they don't have the time, so they instead live vicariously through those who do travel.*

vindictive: adjective – revengeful; unforgiving; bitter; spiteful. *The small claims court judge admonished Sharon for bringing what he considered a clearly vindictive lawsuit; he cited her husband's recent filing of divorce papers as the only justification for the frivolous legal action.*

virtuoso: noun – one interested in the pursuit of knowledge; one with mastery skill or technique in any field. *BK Jackson's saxophone rendition of Prince's Purple Rain was considered a virtuoso performance by many.*

vitriolic: adjective - extremely biting or caustic; sharp and bitter. *Jackson's vitriolic management style created a hostile environment for his employees who did not respond well to his biting and unconstructive feedback and generally surly disposition.*

volatile: adjective – evaporating readily at normal temperatures; changeable; explosive. *The situation in Pattani is quite volatile at the moment, and government officials have warned citizens not to travel there.*

voluminous: adjective – large, bulky; enough to fill volumes. *The hairdresser used lots of hair spray and mousse to make her normally flat and stringy hair appear more voluminous.*

whet: verb – to sharpen; to make stronger; to stimulate. *The executive gave the investors just enough information to whet their curiosities.*

wither: verb – to dry; to shrivel; to cause to lose courage or to be ashamed. *After not being watered for a month, the plants started to wither and die.*

writhe: verb – to twist or squirm, as in pain; to suffer from shame or shyness. *Following his surgery, Antonio spent a week in bed writhing in pain since he refused to take any pain medication.*

zany: adjective – clownish; foolish; funny; absurd. *Jennifer's friends often commented on her zany and eccentric personality since she loves to entertain and tell corny jokes.*

zenith: noun – the point in the sky directly above one; the highest point. *The Shaman Dynasty reached its zenith at the end of the 15th century.*

PREFIXES & SUFFIXES

Prefix	Definition	Example
a	in, on, of, up, to	aloof
an	without, lacking	anaerobic
ad	to, toward	advance
am	friend, love	amiable
ante	before, previous	antebellum
anti	against, opposing	antithetical
auto	self	autonomy
belli	war, warlike	belligerent
bene	well, good	benefit
bi	two	bilateral
chron	time	chronological
circum	around	circumspect
com	with, together, very	communion
contra	against, opposing	contradiction
cred	belief, trust	credible
dem	people	demographic
dia	through, across, apart	diameter
dis	away, off, down, not	disparate
equi	equal, equally	equidistant
ex	out	extract
fore	before, previous	forecast
homo	same, equal	homogenous
hyper	excessive, over	hyperventilate
hypo	under, beneath	hypothermia
in	in, into	invade
in	not, opposing	ineligible
inter	among, between	interconnected
intra	within	intranet
mal	bad, poorly, not	malware

Prefix	Definition	Example
mis	bad, poorly, not	mistake
mono	one, single	monogamy
mor	die, death	morbid
neo	new	neoclassical
non	not	nonsense
ob	against, opposing	obstruct
omni	all, everywhere	omniscient
over	above	overhead
pan	all, entire	panorama
para	beside, beyond	parallel
per	through	permit
peri	around	perimeter
phil	love, like	philosophy
poly	many	polygon
post	after, following	postscript
pre	before, previous	preface
prim	first, early	primary
pro	forward, in place of	propel
re	back, backward, again	revert
retro	back, backward	retrospect
semi	half, partly	semicircle
sub	under, beneath	subterranean
super	above, extra	supersede
sym	with, together	symbiotic
trans	across, beyond, over	transmit
un	not, reverse of	unfit
uni	one	uniform
vis	to see	visible

Suffix	Definition	Example
able	able to, likely	palpable
age	process, state, rank	passage
ance	act, condition, fact	forbearance
ate	having, showing	isolate
ation	action, state, result	occupation
cy	state, condition	clemency
dom	state, rank, condition	kingdom
en	cause to be, become	enliven
esque	in the style of, like	picturesque
ess	feminine	empress
ful	full of, marked by	grateful
fy	make, cause, cause to have	exemplify
hood	state, condition	manhood
ible	able, likely, fit	possible
ion	action, result, state	union
ish	suggesting, like	sluggish
ism	act, manner, doctrine	Buddhism
ist	doer, believer	philanthropist
ition	action, state, result	contrition
ity	state, quality, condition	equality
ize	make, cause to be, treat with	ostracize
less	lacking, without	fearless
like	like, similar	childlike
logue	type of speaking or writing	prologue
ly	like, of the nature of	aptly
ment	means, result, action	engagement
ness	quality, state	eagerness
or	doer, office, action	editor
ous	marked by, given to	momentous

Suffix	Definition	Example
ship	the art or skill of	statesmanship
some	apt to, showing	fulsome
th	act, state, quality	warmth
tude	quality, state, result	magnitude
ward	in the direction of	toward

Made in the USA
Middletown, DE
25 July 2018